Workout

UPPER INTERMEDIATE

STUDENTS' BOOK

Paul Radley
Chris Millerchip

Nelson

Thomas Nelson and Sons Ltd
Nelson House Mayfield Road
Walton-on-Thames Surrey
KT12 5PL UK

51 York Place
Edinburgh
EH1 3JD UK

Thomas Nelson (Hong Kong) Ltd
Toppan Building 10/F
22A Westlands Road
Quarry Bay Hong Kong

© Paul Radley and Chris Millerchip 1993

ISBN 0-17-556465-5

NPN 9 8 7 6 5 4 3 2

Acknowledgements

The authors would like to thank the following:
Kathy Burke and the teachers of the Bell Language Institute; Tom
Dodd and Tamara Berti of the British Council, Milan; Nick Shaw of
Cambridge English Studies, La Coruña; Guy Heath of LinguaSec S.A.,
Madrid; Tom Stableford, Lyn Harris of King's School of English,
Beckenham; Peter Kelly; Suzanne Antonaros; Andrew Kinselle;
Antonella Sanna, and all those who participated in the recordings.

*The authors and publishers are grateful to the following for
their permission to reproduce copyright material on the pages
stated.*

Extracts
Advertisement (12) reproduced by permission of **Accelerated Learning Systems Limited,** 50 Aylesbury Rd, Aston Clinton, Aylesbury,
Bucks, HP22 5AH; COBUILD extracts from the **Collins Cobuild
Student's Grammar** (134-144); *Don't panic* (30) adapted from an
article in **Company Magazine**; *My favourite village* by Gore Vidal (36)
and *Living with my own legend* (44) first published in **The European**;
extract from *The Best Man to Die* by Ruth Rendell (106) reproduced by
permission of **Hutchinson**; *Saved from the turkey by a passion for
fruit* by Sean O'Neill (94) first published in **The Independent** 27/12/
90; extract from *Red Wind* by Raymond Chandler (110) from *Trouble is
My Business*, **Penguin Books** 1950, selection © Penguin Books 1950;
extract from *Valediction* by Robert B Parker (68), **Penguin** 1985 ©
Robert B Parker 1984; biographical notes on Ruth Rendell (106), *A Cure
for Love* by Dr John Collee (64) reproduced by permission of the
Peters Fraser & Dunlop Group Ltd; biographical notes on Alison
Lurie (54) reproduced by permission of **Reed Book Services**; extract
(111) reproduced by permission of Tony Rushton, originally appeared
in **Private Eye**; © Times Newspapers Ltd; **Sunday Times**, *Mr
Guitar's Simple Rule of Strum* (10), *A name in vain* (98); **The Times**,
Stewardess sells home to win her wings (14), *Superman comes down to
earth with a proposal* (70); small ad © **Time Out Magazine**; Technics
Hi-Fi advertisement (97) by permission of **FCO**; Lux Soap advertise-
ment (97) by permission of **JWT**; Dannimac advertisement (97) by
permission of **Robert G Roberts & Jones Limited**; Sony Trinitron
advertisement (97) by permission of **Sony UK Ltd**; advertisements
(102) by permission of the **Health Education Council** and the
Tobacco Advisory Council; extract from *Cry Freedom* by John
Briley (78) by permission of **MCA Publishing Rights**; extract from
James Galway: An Autobiography (56) by permission of **Hamish
Hamilton**; *Road Runners* (24) from **The Face**; extract adapted from
Dressed to Cure (52) by permission of **Essentials**; biographical notes
on Michelle Schocked (11) – **Polygram Music Publishing Ltd**;
extract from *Why?* (84) **Electra/Asylum Records/Warner Commu-
nications Ltd.**

Illustrations
Drawings (30, 100) from 'It's only you that's incompatible!' by Mel
Calman; cartoons (8, 28, 70, 88) reproduced by permission of Grub
Street; cartoons (33, 47, 61, 89) by Nick Newman © Private Eye;
MacLachlan cartoon (108) reproduced by permission of Private Eye.

Photographs
Action Plus: p. 21, 91; Allsport Photographic: p. 21 (2); Amnesty
International: p. 49; Ancient Art and Architecture: p. 13; Aquarius
Picture Library: p. 13 (2), 68 (2), 107; B.T. Pictures: p. 35; Clive Barda: p.
113; Benetton: p. 113; Stuart Boreham: p. 9, 27, 38 (3), 39 (2), 40, 50, 55
(4), 63 (3), 77 (3), 83 (2), 92, 105 (2), 112, 137: Bubbles: p. 9 (2), 22 (2), 27 (3),
112 (2); Bridgeman Art Library: p. 13, 105 (2), 107, 110; Colorific Photo
Library: p. 44; Richard Cook: p. 8; Face Magazine: p. 24; The Ronald
Grant Archive: p. 13, 68 (4), 82, 105 (2), 109; Sally & Richard Greenhill:
p. 38, 86, 87; Hulton Deutsch: p. 13, 27; Hutchinson Photo Library: p. 69
(8); Image Bank Photo Library: p. 7 (3), 21, 35, 41 (2), 55, 63, 77 (4), 12 (2),
137 (3); Independent: p. 94; Bill Kenwright: p. 35; Lever Bros: p. 100; S &
O Mathews: p. 37 (3); National Motor Museum: p. 35; Network
Photographers: p. 9, 21, 41, 63 (2), 83, 91; Popperphoto: p. 35; Rex
Features: p. 10, 41 (2), 44, 56, 81 (7), 83 (2), 91 (4), 105 (3), 107, 108; Chris
Ridgers Photography: p. 21 (2), 27 (3), 55 (3), 63; Sony: p. 97; Frank
Spooner: 11, 13 (2), 27, 82 (2), 91 (2), 105; Still Pictures: p. 7 (2);
Stockphotos: p. 38, 135; Sygma: p. 13 (2), 83 (2), 105, 107; The Times
Newspaper: p. 14; Topham Picture Library: p. 7, 78, 92

*The publishers have made every effort to contact owners of
copyright, but this was not possible in all cases. They
apologise for any omissions, and if any details are sent, will
be glad to rectify these when the title is reprinted.*

Additional artwork
Paul Catherell, Graham Bence, Ian Murray, Sarah Perkins, Eikon,
Illustrated Arts, Pantelis Palios, Peter Schrank

Contents

Map of Workout Upper Intermediate

Unit 1

Topic	*lifestyle*
Listening	*talking about lifestyle; predicting information*
Vocabulary development	*lifestyle words*
Vocabulary building	*compound nouns*
Pronunciation	*vowel sounds - 'e'*
Reading	Mr Guitar's rule of strum
Grammar	*verb tense revision - positive and negative statements*
Writing development	*composition (1)*

Unit 2

Topic	*ambition*
Reading	Stewardess sells home to win her wings
Vocabulary development	*jobs and careers*
Vocabulary building	*verbs ending in -ify*
Pronunciation	*short and long 'a'; intonation in questions*
Listening	*talking about work and ambitions; listening for specific information*
Grammar	*question forms*
Writing development	*informal letters (1)*
Functional target	*starting a conversation*
Learner training	*the right approach*

Unit 3

Topic	*excitement*
Listening	*exciting first experiences; listening for specific information*
Vocabulary development	*1 activities, 2 adjectives of opinion*
Vocabulary building	*adjectives ending in -ed/-ing*
Pronunciation	*the vowel 'i'; the vowel 'u'*
Reading	Road runners
Grammar	*future with* will *and* going to
Writing development	*formal letters (1)*

Unit 4

Topic	*worry*
Listening	*talking about worry; predicting information*
Vocabulary development	*causes and cures for worry; the same word as noun and verb*
Pronunciation	*linking words; the vowels 'oo'*
Reading	Don't panic!
Grammar	*past continuous, past simple, past perfect*
Writing development	*narration (1)*
Functional target	*stating intentions*
Learner training	*speaking*

Unit 5

Topic	*nostalgia*
Reading	My favourite village
Vocabulary development	*where you live*
Vocabulary building	*adjectives ending in -ed*
Pronunciation	*the vowel 'o'; sentence stress (1)*
Listening	*talking about the past; predicting questions*
Grammar	would *and used to*
Writing development	*composition (2)*

Unit 6

Topic	*happiness*
Listening	*talking about happiness; listening for specific information*
Vocabulary development	*happiness*
Vocabulary building	*the suffix -ship*
Pronunciation	*plurals (s, z or /ɪ z /); 'ea'*
Reading	Living with my own legend
Grammar	*modal verbs must, have to, need to, affirmative, negative and interrogative*
Writing development	*informal letters (2)*
Functional target	*remembering and helping people to remember*
Learner training	*Listening*

Unit 7

Topic	*prejudice*
Listening	*talking about types of prejudice; completing information*
Vocabulary development	*types of prejudice*
Vocabulary building	*nouns ending in -ism*
Pronunciation	*hard and soft 'g'; 'th'*
Reading	Dressed to cure
Grammar	*past passive; conditional clauses (1) (if + present + present)*
Writing development	*writing a biographical description*

Unit 8

Topic	*morality*
Reading	James Galway
Vocabulary development	*crime*
Vocabulary building	*nouns ending in -ment*
Pronunciation	*hard and soft 'c'; rising and falling intonation*
Listening	*talking about morality; ordering information*
Grammar	*present perfect and past simple; conditional clauses (2) (if + present + future)*
Writing development	*formal letters (2)*
Functional target	*hesitating*
Learner training	*reading*

Read this!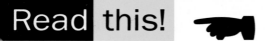

In order to get the best from this book, it is a good idea to read this introduction very carefully.
These are the principal activities in Workout Upper Intermediate.

Speaking

There are increasing opportunities for you to use English to practise new points of grammar and vocabulary and in discussions.

Listening

The authentic interviews on the Class Cassette will improve your ability to understand a wide range of English accents. There are two interviews on each Unit theme on the Class Cassette.

Reading

The range of authentic reading material will improve your ability to read confidently and accurately. For each reading text there is a choice of exercises at the back of the book.

Writing

There is a special writing development section in each Unit covering different writing techniques necessary for the FCE examination.

Vocabulary

There are three types of vocabulary activities:

1 **Vocabulary comprehension**
   These exercises appear after each reading text. They are intended to help develop your ability to understand difficult words. You are not required to use this vocabulary actively.
2 **Vocabulary development**
   These exercises are to extend your active vocabulary. There is plenty of opportunity for you to use these words frequently.
3 **Vocabulary building**
   These exercises are intended to help you increase your vocabulary by categorising words into specific patterns.

Grammar

In this section you will revise and extend your knowledge of the structure of the English language in an active way.

Pronunciation

There are pronunciation activities with every vocabulary and grammar presentation covering the sounds and intonation of English.

Say the right thing

In this section you will be given help in performing particular functions in English. (Starting a conversation, hesitation devices etc.).

Revision

There are revision exercises in the Learning Check sections as well as in the half year and end of year tests.

Learner training

In the learner training sections at the back of the book you will find eight ways of improving your language learning, each section focusing on a particular technique.

Student's Cassette

This is for you to use at home or in your car. Your teacher has the master and you can make copies from it. The cassette contains extra listening material on the theme of the units, extra pronunciation exercises and dictations.

Workbook

The exercises in the Workbook reinforce the grammar and vocabulary presented in the Student's Book. It introduces other grammar points which you will probably have learnt in the past but may have forgotten, has sections on prepositions and English idioms and extra reading texts.

life style, life styles /laɪf staɪl/ also spelled with a hyphen and as one word. The **life style** of a particular person or group of people is the conditions, behaviour, and habits that are typical of them or are chosen by them. EG *They couldn't see that it was their life style that was wrong... this highly urban lifestyle... This is going to affect the life-styles of a great many people.*

Which of these three things do you consider necessary for a satisfactory lifestyle? Discuss your choice with another student.

money   a nice house   a car   friends   exciting holidays
living in town   living in the country   good food and drink
a successful career   a happy relationship

Discuss the following in pairs or groups.

Which of the children in the photos do you think have the happiest lifestyle? Why?
In what ways could the children disagree with you?
Our ideas about what is necessary for a good lifestyle change as we get older. Why is this?

Listening

1 **How much can you tell about a person's lifestyle and attitudes to life just by looking at them?**
Which of these things give you a clue?

facial expression
clothes
way of standing or sitting

Is there anything else which helps you?

"I like a man who knows
where he's going."

Look at the photograph of Richard. Underline the most likely information about him from the choices below.

LIFESTYLE:	satisfied with it – dissatisfied – very happy
RESPONSIBILITIES:	no responsibilities – family responsibilities – responsibility for himself
ABILITY TO PLAN HIS LIFE:	makes plans – doesn't make plans – a combination of the two
AMBITION:	to give his life more purpose – no ambition – to be rich
FUTURE:	has no control over the future – believes your stars affect your future – is in complete control of his future

Compare your information with another student. What points do you disagree about? Can you guess anything else about Richard's lifestyle?

2 **Listen and compare your ideas with what Richard actually said.**
 Circle the correct answers. Did they match your answers?

3 **Listen again and make more detailed notes about what Richard says about how he has planned his life.**

1 ▶

Vocabulary

Vocabulary development: lifestyle words

4 In the interview Richard said that more money and security would improve his lifestyle. Decide which of these things would improve and which would damage your lifestyle.

poverty responsibility stress satisfaction
success travel change luck luxury
security excitement peace possessions
variety money control

Discuss your answers with another student.

Here are some adjectives which describe people's lifestyle.

energetic comfortable relaxed varied
easy-going = outgoing self-centred affluent
miserable

[handwritten annotations: relaxed; = sociable; ego; having lots of money; (not cheerful)]

In pairs check you understand the meaning of these words.

Vocabulary building: compound nouns

5 A compound noun is a word which is made up of more than one noun.

Example *lifestyle*

It is sometimes written with a hyphen, sometimes with a space between the words, and sometimes with either.

Example *life-style, life style, lifestyle*

Make compound nouns with *life* using four of the words below. Check in your dictionary to see if you need a hyphen or not.

jacket book time guard star
insurance boat

Add nouns to the remaining words to make more compound nouns.

Pronunciation vowel sounds: e

6 Listen to the pronunciation of the vowel 'e' underlined in these words.

happen /ə/ immediately /iː/ remember /ɪ/ /e/

3 Listen again and repeat.

Put these words in groups according to the pronunciation of the letter 'e' which is underlined.

less money security result moment series
responsibilities affect rest we deny definitely

Listen and check your answers.

Practice

Invent a sentence

7 In teams. Team A: Read an adjective and noun from exercise 4 to Team B.
Team B: Invent a sentence using the adjective and noun.
Then change over.

Example Team A: *relaxed, security*
  Team B: *It is difficult to have a relaxed lifestyle if you lack security.*

What's their lifestyle like?

8 In pairs. Student A: Choose a photo and describe the kind of lifestyle you think the person has.
Student B: Guess the person and point to him/her.
Then change over.

Speaking

9 **Do you agree or disagree with these statements about learning musical instruments?**

1 If you want to play a musical instrument well you have to start before you are ten years old.
2 It's never too late to learn to play an instrument.
3 You can learn to play an instrument without a teacher.
4 Anyone can play a musical instrument.
5 You have to be able to read music to be a good musician.

Discuss your answers with another student.

Reading

When he was a boy the writer of this article learnt to play the guitar using Bert Weedon's *Play in a Day* Method. Here he is describing a meeting he had with Weedon thirty years later.

10 **Complete a chart with information about 'Mr Guitar' from the text.**

Name:	
Town of residence:	
Age:	
Occupation:	
Publications:	
Hit records:	
TV work:	
Favourite drink:	

Vocabulary comprehension

11 **Here are the definitions of five words from the text. Find the words.**

1 (adj) kind and friendly
2 (n) young men or boys
3 (adv) at a later date
4 (vb) take advantage of
5 (n) a very successful piece of music

Choose three more words which you do not know and which you think are important to understand the text. In pairs try to work out their meaning. Then check the meanings in your dictionary.

Mr Guitar's simple rule of strum

Last week I presented myself at Weedon's home in Beaconsfield, Bucks, as possibly his only failure. A genial and youthful 69, still playing in weekly cabaret, he led me proudly past his gold records to describe the fate I had escaped.

'Impresarios were getting hold of good-looking lads and girls who could sing and were making pop stars of them very quickly.' he said. 'A lot of them were taken advantage of and thrown on the scrap heap. I felt sorry for them.'

Weedon had observed the process closely as a sessions musician with Marty Wilde, Adam Faith, Billy Fury and Tommy Steele. Already a veteran of the big band era, subsequently backing Sinatra and Nat King Cole, he was well positioned to exploit the rock 'n' roll explosion led by Elvis Presley.

'Elvis was not a great guitar player, but he probably got more people playing it than anyone else.' Weedon said. 'I probably came second to Elvis in influencing people. Chappells, the music publisher called me and said, 'You're getting a lot of success, would you like to write a guitar tutor?' I thought, 'Well, I can answer all the questions that a young player would ask. So I took a couple of weeks off and wrote it.'

Widely translated, *Play in a Day* has sold more than 2m copies. Its pupils include Lennon and McCartney, Mike Oldfield, Phil Collins and Pete Townshend. Weedon's recently released video promises tunefulness in 25 minutes.

'Mr Guitar' achieved solo success with the 1959 hit Guitar Boogie Shuffle and subsequent best-selling LPs, but remained a dignified figure who, he admits, 'sold my music and not my pelvis'. He introduced the apple-cheeked Beatles to TV viewers on his show Five O'Clock Club.

'The groupies were never my scene because I was not a sex-symbol type,' he said. 'I have been very sensible. I don't drink very much. I don't smoke and I have never seen any drugs in my career. I am much happier with a glass of lemonade. If a bottle of lemonade cost £15, people would appreciate it more.'

Grammar and pronunciation

> 1 I presented myself at Weedon's home in Beaconsfield.
> 2 Elvis was not a great guitar player.
> 3 You're getting a lot of success.
> 4 'Play in a Day' has sold more than 2 million copies.
> 5 Its pupils include Lennon and McCartney.
> 6 I don't drink much.
> 7 I have never seen any drugs in my career.
> 8 I am much happier with a glass of lemonade.

Grammar: verb tense revision - positive and negative statements

(Grammar reference, page 138)

12 **Look at the sentences in the grammar box. Match the sentence numbers to the verbs below.**

a Present of verb *be*	e Present perfect
b Present simple	f Present perfect (neg)
c Present simple (neg)	g Past of verb *be* (neg)
d Present continuous	h Past simple

Grammar check

13 **Complete the information using words from the box.**

do	present simple	past simple	present perfect	
was/were	*not*	present continuous		*be*
-ed	*not*	*had*	*not*	*never*

1 We use the ____ to talk about repeated actions or habits.
2 Negative sentences are formed with the negative of ____ except for the verbs *be* and *have* where you add ____ to the verb.
3 The ____ refers to temporary situations or to something you are doing at this moment. The negative is also formed by adding ____ to the verb *be*.
4 We use the ____ to describe a situation which began in the past and continued up to the present. The negative is formed by adding ____ or ____ to *have*.
5 The past of *be* is ____. The past of *have* is ____.
6 We use the ____ to describe events completed in the past. The past tense of regular verbs ends in ____.
7 The past simple of all verbs except ____ remains the same for all persons.

Pronunciation: the weak vowel /ə/

14 **Listen to the pronunciation of these words.**

geni**a**l **o**f **a**dvantage Weed**o**n fam**ou**s terr**i**ble

| 4 | Listen and repeat.

What do you notice about the underlined syllable in each word? Is the syllable stressed or unstressed?

Underline the weak vowels in these words.

musician	subsequently	positioned	probably
second	influencing	player	recently
lemonade	appreciate		

Listen and check your answers. Then listen and repeat.

Practice

Michelle Shocked

15 **In pairs. Complete the paragraph about Michelle Shocked using the verbs in brackets.**

Michelle Shocked was born in Dallas, Texas in 1962. Her first introduction to music (*be*) through her father. She (*leave*) Texas in 1983 but (*not be*) able to conform to the lifestyle of people around her. In May 1986 she (*work*) as a volunteer in Kerrville Folk Festival, (*meet*) Pete Lawrence and (*record*) some songs for him.
These songs (*stay*) in the charts for a year. This success (*give*) her the chance to make another album, Short Sharp Shocked and later to work in Hollywood with Pete Anderson. She (*be*) very nervous at first but they (*just complete*) a second album, Captain Swing. Michelle (*learn*) to trust Pete and Captain Swing (*reflect*) that.
The album (*suggest*) that music (*be*) about 'feeling'. The best music always (*have*) that swing.

| 5 | **Listen to check your answers.**
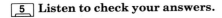

The identity game

16 **Write six sentences (in capitals) about yourself on six separate pieces of paper. Your sentences can be positive or negative. (It is important that no-one recognises your writing!)**

Each sentence should use a different verb tense as follows.

1	Present of verb *be*	4	Past simple
2	Present simple	5	Present perfect
3	Present continuous	6	Past of verb *be*

In groups. Fold all your pieces of paper and mix them up on the desk.

In turn each student takes a piece of paper, unfolds it and reads the sentence. The others have to guess who wrote the sentence.

Writing development

Speaking

17 Look at the advertisement for a rapid language learning method. Have you ever tried to learn a language by a similar method?

In groups discuss and make a list of the advantages and disadvantages of this way of learning a language.

Talk to a member of another group. Compare and discuss your lists.

What other language learning 'methods' have you tried or heard of?

Writing

Composition

18 As a class, discuss how you approach composition writing. What is your technique for planning and organising your work?

Make a list of guidelines for composition writers. Use these headings.

plan
presentation
checking the work

Look at this composition title.

The only way to learn a foreign language is to live in a country where it is spoken. Discuss. (120 - 180 words)

Discuss the title with other students and take notes.
Use your notes to make a plan.
Show clearly what you intend to say in each paragraph.
Read other students' work and compare it to yours.

ambition /æmbɪʃɔ°n/ **ambitions** 1 If you have an **ambition** to be something or do something, you want very much to be it or do it. 2 **Ambition** is the desire to be successful, powerful, rich, or famous: sometimes used showing disapproval. EG *Knowledge of inequality has stimulated envy, ambition and greed.*

Look at the photos. What is or was each person's ambition?
Which definition of 'ambition' above, describes each person?
Was their ambition a positive or negative thing?
Is there any point at which the positive and negative aspects overlap?

In groups choose one of the quotations below and discuss. Does the quotation apply to any of the people in the photos?

'The paths of glory lead but to the grave.'
'The love of power is the love of ourselves.'
'Ambition, in a private man a vice, is, in a prince, the virtue.'

Reading

Before you read

1 Look at the headline of the article.

What do you think the wings are?
Why do you think the stewardess needed to sell her home to win her wings?

While you read

2 What do these numbers from the text refer to?

a	12	e	747
b	26	f	748
c	28	g	40,000
d	44		

Vocabulary comprehension

3 Match the words on the left to their definitions on the right.

1	cockpit	a	obtain
2	former	b	a special case
3	raise	c	the part of the plane where the pilot sits to control the aircraft
4	exception	d	envious
5	gamble	e	one-time
6	guarantee	f	assurance
7	jealous	g	risk

Stewardess sells home to win her wings

First Officer Sally Griffiths, who was told at the age of 26 that she was too old to join a British Airways pilot training course, in the cockpit of a Boeing 747 at Heathrow yesterday (Harvey Elliott writes).

Miss Griffiths, a former air stewardess, sold her flat and car to raise the £40,000 private cost of the 12-month course.

Next week, she will start flying a British Airways Super 748, a 44-seat, turbo-prop airliner, as a qualified pilot on Scottish routes.

Miss Griffiths, now aged 28, said: "I applied to join the British Airways course but was two years too old. I thought they might make an exception as I was a stewardess, but they didn't so I was left with no alternative."

She joined a flying college in Oxfordshire and passed the course with flying colours.

"It was a bit of a gamble. There was no guarantee I would get a job, but I had given up my career as a stewardess so there was no going back", she said.

"It was great being a stewardess, but I was always a little bit jealous and thought I would love to fly the aircraft. I love aircraft and knew I could do it. My ambition is to fly Concorde."

Later this year, Miss Griffiths, of Sonning Common, Berkshire, will marry an officer she met on the course.

14

Vocabulary

Vocabulary development: jobs and careers

4 Put these words under the correct heading in the mind map and check that you understand their meaning. Then in pairs, add four more words to each category.

training   course   energetic   salary
qualify   determination hard working   ambition
promotion   flexible   work
do a course   take exams   timetable
satisfaction qualified   apply

Vocabulary building: verbs ending in -ify

5 Many verbs ending in *-ify* have the adjective form *-ified* and the noun form *-ification*. Fill in the missing words in the following groups.

Verb	Adjective	Noun
qualify	qualified	qualification
modify		
___	clarified	___
___		classification
specify	___	___
___	identified	___

Note: Satisfy, horrify, and *terrify* take a different noun form.

satisfy   satisfied   satisfaction
horrify   horrified   horror
terrify   terrified   terror

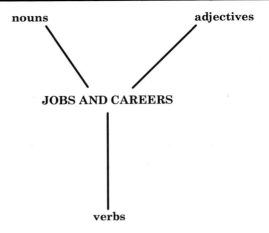

nouns   adjectives

JOBS AND CAREERS

verbs

Pronunciation: short and long 'a'

6 Look at these words from the Reading text.

fl<u>a</u>t   c<u>a</u>r   st<u>a</u>rt   p<u>a</u>ssed   b<u>a</u>ck

Put them under the correct heading.

/ æ /	/ɑː/
flat	car

6 Listen and check your answers.

Now put these words under the correct heading.

cat   arm   can   can't part   last   black
bath half hand basket plan   blanket mankind

Listen and repeat.

Practice

Guess the word

7 In pairs. Student A: Choose one of the words from exercises 4 and 5.
1   Give a synonym for the word.
2   Give the number of letters.
3   Give the first letter.
4   Give the last letter.
Student B: Guess the word. Then change over.

Example Student A: *This adjective has a similar*
                         meaning to contented.
                         It has nine letters.
                         It begins with s.
                         It ends with d.
              Student B: *Satisfied.*
Student B gets 4 points if he guesses after one clue,
3 after two, 2 after three, and 1 after four.

What's my job?

8 Choose a job. Write down six adjectives or nouns connected with the job.

Student A: Read your list.
Student B: Guess the job.
Then change over.

Reading

9 **Questionnaire: Are you over-ambitious?**
Read the questions and choose one option (a, b or c).

1 **Would you stay home from work if you had**
   a a headache?
   b a severe cold?
   c a high temperature?

2 **How many days' work did you miss last month?**
   a None
   b One or two days
   c More than two days

3 **When you leave work do you take extra work home with you?**
   a Always
   b Occasionally
   c Never

4 **Are you prepared to take time off work**
   a to go shopping?
   b to go to a funeral?
   c because you feel tired?

5 **If your boss asks you to work late do you**
   a agree immediately?
   b say it depends what you are doing that evening?
   c refuse?

6 **When starting a new job do you think you should**
   a not do more work than is necessary?
   b try to please but within reason?
   c do anything to create a good impression?

7 **If you found a senior colleague was making a lot of mistakes would you**
   a ask what the problem was?
   b be quiet about it?
   c insist that you took over the job?

8 **If you wanted promotion would you**
   a work really hard to get it?
   b sacrifice your family life if necessary?
   c go to your boss and ask for promotion?

9 **Put these in order of importance.**
   a Family
   b Work
   c Pleasure

10 **Put these in order of importance.**
   a Money
   b Happiness
   c An important job

Look at page 134 to get your score.

Listening

10 **You will hear Louise interviewing Tris about his work and ambitions.**

7 **Listen and find out the following information.**

   1 His present job.
   2 The things he likes about the job.
   3 His ambitions.

Now read these statements. Are they true or false? Listen again and check your answers.

   1 Tris says his job is not very tiring.
   2 Tris works in London.
   3 Tris says his job offers good career prospects.
   4 Tris wears a mask because of the pollution.
   5 Tris says his private life is more important than his work.
   6 Tris will earn a lot of money when he changes job.
   7 Tris thinks it will be an interesting job.

4 ▶

Speaking

11 **In pairs. Look at the illustrations and put the events in order.**
When you have finished, discuss your order with another student. Have you both got the same order?

Grammar and pronunciation

> 1 What's your job?
> 2 What does that involve?
> 3 Why did you choose that job?
> 4 Do you have any regrets about the choice of job?
> 5 Where are you working at the moment?
> 6 Where were you before that?
> 7 Have you ever worked abroad?
> 8 Who worked there with you?

Grammar: question forms

(Grammar reference, page 138)

12 Look at sentences 1-8 in the grammar box. Now use these words to complete the explanation of question formation.

before   order   beginning   infinitive   'wh' word
do   *does*   *after*   questions   past   *did*

We usually form questions by changing the word ____. In most ____ the first verb comes ____ the subject and any other verbs ____ the subject.
We use *do* or ____ to form questions with the present simple and *did* for the ____ simple. The main verb is then in the ____.
When we use a question word (____) to form a question we put it at the ____ of the sentence and then follow the rules above.
When *who* refers to the subject we do not use ____ or ____.

Grammar check

13 Write questions using the following prompts.

Example   *They aren't here. Where .....?*
              They aren't here. Where are they?

1 She's reading. What .....?
2 They've gone on holiday. Where ....?
3 She's crying. Why ....?
4 Mark took us. Who ....?

5 I saw Andrew yesterday. Did ....?
6 They're tired. Why ....?
7 I like music. What ....?
8 Martin got in late last night. When ....?

Pronunciation: intonation in questions.

14 Listen to the first three questions that Louise asked
9 Tris.

- So, what do you do?
- What's your job?
- What does that involve?

When we are asking a simple question in English our voice falls at the end of the question.
Listen again and repeat.

When the voice rises at the end of a question it shows surprise, or is a request for repetition.

Listen to this question and answer sequence.

Where do you live? - In London.
Where? - In London.

Where do you live? - In London.
Where? - In Hammersmith.
Listen and repeat.

Now listen to these questions and say which ones show surprise.

1 What do you do on Saturdays?
2 What do you do on Saturdays?
3 Where do you go?
4 Where do you go?
5 When did you see her?
6 When did you see her?
7 Why are you doing that?
8 Who did you see yesterday?

Listen and repeat.

Practice

Find out more

15 In pairs. Ask and answer questions.
Student A: Look at page 134.
Student B: Look at page 136.
Now write four more questions to ask your partner.

- one in the present simple
- one in the present continuous.
- one in the present perfect.
- one in the past simple.

Ask me another

16 In pairs, choose a topic from the list below. Invent as many questions as possible on that topic. Each question must begin with a different question word and contain a different verb tense. You have five minutes.
Work with another student. Ask the questions you prepared and answer the other student's questions.

Travel / transport   Medicine   Family   Education
Free time

Writing development

Speaking

Rules for effective language learning

17 Answer these questions.

Why are you studying English? (personal interest? work? studies?)
What do you expect from your English lessons?
What things are your teacher's responsibility?
What things are your responsibility?

In groups. Compare and discuss your answers.

18 In groups. Produce a list of rules for inside and outside the classroom to make language learning more effective during your course.
Look at these things.

not missing classes   arriving on time   using your own language
homework   self-study

Writing

Informal letters (1)

19 Rewrite the letter below in the correct order.

20 Now write another letter telling a friend about your English course. Write about the number of lessons a week you have, the other students, your teacher, the books you use, your opinion of the course etc. Begin and end your letter in the correct way for an informal letter. Your letter should contain 150-180 words excluding the address.

Perhaps you'd like to come and visit me one weekend.

It's lots of fun

Walthamstow

29 Oxbridge Road

London

Lessons start at 9 o'clock every day and finish at 4 o'clock with an hour and a half for lunch.

26-5-93

Thanks for your letter which I got yesterday.

Dear Margaret,

Love

It was good to hear that things are going well for you and that you are enjoying your new job.

As you can see I'm in England.

He needs it: we aren't very good students.

James gives us homework every day so I haven't much time to go out in the evenings.

I'm studying English at a school in Walthamstow.

The teacher's very nice too.

There are eleven other students in the class who come from six different countries.

Carlos

You know you're always welcome. Hope to hear from you soon.

His name is James Clavell - he's about 35 years old and he's got a very good sense of humour.

Say the right thing!

Starting a conversation

1 Choose appropriate ways of starting a conversation in these situations.

a Hi, Alison! Haven't seen you for ages. What have you been up to?

b Excuse me, is this seat free?

c Lovely day, isn't it?

d Pleased to meet you.

e Do you mind if I borrow your newspaper?

f Hello, how are you today?

g How do you do?

h Oh, hello. I didn't expect to see you here!

Now write a suitable reply to each conversation opener.
Choose one situation and add two or three exchanges to develop the conversation.

2 Now listen to these four dialogues. Write down any phrases or
10 expressions you think will be useful when you use this language later.
Compare your expressions with another student. Add these to your
conversation if appropriate. Practise your finished conversation with
another student.

Vocabulary

Lifestyle

1 **Read the definitions and write the words.**

Example   *The state of being extremely poor* (n) (7 letters)
Poverty

1 A feeling of being safe and not having fears or worries. (n) (8 letters - S...)
2 A word to describe a lifestyle that makes you feel unhappy or depressed. (adj) (9 letters -M...)
3 A word to describe a lifestyle in which you have enough money to live without financial problems. (adj) (11 letters - C...)
4 The ability to make something behave as you want it to. (n) (7 letters - C...)
5 A force or quality that seems to cause good things to happen to some people and not others, without any reason. (n) (4 letters - L...)
6 A word to describe someone who is very friendly and open. (adj) (8 letters - O...)

Use each of these words in a sentence to show you understand the meaning.

Jobs and careers

2 **Complete the paragraph with these jumbled words from Unit 2.**

David's (*nbtoaiim*) was to become a doctor. He was very (*darh nkoirwg*) at school and then (*ilpeapd*) for a place at university. At the end of the (*eorcsu*) he (*adueliqfi*) as a doctor and got a (*obj*) at the local hospital. His (*iaettebml*) was not good and neither was his (*aylasr*) but he got a lot of (*cfnataosisit*) from working with people who were sick and knew that his (*eacerr*) prospects were good.

Grammar

Verb tense revision: positive and negative statements.

3 **Put the verbs in brackets in the correct tense.**

Example   *I (not go) because I (get up) late.*
I didn't go because I got up late.

1 She (*go*) to France twice a year.
2 I (*not like*) Maths when I (*be*) at school but now I do.
3 He (*never visit*) Wales but he (*hope*) to go next year.
4 She (*live*) with her parents while she (*look*) for a flat.
5 She (*not come*) last night as she (*be*) ill.
6 I (*hate*) parties where they (*want*) you to play games.
7 They (*live*) there since 1990.

Verb tense revision: question forms

4 **Here is some information about Rachel. What questions were asked to get these answers?**

Example   *What's your name? - My name's Rachel.*

1 I was born in Maidstone.
2 In the south-east of England.
3 Yes, I speak it fluently.
4 Yes, I went to school in Italy until I was sixteen.
5 After that I went to school in England.
6 Yes, I did. I went to Liverpool University.
7 Medicine.
8 I qualified in 1991.
9 I'm working in a hospital in Liverpool.
10 I've been there since I qualified.
11 Yes, I love it.

Guide to better language learning
Part 1 - The right approach

If you have difficulty knowing how to approach language learning, or want to improve your technique look at page 117.

excited /ɪkˈsaɪtɪd /. If you are **excited**, you are so happy that you are full of energy and cannot relax, especially because you are looking forward to an enjoyable and special event and cannot stop thinking about it. EG *He was so excited he could hardly sleep.*

excitement /ɪkˈsaɪtmənt/, excitements. **Excitement** is the state of being excited; also used of something that causes you to be excited. EG *Struggling to conceal his excitement he accepted her invitation.*

What are these people doing?

Which of these things have you done? How did you feel about it? How exciting do you find the activities in the photographs? Give a mark from 1 - 10 (1 = not very exciting; 10 = very exciting), then compare your answers in groups.

Class survey

Make a note of the three most exciting things you do/have ever done. Work in groups. Find out the exciting activities that your group has in common. When you have finished compare results with other groups and find out the three exciting activities which are most popular in your class.

Discuss in groups.

Why do people need excitement?
How much excitement do people need?
What is excitement for you?
What's the relationship between excitement and danger?

Listening

Before you listen

1 **You often feel excited when you do something for the first time, like riding a bicycle or learning to swim.**
Think back to your childhood and write down three 'first time' experiences and the age at which you did them.
Discuss your experiences in pairs.

While you listen

2 **Which of these things did Giles find exciting when he was younger?**

`11`

a   going swimming   f   playing football
b   competing in sports   g   driving a car
c   going skiing   h   going camping
d   riding a bicycle   i   travelling
e   rock climbing

Listen again. What is the most exciting thing he has done recently? What was particularly exciting about it?

 5

Speaking

3 **Excitement is often linked with danger. In groups. Look at the class survey you did on page 21. Which exciting activities were linked to danger? What other factors made them exciting? How does somebody's concept of excitement change between childhood and adulthood? Can you think of any reasons for the change?**

Vocabulary

Vocabulary development 1: activities

4
13 Listen to the definitions of these words. Match the definition to the word.

a	playing chess	g	horse riding
b	dancing	h	painting
c	hang-gliding	i	fishing
d	rambling	j	sailing
e	mountain biking	k	windsurfing
f	skating	l	dressmaking

In pairs. Try to find the names of another ten activities.

Vocabulary development 2: adjectives of opinion

5
14 Listen to the list of adjectives and write them under the correct heading

	Positive	Negative
Example	*exciting*	*boring*

Can you think of any other adjectives which fit into either of the two categories?

Vocabulary building: adjectives ending in -ed/-ing

6 Look at these two sentences.

She was *shocked* when she heard the news.
The news was really *shocking*.

Which of the adjectives in italics describes a person's feelings and which describes the thing or person that produces those feelings?

Give the adjectives ending in -ing and -ed for these verbs.

Example *shock   shocking   shocked*

shock   excite   bore   interest
frighten   amaze   terrify   thrill

Pronunciation: vowel i

7
15 Listen to the pronunciation of the letter *i* in these words.

1 exc<u>i</u>tement /aɪ /   2 f<u>i</u>shing /ɪ/

Now add the following words to the correct list.

cl<u>i</u>mb   <u>i</u>nteresting   gl<u>i</u>ding   thr<u>i</u>ll   wr<u>i</u>te
d<u>i</u>ve   d<u>i</u>scuss   act<u>i</u>vity

Listen and repeat.
Note: An exception to these pronunciations of *i* is
ski - skiing /iː/ .

Practice

Connections

8 In pairs. Student A: Choose two words.
            Student B: Find a connection between them.
Then change over.

Example   *playing chess and painting*
                These are two activities you can do at home.

Student B gets a point if he/she can find a connection. Otherwise Student A can find a connection and get the point.

painting   sailing   playing chess   fishing
windsurfing   swimming   hang-gliding   dancing
skating   walking   horse riding   dressmaking
mountain biking

Feelings

9 Look at the two sentences in exercise 6 again.
In pairs. Student A: Make a sentence using an adjective ending in -*ed* and one of the activities in exercise 4.
Student B: Make a sentence using the corresponding adjective ending in -*ing* and one of the activities in exercise 4. You have a time limit of thirty seconds.

Example Student A: *I get really bored when I go fishing.*
            Student B: *I certainly think chess is a boring activity.*

Student B: Choose an adjective and and activity and make a sentence.

Speaking

10 **Why do you think people take part in dangerous activities?**

1 Because they need danger in their lives to stop them getting bored.
2 Because they want to prove that they are stronger and braver than others.
3 Because they need to prove that they are individuals and not just the same as everybody else.

In groups decide which, if any, of these reasons are accurate. Think of three more reasons. Compare your lists with other students.

Reading

Before you read

11 **Look at the photograph and discuss these questions.**
What is the person in the photograph doing?
Where is he?
What do you think the problems are with a sport like this?

While you read

12 **Find out the following information about 'land luging'.**

1 The names of the people who started it.
2 The country where it originated.
3 The type of countryside where the sport is practised.
4 The cost of equipment.

Note: a *shredder* is an American word for someone who rides a skateboard.

Vocabulary comprehension

13 **Which of the two meanings of these words is correct in the context of the article?**

steepest	a	sloping at the sharpest angle.
	b	most expensive.
catch on	a	understand and learn.
	b	become popular.
snakes	a	long thin reptiles with scales on their skin.
	b	moves in long winding curves.
barren	a	very dry and bare.
	b	not producing any successful results.
thunder	a	make a very loud noise, usually continuously.
	b	go along quickly and with a lot of noise.
flat	a	level and horizontal, rather than sloping, curved or round.
	b	not very tall or deep in relation to its length and width.
tracks	a	footprints or other marks which people or animals make on the ground.
	b	pieces of ground which have been specially prepared for racing.

6 ▶

road runners

Thrill seekers of the world unite, it's time to check out a sport that's *really* dangerous: land luging

What's an ageing shredder to do when he's outgrown his skateboard? In California, the answer is an activity that's exploring the outer limits of the danger
5 zone: land luging. The rules are simple: drive to the top of the longest and steepest road you can find, strap yourself to an eight-foot wheeled aluminium board that is barely inches off the tarmac, and let gravity pull you to speeds of up
10 to 90mph. If it sounds suicidal, that's because it is: bob-sleigh racing is kid's stuff by comparison.
    The pioneers of this dangerous game are Bob Pereyra and skateboard accessories company owner Ron Amos, who have spent a small
15 fortune testing and designing equipment in the belief that the land luge will catch on as the next big sports craze. We meet at the top of a two-and-a-half mile stretch of road that snakes down the barren, windy San Gabriel mountains, 50
20 miles north of Los Angeles. Pereyra's neighbour, Jeff Levy, completes the party.
    The land luge board, Pereyra tells me, is incredibly manoeuvrable, and riders, using their feet as brakes, can skid to a stop from
25 60mph within the length of a telephone pole. The chief danger comes in the form of the cars and lorries which thunder down the road alongside the lugers.
    A car detailer by trade, Pereyra tried racing
30 bikes and cars professionally for a while, but decided he preferred the hassle-free, inexpensive simplicity of the padded aluminium luge board, which costs just a few hundred dollars.
    Once all the bugs are worked out, Amos, a
35 skate wheel and snowboard entrepreneur, envisions an international Luge Roadracing Association with racing events around the globe within five years. "It's the sport of the Nineties," he says. "We're going to get it out there to
40 the public and it's going to be like BMX biking. You can't do it on flat land, but most of the world has mountains, and tracks can be built."

Grammar and pronunciation

1 The land luge *will* catch on as the next big sports craze.
2 ...and it's *going to* be like BMX biking.
3 I think they'*ll* come round after the concert.
4 He's very pale: I think he's *going to* be sick.
5 I'*ll* ring you tonight.
6 They're *going to* buy a sailing boat.
7 I'm *going to* take up skiing.

Grammar: future with *will* and *going to*
(Grammar reference, page 139)

14 Look at the sentences in the grammar box. Which sentences match the explanations?

a When you are making predictions about the future you sometimes use *will* and sometimes *going to*.
b When you are making predictions about the future and there is evidence in the present you use *going to*.
c When you are talking about your own intentions you use *going to*.
d When you are stating an intention which you have just decided you use *will*.
e When you are saying what someone else has decided to do, you use *going to*.

Grammar check

15 Complete the sentences with the correct form of *will* or *going to*.

1 I'm very hot. I ____ open the window for you.
2 Don't worry, I'm sure you ____ pass your exam.
3 Have you decided what to do with the money? Yes, I ____ buy a new car.
4 If you don't hurry you ____ be late.
5 I'm tired. I think I ____ go to bed.
6 He's got his racquet with him so I expect he ____ play tennis.
7 Oh no, look at those cars! They ____ crash!

Pronunciation: vowel 'u' /ʌ/ /ʊə/ /uː/ /ɜː/ /aɪ/

16 There are five different ways of pronouncing the letter 'u' in these words. Find the pairs of words.

guy
up   rules
put   suicidal   fortune
pull   thunder
using   buy

Listen and check your answers.
When you have finished, listen and repeat.

Practice

Intentions

17 In pairs. Use the table to ask questions about your partner's intentions. Discuss any of your partner's statements which you find particularly interesting.

Do you think you'll Are you going to Will you	watch television go skiing try skydiving read a book go riding eat out in a restaurant go mountain biking windsurf go and see a film take up a new hobby	this evening? at the weekend? next summer? this year? next winter?

Debate

18 The citizens of a small town in the San Gabriel mountains have complained to the police about land-luging. The mayor decides to call a meeting so that the land-lugers and the townspeople can discuss the problem.

In groups. Act out the meeting. There are four roles.

Mayor of Brownsville. Your role information is on page 134.
Citizens of Brownsville. Your role information is on page 135.
The police. Your role information is on page 136.
The land-lugers. Your role information is on page 137.

When you have finished preparing your roles the mayor will start the meeting for which there is a time limit of fifteen minutes after which the mayor will have to decide whether to impose a ban on the new sport or not.

Writing development

Speaking

Studying in Britain

19 In groups. You are going to Britain for a one month English course next summer. You can only take ten things with you apart from clothes and toiletries. Choose ten things which you think are absolutely essential. Decide which is the most important item on your list. Exchange lists with another group. Which is the most important item on their list?

Check with the other group. Did they choose the same item as you?

Writing

Formal letters (1)

20 Answer the questions about formal letters.

1 Where do you write your address?
2 Where do you write the address of the person you're writing to?
3 How do you begin a formal letter when you know the name of the person you're writing to? And when you don't?
4 How do you start a formal letter when you want to refer to previous correspondance?
5 What do you know about the way paragraphs are laid out in formal letters?
6 Can you name three possible ways of ending the last paragraph of a formal letter?
7 How do you end a formal letter?

21 You are the secretary of a school which organises language courses in Britain. Write a letter to students giving details of a course starting in July. Include the following information.

- the starting date of the course — 1st July
- the date by which to send in their application — 15th May
- what is included in the price — lessons, lunch, a weekly excursion, parties at the beginning and end of the course, social programme.

Exchange your letter with other students and read their letters. Correct any mistakes that you find. Discuss them when you give the letter back.

worry /wʌrɪ/ worries, worrying, worried 1
If you **worry** you keep thinking about problems that
you have or about unpleasant things that might
happen. EG. *Don't worry, Andrew, you can do it …*
I worried that when I got back he wouldn't be there.
People worry about the safety of nuclear energy.

2 **Worry** is the state or feeling of anxiety and
unhappiness caused by the problems that you have
or by thinking about unpleasant things that might happen.
EG *She would be free of all financial worry…*

In pairs look at the photos and decide what worries they represent.

Example   *a car crash: worry about having an accident.*

In groups discuss which worries you think are common to most people.

Listening

Before you listen

1 You are going to hear a conversation about worry. Which things do you think Shai worries about? Which things is she not very worried about?

1 World problems
2 Family
3 Work
4 Illness
5 Personal relationships

While you listen

2 Check your predictions in exercise 1.

17 Now listen again and answer the questions.

1 What does Shai think she can do to solve her problems?
2 What physical symptoms does she have?
3 Does Shai believe that worry can be the cause of illness?
4 What advice does her doctor give her?

Speaking

3 In groups discuss the following.

1 Are you more worried about world problems or personal things?
2 What problems at work or in the family make you worry?
3 What physical reactions do you have when you worry?
4 What do you do to stop yourself worrying?
5 In your opinion is it better to 'talk about it' or 'forget about it'?

**"Don't start looking for
your glasses at 80 mph."**

Vocabulary

Vocabulary development: causes and cures for worry

4 **In pairs, complete the mind map. Use these words and any others you can think of.**

work   a holiday   panic   cold sweat   family
anxiety   exercise   fear   nausea   busy life
illness   phobia   a drink   pain   relaxation
depression   talking to people

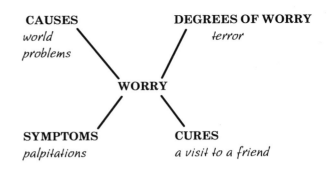

CAUSES
world
problems

DEGREES OF WORRY
terror

WORRY

SYMPTOMS
palpitations

CURES
a visit to a friend

Vocabulary building: the same word as noun and verb

5 **Sometimes the same word can be used in English as a noun and a verb. Sometimes the meaning is similar.**

Example *worry*.

Sometimes the meaning is completely different.

Example *train*.

Find another two words in exercise 4 which can be used as nouns and verbs.

Which of these words can be used as both nouns and verbs?

accompany   life   play   book   behaviour   study
college   train   visit   see

Make sentences with these words as nouns and as verbs.

Example *People sometimes worry unnecessarily about the future.*
Money is a constant worry for some people.

Pronunciation: linking words

6 **Look at the way these sentences are joined.**

I'd like to ask you.
Not that much but they do.
Can you see any way of trying to solve that problem?
I don't think there is.
Worrying a great deal can actually cause illness.
I'm afraid to say I'm the sort of person who really worries a lot.

19 **Now listen and repeat.**

Practise these sentences.
What did you do?
It rained during the day.
He caught the train.
We listened to the radio.
Stop playing with that telephone.

Put a link symbol (‿) between the words that are linked as in the example phrases.
Now listen and repeat.

Practice

Guess the word

7 **In pairs.**
Student A: Choose a word from exercise 4.

1 Give an explanation of the word.
2 Give the number of letters.
3 Give the first letter.
4 Give the last letter

Student B: Guess the word.
Then change over.

Example Student A: *You do this if you keep thinking about your problems.*
It has five letters.
It begins with 'w'.
It ends with 'y'.
Student B: *Worry*

Phobias

8 **Student A: Look at page 134.**
Student B: Look at page 136.
In pairs, spot the invented phobias.

Student A: Read a definition of a phobia from your list.
Student B: Say if the phobia exists or not.
Then change over.

Example Student A: *Linguaphobia is the feeling of panic you experience when you have to speak a foreign language.*
Student B: *I think it's false.*
Student A: *Yes that's right.*

When you have finished write your own true or invented phobias to try out on other students.

Speaking

9 In pairs. Look at the cartoon. Is the fear of flying a real or an irrational fear?
What do you think is the difference between real and irrational fears?
Give more examples and discuss them.

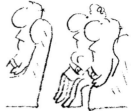

Reading

10 This is a letter about irrational panic attacks which was written to a magazine. The letter is jumbled up. Read the paragraphs and put them in the right order.

Vocabulary comprehension

11 Find these words in the text.

1   A noun beginning with 'p' which describes fast, irregular beats of the heart.
2   A noun beginning with 'n' which has a similar meaning to 'sickness'.
3   An adjective beginning with 'p' which has a similar meaning to 'stressful'.
4   An adjective beginning with 'e' which has a similar meaning to 'outgoing', 'friendly'.
5   A noun beginning with 'e' which means 'extreme tiredness'.
6   A compound noun beginning with 'a...d...' which are drugs.
7   An adjective beginning with 'o' which has a similar meaning to 'uncontrollable'.
8   A noun beginning with 'd' which has a similar meaning to 'vertigo'.
9   An adjective beginning with 'w' which has a similar meaning to 'cautious'.
10   A noun beginning with 'd' which has a similar meaning to 'fear'.
11   A verb beginning with 'p' which means 'thought about'.

8 ▶

Speaking

12 The woman in the text began to feel much better after she moved out of her parents' house.

In what ways do you think living with her parents contributed to her problems?

What are the advantages and disadvantages of living with your parents?

Don't panic!

A
Over the months I forced myself to go out more and more, but felt I still had limitations that were ridiculously stupid. I often ended up in tears at my own inability to conquer a self-made fear. Eventually I took my biggest step of moving out of my parents' house and buying a house with a friend. In doing this I knew I would be losing all the security that made me feel safe and wanted. After nine months I am still there - and have never been happier.

B
Two years ago, I suffered suddenly from heart palpitations, nausea, dizziness, sweating - and utter fear. I was working in London as a PA in a highly pressurised position, my boyfriend had just left me, and my parents' relationship had never been worse.

C
After a week when suddenly, to my horror, I could no longer get on a train, go on the underground or relax in public, I went to the doctor. Although she helped by clarifying my situation as mental exhaustion rather than anything physical, all she offered me was a course of mild anti-depressants, which I refused to take.

D
In one week I went from an extrovert, confident personality to a broken shell, but I could not tell anyone how I felt. I genuinely believed I had some terrible physical illness - and that I was going to die when I was alone.

E
For a further week I stayed in the house and thought that if I went out I would become ill and die. Despite this, the overwhelming fear of being stuck in a house for the rest of my life frightened me more, and I knew I had to get in my car and go somewhere, *anywhere* - I got two miles before I panicked.

F
Many times I wish I had been able to speak openly about my feelings - if only someone could say, 'Yes, you've done well, you will get there.' Any encouragement would help and maybe stop me feeling so inadequate. I pondered greatly on writing this letter to you but now feel I have the determination to deal with all shops, trains, pubs and so on. Thank you for letting me know I am not alone. *AV, Rochester*

G
Today I still feel *extremely* wary in shops when I am alone, and have yet to get on a train to London (despite the fact that I long to do so). Sometimes when I am on my own in the house the old feelings of dread come back, but I tell myself that they will soon go away.

Grammar and pronunciation

> 1 I was working in London as a PA in a highly pressurised position...
> 2 She was feeling really ill when she decided to go to her doctor.
> 3 She was looking really ill and wasn't getting any better.
> 4 Two years ago I suffered suddenly from heart palpitations.
> 5 In one week I went from an extrovert, confident personality....
> 6 She soon realised she needed help.
> 7 My boyfriend had just left me.
> 8 My parents' relationship had never been worse.

Grammar: past continuous, past simple, past perfect.

(Grammar reference, page 139)

13 **Look at the sentences in the grammar box. Do these statements refer to the past continuous, past simple or past perfect?**

a This tense describes actions which were in progress at a time in the past.

b This tense describes actions which began and finished in the past.

c This tense describes something which had already happened before a particular time in the past.

d This tense describes duration and change.

e This tense describes actions, situations, or events in the past.

Grammar check

14 **Put the verbs in brackets into the appropriate tense: past simple, past continuous, or past perfect.**

I (*go*) into the house and (*walk*) towards the living room. Just as I (*put*) out my hand to switch on the light I (*hear*) a noise behind me. I (*turn*) round. A man (*stand*) there pointing a gun at me. At that moment the door (*open*) and two policemen (*come*) in. My neighbour (*see*) the burglars break the window and (*phone*) the police!

Pronunciation: the vowels 'oo' /uː/ and /ʊ/

15 **Listen to the pronunciation of the words with 'oo'**
20 **from sentences 3 and 6 in the grammar box.**

looking /ʊ/   soon /uː/

Which pronunciation do these words have?

took   cool   stood   foot   moon
pool   cook   fool   book   wood

Listen to check your answers. Then listen and repeat.

Practice

Find out more

16 **Student A: Read the information on page 134.**
Student B: Read the information on page 136.
Take turns to ask questions. Student A starts.
When you have finished check your completed paragraphs.

Dreams

17 **In groups, talk about dreams you have had. Remember to talk about these things.**

Where you were in your dream.
What you had done before going to bed.
What was happening at the beginning of the dream.
What happened next.
How you reacted.

The students who are listening can ask as many questions as they wish.

Example Student A:	*I remember I dreamt I was driving along an empty road in the snow.*
Student B:	*What were you doing out in the snow?*
Student A:	*I think I'd been to a party or something.*
etc.	

Writing development

Speaking

Problem solving

18 **Read the story.**

Ask your teacher questions to find out why.

Your teacher can only answer 'yes' or 'no'.

In pairs. Student A: Read the story on page 134 to Student B.

Student B: Ask questions to find out the solution to the story.

When you have finished:

Student B: Read the story on page 136 to Student A.

Student A: Ask questions to find the solution.

One day a young man was driving in his car with his father when he lost control of the car and it left the road and hit a tree. The young man's father was killed and the young man was badly injured. An ambulance took him to hospital where he was rushed to the operating theatre. The surgeon looked at the young man and said, 'I can't operate on him.' and left the operating theatre. Why?

Writing

Narration (1)

19 **Read this account of the plot of the film *Nikita*.**

The film started with a gang of juvenile delinquents robbing a chemist's looking for drugs. They shot the owner of the chemist's who was the father of one of the gang. Then the police arrived. In the gun battle which followed all the members of the gang were killed except for a very violent girl called Nikita. One of the policemen approached her so she shot him too and as a result was put in prison and convicted of murder. The prison guards gave her an injection to make it look as though she had committed suicide, but she wasn't in fact dead.
A government department retrained her as an assassin, gave her a new identity, a flat and some money to live on, and then used her for various secret missions. She fell in love with a man she met in a supermarket and he moved into the flat with her. Eventually he found out what her real job was. After an unsuccessful attempt to steal some documents from the Russian Embassy, during which one of her colleagues was killed, Nikita ran away, presumably to start a new life. The film ended with a conversation between her lover and the man who had trained Nikita, who had also fallen in love with her.

Joining sentences

There are various ways of making sentences more interesting in English. For example you can join two short sentences with a coordinating conjunction (e.g. *and*) or a relative pronoun (e.g. *who*). Read the plot of *Nikita* again and underline the coordinating conjunctions and the relative pronouns.

20 **Complete these sentences with the correct relative pronoun or coordinating conjunction. You can use each word more than once.**

and	then	or	but	so
which	who	whose	whom	

1 The man ____ found the wrecked coach first went back to the village ____ asked for help.

2 She felt very ill the next morning ____ she still went to work, ____ surprised me.

3 When the police arrested him he didn't put up a struggle ____ make a fuss.

4 First they went to Madrid ____ they took a plane to Seville.

5 The last bus had gone ____ he had to hire a car, ____ was very expensive.

6 The couple ____ daughter was kidnapped went to the police ____ told them what had happened, after ____ they gave an interview to the newspaper reporters.

7 The two women, one of ____ I was at school with, climbed the mountain in record time.

8 She was the woman ____ stole the car from the garage.

Now write the plot of a film that you have seen recently (150 - 200 words). Use the coordinating conjunctions and relative pronouns that you have studied.

Say the right thing!

Stating intentions

There are various ways of saying what you intend to do in English, depending on who you are talking to and how you feel about what you are intending or not intending to do.

1 **Look at this jumbled list of ways of stating intentions. Separate the list into positive and negative intentions.**

a I'm going to...
b I don't think I'll...
c I'm certainly going to...
d I thought I might...
e I probably won't...
f I'm thinking of...
g I don't really feel like...
h I'm definitely not going to...
i I'll probably...
j I'm hoping to...
k I think I'll...

Which of the intentions is the *most* positive and which the *most* negative? Compare and discuss your answer with another student. Do you agree? (1 = most positive   11 = most negative)

2 **The phrases in exercise 1 are used when you are stating your intentions spontaneously and not necessarily in response to a question. Now look at this question.**

Are you going to the party at the weekend?

Convert the phrases above so that they are answers to the question.

Example   c   *No, I'm certainly not going.*

21 **Now listen and check your answers.**

It is important to use the correct intonation in these answers if you want to avoid offending people, particularly if the answer is negative. Listen again and repeat, concentrating on accurate intonation.

3 **Choose one of the activities below to do on Saturday evening.**

1 Go to Ann's birthday party
2 Go and see a film
3 Go out for a meal
4 Go to a club
5 Go dancing
6 Stay at home

Now find two other people in your class who intend to do the same thing. Ask questions beginning: Are you...? Give a variety of replies when answering other students' questions.

"We're not going to take this sitting down"

Vocabulary

Activities

1 Write down the names of

1 three sports or activities which you do regularly.
2 three exciting sports or activities from Unit 3 which you have never tried but would like to try.
3 three exciting sports or activities from Unit 3 which you have never tried and don't want to.

Adjectives of opinion

2 Write down three positive (e.g. exciting) and three negative (e.g. boring) adjectives of opinion.
In pairs. Take it in turns to say one of the adjectives. The other student has to make a sentence using the adjective giving an opinion of a sport or activity and justify this opinion.

Causes and cures for worry

3 Complete the paragraph using vocabulary from Unit 4.

Janet leads a very b ____ l ____ , working and looking after the f ___ and she is often tense. When she left w ____ on Friday evening she didn't feel very r ____ because she and Tim were going on h ____ the next day. The next morning Janet woke early with a feeling of n ____ in her stomach. She immediately understood what it was, the old feeling of p ____ that she always got when she had to go in an aeroplane. She had come out in a c ____ s ___ , suffered from p ___ and decided she couldn't possibly go away. Her husband understood the s ____ made her a cup of tea and started t ____ about all the things they were going to do when they got to Spain. She gradually became c ____ , made herself get on the plane, closed her eyes as they took off and then really enjoyed herself for the rest of the journey.

Grammar

Future with *will* or *going to*

4 Write the questions for these answers.

1 This time next year I'll be in Brazil. (*Where?*)
2 I'm going to watch TV this evening. (*What?*)
3 Golf will be the next big sports craze here. (*What?*)
4 We're going to spend our holidays in France. (*Where?*)
5 I'll probably study German next year. (*What?*)
6 Next weekend? I'm going to visit friends in Istanbul. (*What?*)
7 I don't know what I'll do when I retire. (*What?*)
8 I'll be forty on my next birthday. (*How old?*)

Now write your own answers to the questions you wrote.

5 Make two predictions for each of the following categories.

A Sport   B Science   C Politics

Example   *Ayrton Senna will win the World Formula One car racing championship next year.*

Past continuous and past simple

6 Write the beginnings to these sentences.

Example   *... when the lights went out.*
          We were having dinner when the lights went out.

1 ... when the police arrested him.
2 ... when she fell asleep.
3 ... when I found a £50 note.
4 ... when his car suddenly stopped.
5 ... when she heard a strange noise.
6 ... when it started to rain.
7 ... when she felt a terrible pain in her back.
8 ... when she got the news.

Past perfect

7 Look at this sentence using the past perfect tense. Make six new sentences by substituting words for the words in italics.

I had *learnt* to swim by the time *my sister* was *born*.

Guide to better language learning
Part 2 - Speaking

If you have problems with speaking, or want to improve your technique look at pages 117 - 118.

nostalgia/nɒstældʒɪə/ is a slightly sad and very affectionate feeling you have for the past, especially for a particularly happy time. EG ... *nostalgia for the good old days* ...

Look at these photographs. Which decade (twenties, thirties etc.) of the twentieth century are the objects originally from?

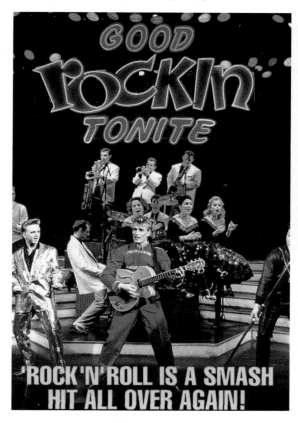

How can you explain nostalgia? Choose one of these statements that you agree with.

- People are nostalgic about the past because it reminds them of their youth.
- Nostalgia is encouraged by the media and the fashion world to make people buy old things.
- People are nostalgic about things from their youth because they like to believe that they were of a higher quality than what we have today.
- Nostalgia is an unhealthy preoccupation with the past usually experienced by people who are afraid of the future.

Can you think of any other reasons for nostalgia?
Is there anything you possess which you keep out of nostalgia? Why? Describe the thing and explain when you acquired it and why you feel nostalgic about it.

Reading

Before you read

1 **What makes people buy a certain house rather than another one? In groups, look at the list of factors and choose the most and least important ones for these people.**

1   a person living alone   3   a young couple with small children
2   a middle-aged couple   4   a retired couple

a   near to the shops   f   pleasant neighbours/   j   land included in
b   low overheads   local residents   price
c   good services   g   interesting history   k   near to public
d   large rooms   h   garage   transport
e   beautiful views   i   cheap

Can you add any more to the list?

While you read

2 **Gore Vidal feels very nostalgic about Ravello and the house he bought there. Read the text quickly and find out why he bought the house.**

Vocabulary comprehension

3 **Find the words in the text.**

1   A noun in paragraph 1 which means the parts of a building which remain after the rest of it has fallen down.

2   A noun in paragraph 2 which means a very bright light which comes suddenly and disappears immediately.

3   A noun in paragraph 3 which means a period of one hundred years.

4   A verb in paragraph 3 which means disappeared suddenly.

5   An adjective in paragraph 4 which means so strong or powerful that you cannot resist something.

6   A noun in paragraph 4 which means the route taken by a vehicle especially a ship or aircraft.

7   An adjective in paragraph 6 which is used to describe a road, hillside etc. that slopes at an angle so that it rises or falls sharply.

8   An adverb in paragraph 8 which means 'certainly not'.

Speaking

4 **Discuss in groups. How do you feel about the place where you live? What are the good and bad things about your flat or house?**
How did you come to live there: by choice or for other reasons?

MY FAVOURITE VILLAGE
GORE VIDAL on RAVELLO

1   In 1948 Tennessee Williams and I drove down in his jeep from Rome to Naples, where the harbour was still torn up from the war. The villages were in ruins, the people poor, but busy. Tennessee was the world's worst driver.

2   "I am for all practical purposes blind in one eye," he would say, serenely making his way down the middle of the Amalfi drive, the last flash of beauty many a tourist sees as he falls into the sea. But we made it into the hills, to Ravello.

3   In the days when I answered silly questions posed by magazines, I was asked by *Esquire*: "What is the most beautiful place you ever saw?" And I said: "Ravello." Specifically, the belvedere of the Villa Cimbrone, where on a bright, cold February day, at the end of an alley of cypresses (planted in the last century by Lord Grimthorpe), the sky and the sea were so startlingly blue the horizon had vanished.

4   In 1972, I acquired the villa of Lord Grimthorpe's daughter, built by her in the year of my birth, 1925. It is called the Swallow's Nest, *La Rondinaia*, and I spend several months here in summer. For the other part of the year, I used to live in Rome. Now I spend it in Los Angeles, where I am political. I have always liked Magna Graecia, which is to Greece what the US is to Europe - vast, rich, a bit overpowering. Ravello is at the heart of Magna Graecia. The locals still point to where Odysseus got lost on our coast, which

would mean that he is an even worse sailor than Homer suggests to be so far off course. But we have Siren islands, the Cyclops cave and the rest.

5   I own the house because I own books and they must be somewhere. I don't like possessions, but the books require far more room than I do. I know most of the people hereabouts and a few years ago they made me an honorary-citizen of Ravello - the name comes from the Latin for 'rebel'.

6   The Swallow's Nest is a steep, four-hectare farm where we make our own olive oil and wine. I grow all my own vegetables and roses too. If I eat out, the best restaurant is Zaccharia, between Amalfi and Atrani. The tourists here are mostly sedate, middle-aged English school-teachers and so on, rather pleasant people. The town would prefer swingers but it is a mystery and joy to me, if not to the hoteliers and restaurateurs of this so-called Divine Coast, that it has never been fashionable.

7   My father's family are from the Friuli, north-east of Venice - my great-grandfather came to the US. I speak, but never learned, Italian, so I can do no more than, let us say, a light TV interview. Nothing intelligent. I know only Italians in Ravello.

8   The special pleasure of living here is that it is the most beautiful place I have ever seen. Although, an Australian once observed, it is hardly Adelaide.

Vocabulary

Vocabulary development: where you live

5 In groups. Write down as many words as you can for each of the following categories.

	Types of countryside		Urban areas	
	Adjectives	Nouns	Adjectives	Nouns
Example	*wooded*	*hillside*		
	Types of houses		Rooms in houses	
	Adjectives	Nouns	Adjectives	Nouns

22 Now listen and write the words you hear under the correct heading.

Vocabulary building: adjectives ending in -ed

6 Some adjectives ending in *-ed* are formed from nouns.

Example   *wood - wooded*
            population - populated

Others are past participles used as adjectives.

Example   *thatch - thatched*

Some participles ending in *-ed* combine with adverbs to form compound adjectives.

Example   *populated - densely populated*

Which of the words from exercise 5 fit these categories?

Now make the following verbs and nouns into adjectives ending in *-ed*.

detach   beard   excite   bore   escape   cramp

Write a sentence for each adjective to show you understand the meaning.

Pronunciation: the vowel 'o'

7 Look at the phonetic symbols for these pronunciations of the letter 'o'.

23 Listen and repeat the sounds.

/ə/   /əʊ/   /ɒ/   /ʌ/   /ɔː/

Listen to the pronunciation of these words and say which phonetic symbol the word comes under.

torn   drove   months   lost   political

Add these words to the correct column.

on   Monday   most   born   own   know
comes   olive   nothing   observe

Listen and check your answers.
Listen and repeat.

Practice

Word pairs

8 Prepare a list of nouns and suitable adjectives to describe them using the words in exercises 5 and 6.

Example	**adjective**	**noun**
	thatched	*cottage*
	wooded	*hillside*
	three-bedroomed	*bungalow*

In pairs. Take turns to say an adjective. Your partner has to give an appropriate noun. For each appropriate pair you get one point.

Descriptions

9 In pairs. Student A: Choose one of these photographs.
Describe your photograph in detail to Student B.
Student B: Guess which photograph it is.
Then change over. Look at page 135 for Student B's photographs.

Speaking

10 People often say that childhood is the happiest time of your life, but it can sometimes be a difficult and unhappy time too.

Look at these periods of life and make a note of an advantage and disadvantage of each.

Discuss your notes with another student.

childhood	adolescence	young adulthood
adulthood	middle age	old age

Example *Young adulthood - advantage: freedom*
disadvantage: pressure to succeed

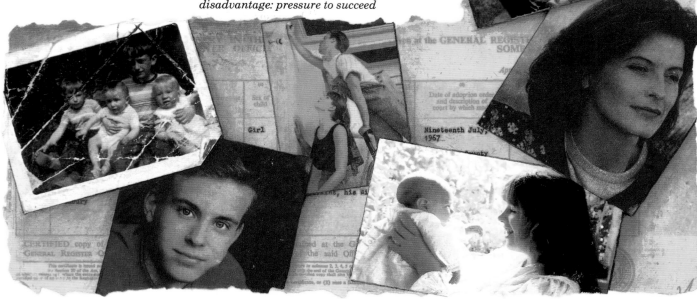

Listening

Before you listen

11 You are going to hear a conversation about a place where one of the speakers used to live and spend his holidays as a child.

Look at the photo of the speaker when he was a child. Make a note of four questions that you would ask the person about this place if you were the interviewer.

While you listen

12 The first time you listen, make a note of the questions asked. Were
24 they the same as the ones you listed in exercise 11?

Listen again and make a note of the answers to the questions. Check your answers with another student.

10 ▶

Speaking

13 In pairs use the questions from the listening to ask each other about holidays you had when you were a child.

Grammar and pronunciation

1 I *used to* live in Devon.
2 We never *used to* really go anywhere away from Devon, but instead we'*d* go to the seaside.
3 We'*d* have a good time.
4 For the other part of the year I *used to* live in Rome.
5 'I am for all practical purposes blind in one eye,' he *would* say.

Grammar: *would* and *used to*
(Grammar reference, page 139)

14 **Look at the sentences in the grammar box. Use these words and phrases to complete the explanation of the use of *would* and *used to*.**

time	habit	would	happy	common
used to	past	Would	events	
past	used to	state	cannot	

1 When you talk about ____ habits you can use ____ or ____ instead of the past simple.
2 ____ normally requires a ____ expression, for example: *often / once in a while / every day.*
3 If the ____ you are referring to are ____ memories *would* is slightly more ____ than *used to.*
4 You cannot use *would* to begin reminiscing. You set the scene with the ____ simple or ____.
5 WARNING: You ____ use *would* to talk about a discontinued ____ or past ____ .

Example *She used to have black hair. (NOT: She would have black hair)*
He used to drink wine; now he drinks lager.
(NOT: He would drink wine; now he drinks lager)

Grammar check

15 **Underline the appropriate word to complete the sentences. If both are possible underline both.**

My sister and her husband (*used to/would*) live in Spain when they were first married. They (*used to/would*) work in the centre of Madrid but at the weekend (*used to/would*) often go into the mountains where they (*used to/would*) go walking in summer and skiing in winter. They (*used to/would*) enjoy climbing too but had to give this up when they had their first child.

Pronunciation: sentence stress (1)

16 **English is a stress-timed language, which means that the rhythm of a sentence will depend on the stressed words.**

In any spoken English sentence there are stressed and unstressed words. The stress depends on the importance of the words in the sentence.

26 **Listen to sentence 1 in the grammar box and mark the stressed words.**

Now do the same for the other sentences.
Listen and repeat.

Practice

Bluff!

17 **Write four sentences with *would* and four with *used to* about habits and events when you were younger. Five of the sentences must be true and the other three untrue.**

Example *When I was 16 I used to dye my hair orange.*
When I was a child my father would bring me a cup of tea in bed every morning.

Think about the following topics.

habits	food	holidays
school	free time	family

In pairs take turns to read your sentences. Try to guess which of your partner's sentences are untrue.

Favourite places

18 **Make notes about a favourite place that you used to visit or a house where you used to live during your childhood. What did you do/used to do there that evokes such happy memories?**

Use the vocabulary of descriptions that you studied in exercises 5 and 6.

Now discuss the place with another student. Find out as much as you can about each other's favourite place.

Writing development

Speaking

Town or country?

19 **In groups of three.**
Students A and B are estate agents (people who buy and sell houses).
Student C is a client who wants to buy an unusual house.
Student A wants to sell C a castle on a secluded island.
Student B wants to sell C a mansion in the centre of the town.
Student C is undecided where to live.

1 Students A: Get together in groups and look at the castle on page 135, which you are going to try to convince C to go and see. Think of the advantages of this type of accommodation and living on a lonely island.

  Students B: Get together in groups and look at the mansion on page 137, which you are going to try to convince C to go and see. Think of the advantages of this type of accommodation and living in the town.

  Students C: Get together and discuss the advantages and disadvantages of living in the town and on a secluded island.

2 In groups. Student A: Describe the place that you would like Student C to go and see. Try to convince Student C of the advantages of living in this sort of property and the beauty of the island. When A has finished Student B does the same with the mansion in town. Student C can ask any questions which he or she wants to.

  Students A and B: Criticise each other's proposal and make a last attempt to convince C which place to go and see.
  Student C: Decide which one to go and see.

3 After Student C's decision, all look at the photographs of the two places. Would Student C have made the same decision if she or he had seen the photographs?

Writing

Composition (2)

20 Look back at page 12 for guidelines on composition writing or at the *Guide to better language learning* section on pages 119 -120.

In pairs. Make notes for a composition (150 - 180 words) with this title:

City life is a nightmare. The only way to have an acceptable life style is to live away from the crowds.

Order your notes into paragraphs and make a detailed plan of the contents of each paragraph before you begin writing. Include your plan when you hand in your composition.

happy /ˈhæpɪ/ **happier, happiest** 1 Someone who is **happy** has feelings of pleasure for example because something nice has happened or because they feel satisfied with their life. **happiness** is a derivation of **happy**.

Look at the photographs. Why are these people happy?

In pairs or groups. Discuss the following.

Do you remember feeling happy at any of the times shown in the photographs?
Which one do you identify with most?
Describe something else which makes you feel particularly happy.

Write your own definition of happiness. Compare your definition with those of other students.

41

Listening

1 Read the quotes about happiness. Then listen to Louise and Togo
27 talking about them.

A lifetime of happiness! No man alive could bear it: it would be hell on earth.
George Bernard Shaw

We have no more right to consume happiness without producing it than to consume wealth without producing it.
George Bernard Shaw

There is no greater sorrow than to recall a time of happiness in misery.
Dante

A large income is the best recipe for happiness I have ever heard of.
Jane Austen, Mansfield Park

Travelling is the ruin of all happiness! There's no looking at a building here after seeing Italy.
Fanny Burney

It is better that some should be unhappy than that none should be happy.
Samuel Johnson

Happy is that city which in time of peace thinks of war.
Anon

2 Answer the questions.

1 Which two quotes did Togo choose?
2 What comment did he make about the first one?
3 Why?
4 What comment does he make about money?
5 What three things mean happiness for Togo?

Speaking

3 In pairs. Ask each other these questions from exercises 1 and 2.

1 Which of the quotes were you most interested to read?
2 Why?
3 What do you think people's happiness depends on?
4 What about your quote? Could you define happiness?

Vocabulary

Vocabulary development: happiness

4 **In groups. Add more categories to complete the mind map. Check your completed maps with other groups and add any extra words to your map.**

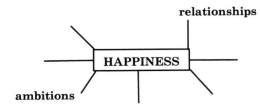

relationships

HAPPINESS

ambitions

Vocabulary building: the suffix -*ship*

5 **The suffix -*ship* is sometimes added to nouns to form new nouns.**

1 **It can be added to nouns which refer to people in a particular occupation or position. The new noun can refer to the state of having that occupation or position:**

Example *owner* (possessor of something)
ownership (the state of owning something)

or to the skill used when people do that job.

Example *sportsman - sportsmanship*

2 **It can also be added to nouns which refer to a relation between two or more people and things.**

Example *comrade - comradeship*

Complete the sentences using one of these nouns in its -*ship* form.

leader   member   craftsman
          relation   friend

1 The way in which two people or groups of people behave towards each other and feel towards each other.
2 The position or state of directing or being in control of a group of people.
3 A relationship between friends.
4 The skill that someone uses when they make something beautiful with their hands.
5 The state of belonging to an organisation.

Pronunciation: plurals (s, z or ız)

6 **Listen to the pronunciation of the final '*s*' in these**
29 **words and note the phonetic symbol.**

relationships(s)   ambitions(z)   houses(ız)

Now listen to the following words.
Which pronunciation does each word have?

books	valleys	flashes	moths	eggs
ducks	noises	lakes	notes	boots
buses	clothes	rings	rooms	hobbies
sports	cases	mountains		

Listen and repeat.

Practice

Guess the word

7 **In pairs.**
Student A: Choose one of the words from the mind map.

1 Give an explanation for the word.
2 Give the number of letters.
3 Give the first letter.
4 Give the last letter.

Student B: Guess the word.
Then change over.

Example Student A: *This is something you use when you buy things.*
It has five letters.
It begins with 'm'.
It ends with 'y'.

Student B: *Money*

Happiness is...

8 **Group poem**
Students sit in groups of six, and each member of the group has a piece of paper. At the top of the paper they write the first line of the poem.

Example *Happiness is sitting by a fire on a cold evening.*

They fold back the paper and pass it to the next student to write the next line without reading what the previous student wrote. The chain continues until each student has the first piece of paper they wrote on. They read out their 'poem' to the group, choose the best six lines and rearrange them to compose a new group poem. They must also think of a title for their poem.

Groups take it in turns to read their poem aloud.

Speaking

9 We often have very strong opinions about famous people without really knowing them at all!

Make a list of famous people you feel strongly about and say what you think about them.
Do you think they're happy?

Reading

Before you read

10 Make a list of the advantages and disadvantages of being Boris Becker. Do you think he's happy?

While you read

11 Find out if the text mentions the same things.

Vocabulary comprehension

12 Word pairs. In each pair one word (marked with a *) is from the text. Find them and say if they are a noun or an adjective. Then try to find a word which has a similar meaning.

prosperity   unseeded*
living   worldly   brand name*
spiritual   glare of publicity   make   material*
wealth*   inner*   unclassified
limelight*   survival*

13 Find expressions in the text to complete each of these sentences.

1 I was astonished: it didn't ____ that you would do such a thing.
2 We drove along the road until we came to ____ and couldn't go any further. We had to turn round and go back.
3 It was just another in ____ of disasters.
4 Although she seemed in control she was just ____, as others made all the decisions for her.

Speaking

14 People who become famous when they are very young often have problems. Why do you think this is?

Do you think Boris Becker will ever be a really happy person? Give reasons for your opinion.

Are famous people often unhappy? Explain why, or why not.

Is it possible for them to avoid unhappiness or change the situation?

Living with my own legend

It all began in September 1987. I was rich, I had all the material things one dreams of - money, wealth, cars, women. I had everything, but I was no longer really successful in tennis. My values were wrong, my tennis was wrong, everything was wrong. I was at a dead end - a street going nowhere. I had won Wimbledon twice, once as the youngest unseeded player. I had a string of successes behind me. However, I was unhappy. It was the old story of movie and pop stars who commit suicide. They have everything - and yet they are so unhappy. They are a lesson to me: Elvis Presley, James Dean and Marilyn Monroe. Their examples cross my mind again and again - and for this reason I read their biographies. I learn from their mistakes and I learn from their strengths. I can only learn from those who are in the limelight because only they live a life comparable to mine.

I shall never forget how I drove back to the hotel the night after Flushing Meadow, across a bridge and around Manhattan, saying to myself: "You're on the wrong path. You must get out. You must change something."

That I did it was a matter of survival to me. I recognised that there are no clear goals for me any more, that the path alone is the goal. My goal was to win Wimbledon - and I did. But the next day, life had to go on. Yet that is not possible if you have reached the goal of your lifetime. You suddenly become depressed. You're the unhappiest man in the world.

I thought about all of this and then I decided that I would only do what I considered correct and what I myself believed in. That year I also realised what was wrong. I recognised why I had no inner peace. I was a product - a puppet on a string.

Maybe my 1987 Wimbledon defeat saved my life. At least it turned me into a different human being. I changed - and I'm still working on it. I changed from the brand name product Boris Becker to the human being Boris Becker.

Grammar and pronunciation

1 You *must* get out. You *must* change something.
2 You *have to* work hard to realise your ambitions.
3 You *need to* live in peace to be happy.
4 You *mustn't* think wealth is more important than good health.
5 You *don't have to* be rich to be happy.
6 You *needn't* be rich to be happy.
   You *don't need to* be rich to be happy.
7 Do you *have to* go now?
   Have you to go now?
   Must you go now?
8 Do you *need to* go now?

Grammar: modal verbs *must, have to, need to*
(Grammar reference, page 140)

15 **Look at sentences 1-3 in the grammar box.**
Which modal is used when the speaker is saying what he/she thinks is necessary?
Which modals often have the same meaning?
Which modal is used for obligation in general?
Which modals show obligation and which necessity?

Look at sentences 4-6 in the grammar box.
Which modal shows obligation not to do something?
Which modals shows that it is not necessary to do something?
Which modal has two forms in the negative?

Look at sentences 7-8 in the grammar box.
Which modals take *do* in the question form?
Which modal can be used with or without *do* in the question form?
Where in the question do you put the modal?

Grammar check
16 **Use information from the table to make true sentences.**

Diabetics British children Overweight people	mustn't need to must have to don't have to	exercise more. stay at school all day. eat too much sugar. go to school on Sundays. ride their bikes on the left.

Pronunciation: 'ea'
17 **In the text about Boris Becker you saw these words which contain 'ea'. They can be divided into three groups.**

r<u>ea</u>lise /ɪə/   p<u>ea</u>ce /iː/   w<u>ea</u>lth /e/

Find six more words in the text which contain 'ea' and add them to the correct group.

30 **Listen and check your answers.**
Which verb can go in two columns depending on the tense?

Practice

Enjoy your free time
18 **In pairs. Complete these sentences and suggest how to make the most of your free time.**
These ideas may help you.

be interested in a lot of things   take up new hobbies
attend courses   watch TV every evening

You must ...   You needn't ...
You mustn't ...   You have to ...
You need to ...   You don't have to ...

Compare your sentences with other students. Add to your list any that you like better.

Giving advice
19 **Student A: Choose an activity that you know a lot about. (Refer back to Unit 3 if you like.)**

Student B: Ask for advice about what you have to do if you want to practise the activity.

Example   *Playing tennis*
Student A   *Do I have to buy an expensive racquet?*
Student B   *No, but you need to buy one which is the right weight for you.*

Then change over.

Writing development

Speaking

20 **What sort of person are you?**

Try our 'Opinions' questionnaire. Circle the letter which coincides with your opinion. Then discuss your answers with another student. Give reasons for your opinion and be prepared to argue!

Key: A = I agree   B = I don't agree   C = it depends

People were happier in 'the past'.	A B C
Strikes are never justified.	A B C
Some jobs can never be done by a woman.	A B C
The quality of life in the country is better than in town.	A B C
Everybody needs a busy social life.	A B C
Caring for old people is the responsibilty of families.	A B C
Planning for the future is a waste of time.	A B C
In thirty years' time nobody will get married.	A B C

In pairs. Prepare a similar questionnaire on one of the following topics.

Entertainment - cinema, music
Food

When you have finished try out your questionnaire on another student. Then write a sentence describing your partner's tastes in music, cinema, or food.

Writing

Informal letters (2)

21 **Answer these questions about letters you write to a friend.**

1 Where do you write your address?
2 Where do you write the date?
3 How do you start a letter to a friend?
4 How do you end the letter? Give three examples.
5 In what ways is the language and layout of a letter to a friend different from a business letter? Give two examples of language and three examples of layout.

22 **Now write a letter to a friend telling him/her about a meal you had, a film you saw, or a concert you went to recently. Include the following points.**

A general paragraph of introduction saying how you and the family are and asking after your friend's health.
A paragraph in which you give your opinions about the meal, film, or concert.
A third paragraph in which you invite your friend to a meal, film, or concert with you.

Say the right thing!
Remembering and helping people to remember

"I remember when we used to do it because it was there. . ."

1 **When people are remembering the past they often begin with the
expression '*I remember...*'.**

I remember breaking a window in my grandmother's house when I was a child.
I remember that house very well.

**Match the first and second halves of the sentences to describe the event.
The first halves on the left are in the correct order.**

1	I remember I was ...	a	cleaned up the mess.
2	Well, the next thing I did was ...	b	she wasn't really angry.
3	Then I ...	c	playing football in my grandmother's garden.
4	Yes, I still remember ...	d	insisted on paying for the window.
5	As far as I can remember ...	e	to kick the ball really hard and break the window.
6	I think I ...	f	the look on my grandmother's face!

**When we are interested in what someone is telling us we ask questions to
have more information. These questions and comments could prompt the
sentences above.**

In pairs use the questions and comments to practise the dialogue.

Example   *I remember I was playing football in my grandmother's garden.
That was a bit dangerous! Did anything happen?*

Oh, yes? What happened?
Oh no! What did you do then?
Did your grandmother see you?
I don't suppose she was very pleased!
Did she punish you?

2 **Listen to the speaker remembering something that happened.**
31 **Make a note of the ways of encouraging the person to go on.**

3 **Write a true sentence about something you remember from your
childhood.**

Example   *I remember falling into a river once.*

In groups. Student A: Say what you remember doing.
**The other students ask as many questions as possible to help Student A
remember the incident.**
Then change over.

Vocabulary

Where you live

1 **Look at the six pictures and describe the scenes.**

Example   *1 A sleepy village on a river in the country.*

In pairs. Compare your sentences. Look at the pictures again. Can you add any more adjectives or nouns and expand the description of each picture using the words you studied in Unit 5?

Happiness

2 **Where do you find most happiness and satisfaction? In your family life, your surroundings, your work or your social life? Write a paragraph saying where you find most happiness and why. Use the vocabulary you studied in Unit 6.**

Grammar

Used to and *would*

3 **Use an element from each column to make as many true sentences about yourself or your family as you can. (You may need to add a time expression in some cases.)**

Example   *I'd sometimes have terrible nightmares when I was younger.*

I My	father mother sister brother	used to would/'d	be overweight as a child. have a cat. sleep with the light on. walk in my/his/her sleep. smoke more than ten cigarettes a day. have terrible nightmares. walk to school every day. play the piano. have long hair as a child. copy my/his/her homework from other children.

Modals: *must, have to, need*

4 **Choose the best alternative for each sentence. Sometimes both are possible.**

1 Look at the notice. It says you *don't have to/mustn't* smoke.
2 David didn't pass his exams: he *has to/must* study harder.
3 After an accident you *have to/must* phone the police.
4 You *mustn't/needn't* come if you don't want to.
5 You *don't need to/mustn't* go yet: it's still quite early.
6 We *don't have to/needn't* go to work tomorrow as it's a public holiday.
7 You *must/need to* get your hair cut: it's looking very long.
8 You *must/need to* give me all your news when we meet.

Guide to better language learning
Part 3 - Listening

If you have problems with listening, or want to improve your technique look at pages 118 - 119.

prejudice /ˈprɛdʒʊdɪs/ 1 **Prejudice** is an unreasonable dislike of or preference for something, for example a particular group of people in society.

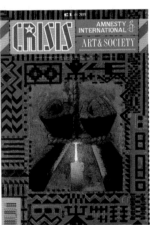

What do you think makes us prejudiced against certain people?
Make a list of five possible reasons.
To what extent is our prejudice conditioned by our upbringing?
Describe what is happening in the pictures and discuss what kind of prejudice the people are encountering.

32 Listen to these people discussing the pictures. Did they come to the same conclusions as you?

Listening

1 **Listen to Dave talking about prejudices. Complete the sentences.**

 1 When Dave was teaching he had to wear a ____ but didn't have to
   wear a ____.

2 He thinks ____ people should wear clothes they feel ____ in.

3 He thinks people form ____ about other people's ____ and ____ from the clothes
   they wear.

4 ____ prejudice is stronger in ____ than in other parts of ____.

5 He also thinks ____ and ____ prejudice still exist in Britain.

6 If he was ____ on a train late at night and saw a man with very ____ hair and
   ____ enter the compartment he would immediately feel ____.

Speaking

2 **Steve and Janet decided to reverse roles after the birth of their first child.
Janet continued her job as a social worker and Steve gave up his job to
look after the baby.**

**In groups. Discuss what sort of prejudices they might have encountered.
Think about the people involved.**

Steve: Can a man successfully substitute a woman as the person most
responsible for looking after the baby?
What difficulties is he likely to encounter?
What about the attitude of his neighbours?
What about his own social life?

Janet: Is it natural for a woman to hand over the care of a small child to a
man?
What difficulties is she likely to encounter?
What difference will it make to her relationship with her husband?

The baby: Will their child suffer in any way?

50

Vocabulary

Vocabulary development: types of prejudice.

3 **In pairs write down as many kinds of prejudice as you can think of. Check your answers with other students.**

Example *class prejudice*

35 **Listen to these people talking about prejudice and add any you haven't got to your list.**

Vocabulary building: nouns ending in -ism

4 **The suffix *-ism* occurs in nouns which refer to particular beliefs or to behaviour based on these beliefs.**

Example *Feminism is the belief that women should have the same rights, power and opportunities as men.*

Read the definitions of words which end in *-ism* and write the missing words.

racism   sexism   cynicism   optimism
pacifism   terrorism

1 This is the belief that members of one sex are inferior to members of the opposite sex.
2 This is the feeling of being hopeful about the future.
3 This is the belief that war and violence are always wrong.
4 This is the belief that some races are inferior to others.
5 This is the use of violence to achieve political aims.
6 This is an attitude towards people in which you expect them to behave in a selfish way.

Can you add any more words ending in *-ism* to the list?

Pronunciation: hard and soft 'g'

5 **Listen to the pronunciation of the letter 'g' in these**
36 **words.**

extravagant /g/ (hard)   age /dʒ/ (soft)

Do these words contain a hard or a soft 'g'?

intelligent   against   lodge   give   get
argument   generous   gin   change   recognise

Listen and check your answers.
Now listen and repeat.

Practice

Connections

6 **In groups. Students take turns to choose two words from the list below, and explain the connection. The group decides if the connection is reasonable.**

war	women	work	black	optimism
appearance	sex	violence	race	peace
terrorism	class	feminism	clothes	guilty
society	pacifism	colour	political	belief

Example *war - peace (war is the opposite of peace)*

Beliefs and characteristics

7 **In groups. Choose four words from exercises 3 and 4, discuss them and write four sentences about each one describing the characteristics.**

Example *(Racism) Black people are often refused work on the basis of the colour of their skin.*

Compare sentences with other students. Add new sentences to your own where possible.

Speaking

8 **Is it important what clothes people wear?**
How are the following people dressed when they are working?

a shop assistant   a doctor
a bank manager   a labourer
a member of a pop group   a chauffeur
a student

Would it matter if they wore different clothes? Discuss and give reasons for your opinion.

Reading

Before you read

9 **Look at the headline.**
What do you think the article is about?

While you read

10 **What clothes do most people in the survey expect**
a) male b) female doctors to wear?

Vocabulary comprehension

11 **Look at the words below and find them in the text.**
Replace each of the words or phrases underlined
with one of these words.

trendy   GP   conservative   research   outfits
smart   casual   confidence   stylish   surgery

1 He decided to go to his <u>doctor</u> because of his persistent cough.
2 She always wore very <u>fashionable and modern</u> clothes.
3 She wears <u>informal</u> clothes when she's at home.
4 The air stewardesses looked <u>pleasantly neat and clean</u> in their new uniforms.
5 She always wears <u>smart, elegant, distinctive</u> clothes.
6 The <u>clothes</u> she wears are always immaculate.
7 I have a lot of <u>faith</u> in his ability to do a good job.
8 Our doctor has his <u>consulting room</u> at the back of the house.
9 My father detests fashionable clothes and always dresses in a very <u>traditional</u> way.
10 After getting his degree he did some <u>detailed study</u> on an aspect of his thesis.

14 ▶

DRESSED TO CURE

Doctors don't normally spring to mind when we think of trendy professionals, but by all accounts that's just as well.
5 We like our GPs to dress conservatively, men preferably in a suit and tie, and lady doctors in a skirt.

These findings come from
10 new research by a Scottish GP, who showed pictures of doctors wearing different outfits to 475 patients. They were asked to rank the outfits in
15 order of preference.

The results showed that most people preferred male doctors to wear a dark suit, or a jacket and tie, while female
20 doctors got the thumbs-up when wearing a white coat or smart skirt and jumper. Older patients and those in
25 the highest social classes were keenest on such conservative wear.
30 Over 60 per cent of the patients said that the appearance of their doctor was important, and
35 more than a quarter of them admitted that they would be unhappy
40 about consulting one of the doctors pictured (usually the woman doctor wearing trousers, or the

45 male doctor in jeans or casual trousers).

Reporting this study in the British Journal of General Practice, the researchers
50 pointed out that it was logical for doctors to dress in a way that inspires confidence in their patients. So, if any stylish doctors are reading this, keep
55 the jeans out of the surgery, please!

Grammar and pronunciation

1 They *were asked* to rank the outfits in order of preference.
2 The research *was conducted by* a Scottish GP.
3 Studies *were carried out with* the help of 475 patients.
4 ... if any stylish doctors *are reading* this, keep the jeans out of the surgery, please!
5 What *do* you do if you *don't agree* with them?

Grammar: past passive
(Grammar reference, pages 140 - 141)

12 Look at sentences 1-3 in the grammar box.
When do you use the past passive?

1 To talk about a person or thing that performed an action?
2 To talk about the person or thing affected by an action?

Choose the correct alternative in italics.

When you use the *active / passive* form you often do not mention the person or thing that performs an action.

***By* or *with*?**
Which word do you use in the passive to mention the person or thing that performs an action?
Which word do you use to mention the thing that is used to perform an action?
What change do you make to put a present passive into the past passive?

Grammar: conditional clauses (1) (If + present + present)
(Grammar reference, page 141)

13 You use conditional clauses to talk about a situation that might happen and to say what its results might be.

Look at sentences 4-5 in the grammar box.
Which tense is used in the *if* clause?

Which tense is used in the other clause?
Which of the following situations does this conditional describe?

Events and situations
- that happen often?
- that may happen in the future?
- that could have happened in the past but did not happen?
- that are unlikely to happen at all?

Grammar check

14 **Complete the sentences with the verbs in brackets. Add *by* or *with* if appropriate.**

1 Rome (*not build*) in a day.
2 He (*present*) a gold watch when he had been with the company for 25 years.
3 They (*give*) a lot of help when they first arrived.
4 The table (*make*) the best wood available.

Complete these sentences using the conditional (*if* + present + present)

1 If I ____ to bed late, I ____ tired all day.
2 What ____ ____ ____ if you ____ late?
3 I usually ____ if I ____.

Pronunciation: *th*

15 **Listen carefully to the pronunciation of 'th' in these**
37 **words from the text.**

think /θ /   these /ð/

Look at these words which contain 'th'. Which pronunciation do they have?

| that | father | three | thumbs |
| this | thank | though | bath |

Listen and check your answers.
Now listen and repeat.

Practice

Difficult situations

16 In pairs. Ask each other what you do in certain difficult situations.
Student A: Look at page 135.
Student B: Look at page 137.
Now invent four more sentences and try them out on other students.

Discrimination or bad luck?

17 Brendan Clark, a successful artist, saw an advertisement for a house in a residential area of Cambridge. He went to see the house, liked it, put down a deposit and at the last minute realised that somebody else had got it. He was not satisfied with the reasons given and took the case to court.
The case is now being discussed.
In groups of four. Look at page 135. Each choose a role. Make notes about yourself, inventing new information where possible. Now act out the situation.

Writing development

Speaking

18 Think of a person who is close to you. It can be a member of your family or a close friend. Imagine you are going to introduce this person to someone. Write down two or three sentences to introduce the person (name, age, profession etc.).

In groups. Sit in a circle and leave one chair empty. The person who is on the right of the space (Student A) has to read the sentences introducing his or her person to the group.

Example *This is my brother. He's twenty five and he's a photographer.*

Everyone else in the group now writes down four questions that they would like to ask this person. They write the questions with *you*.

Example *What sort of photographs do you take?*

(Student A) now sits in the empty chair and 'becomes' the person he or she has introduced. The other members of the group now ask their questions and the person in the chair replies as if he or she were the person he has introduced.

When all the questions have been asked, another student sits next to the empty chair and introduces someone else.

Writing

Writing a biographical description.

19 A biography usually contains the following information.

Date of birth	Place of birth	Education
Work	Hobbies	Town and country of residence

Read this biography of the writer Alison Lurie.

Alison Lurie was born in Chicago, Illinois in 1926, but grew up in New York. A graduate of Radcliffe College, she has received both Guggenheim and Rockefeller grants for her work, and currently teaches and studies children's literature at Cornell University. *Love and Friendship*, her first novel, was published in1962, followed by *The Nowhere City* (1965), *Imaginary Friends* (1967), *Real People* (1970), *The War Between the Tates* (1974), *Only Children* (1979), and a non-fiction work, *The Language of Clothes* (1982). Her most recent novel is *The Truth About Lorin Jones*.
Alison Lurie is based in New York but divides her time between New York, London and Florida.

Now write a similar biography of the astronaut Neil Armstrong using these notes.

Place of birth:	Wapakoneta, Ohio
Date of birth:	1930
Childhood spent in:	Wapakoneta
Education:	Purdue University. Studies interrupted by Korean War
Work:	1955 research pilot
	1962 joined space program
	July 16 1969 Apollo 11 to the Moon with Edwin (Buzz) Aldrin and Michael Collins
	July 20 landed
	21 hours and 37 minutes on moon
	July 24 splashdown in Pacific
	tour of 27 nations

Write a biography of the person you introduced to the other people in your group in exercise 18. (150 — 180 words)

morality/mərælɪtɪ/ **moralities**. Morality is the idea
that some forms of behaviour are right, proper and
acceptable and that other forms of behaviour are bad or
wrong, either in your own opinion or in the opinion of society.

Look at the photos.

Decide if they are examples of mischief, delinquency, vandalism, or stealing.

If they do not fit any category put a question mark.

In groups discuss your answers. Try to agree on a category for the ones with question marks.

Where do you draw the line between 'innocent' fun and serious offences?

Is it a question of age?

Is it a question of degree of seriousness?

Can you really draw the line between them?

Reading

Before you read

1 **In this extract from his autobiography, James Galway, the flute player, describes some of the things he and his friends did when they were young. In groups discuss and make a list of the kind of naughty or mischievous things children might do.**

While you read

2 **Find out if James Galway and his friends did any of the things you listed. Find out what they took and what they did when they got them.**

Looking back, I seemed to have the makings of a delinquent - although to be serious, I suppose there is a wide gulf between delinquency and the simple pranks I got involved in. Near our street were two establishments that intrigued us. One was Johnny Rankin's rag store which was full of old rabbit skins and things like that which we delighted in occasionally nicking, and the other was Mercer's Bakery where you could actually see them baking the bread as you walked past the window. Eventually I figured out that the back wall of Mercer's adjoined the top of our street. So a bunch of us got hammers and, when it got dark, knocked a few bricks out of the wall and got into the bakery where we proceeded to nick some of the cakes and buns. After this we would pinch a few potatoes, carrots and things like that from somewhere, light a wee fire and have a real banquet. It was days before Mercer's cottoned on to the fact that somebody was climbing in at the back and lifting their buns. The wall was then bricked up again and 'inquiries', as they say, were made, but we were never found out.

Vocabulary comprehension

3 **Find the words on the left in the text and match them to the appropriate word or phrase on the right.**

1	gulf	a	shop
2	pranks	b	was very close to
3	establishments	c	steal
4	store	d	small
5	nicking	e	foolish tricks
6	figured out	f	began to understand
7	adjoined	g	stealing
8	bunch	h	stealing
9	pinch	i	significant difference
10	wee	j	feast
11	banquet	k	group
12	cottoned on to	l	shops or businesses
13	lifting	m	discovered by thinking
14	found out	n	discovered

Vocabulary

Vocabulary development: crime

4 **Put the words below under the appropriate heading.
Add any other words you can think of to the lists.**

burglary   steal   theft   pick up   pick-pocket
take   crook   robbery   find out   burglar
nick   catch   lift   thief   imprison   pinch
vandal   delinquent   rob   arrest   criminal
mugging   robber   shop-lifting

Crimes	People	Crime verbs	Possible Results

Vocabulary building: nouns ending in -ment

5 **The suffix -ment is sometimes added to verbs to form
nouns. These nouns usually refer to the process of
making or doing something, or to the result of this
process.**

Example   *imprison*   *imprisonment*

**Write the verb and the noun for the following. You can
use your dictionary to help you.**

1   Succeed in after a lot of effort
2   Give someone money for something
3   Give work to someone
4   Disagree with someone
5   Make something better

**Make a list of other words that you know ending
in -ment.**

Pronunciation: hard and soft c

6 **Listen to the pronunciation of the letter 'c' in these
words from the text.**

occasionally (k)   proceeded (s)

Do these words have a hard 'c' or a soft 'c'?

Mercer's   could   actually   cakes   fact
civil   became   decide   secure   clever

Listen and check your answers.
Listen and repeat.

**The pronunciation of 'c' always depends on the letter
which follows it.**

1   Before which vowels is 'c' pronounced 's'?
2   Before which vowels is it pronounced 'k'?
3   What is the pronunciation of 'c' before a consonant?
4   Does the rule change when 'c' is at the beginning of the
    word?

Practice

Invent a sentence

7 **In teams. Choose verbs from the list on page 136.
In turns read one of your verbs to the other team.
They give the noun formed from the verb and invent a
sentence including this noun. (You can only use a verb
once.)**

**If they get the noun they get one point. If the sentence
is logical and correct, they get another point. The
team with most points is the winner.**

Example   *improve - improvement*
              It had rained all day but showed signs of
              improvement towards evening.

Guessing meanings

8 **In pairs.**
Student A: Choose a word from exercises 4 and 5.
Define the word.
Student B: Guess the word.
Then change over.

Example   **Student A:**   *This is a person who breaks
                            into a house to steal something.*
              Student B: *A burglar.*

Listening

9 Listen to Togo and Tony talking about morality.

39 Which of the things pictured here has Tony done? Put the things he has done in the order he talks about them.

Listen again. What does Tony say about stealing by children and stealing by adults?

▶ 16

Speaking

10 Look at the illustrations. Choose one of the things which you have done. Talk about it to another student.
Say:
when it happened
what exactly you did
if you were caught
if you ever did it again

Grammar and pronunciation

1 Have you ever driven the wrong way up a one-way street?

2 Yes I have. I did it last week.

3 If you see some Mars bars on your way home tonight what will you do?

4 I'll definitely take one or two.

Grammar: present perfect and past simple
(Grammar reference, page 141)

11 Look at sentences 1 and 2 in the grammar box.

Why does the speaker use the present perfect tense in question 1?

Why does the speaker in sentence 2 use the past simple in the answer to question 1?

Which of these words is usually used with the present perfect and which with the past simple?

since   ago   ever   never   once
yesterday   recently   from ...   to ...

Grammar: conditional clauses (2) ('if' + present + future)

(Grammar reference, page 142)

12 **Look at sentences 3 and 4 in the grammar box. When do you use this conditional?**

1 To talk about a situation which may exist in the future?
2 To talk about a situation which you know does not exist?
3 To talk about a situation where the result is generally true or happens often?

Grammar check

13 **Choose words from each column and write sentences.**

We
They
I
	have been
	went
	have never
	  studied
	have seen
	saw
	lived
	played
		in/to the
		  mountains
		a lovely car
		in/to Paris
		tennis
		a good film
		Greek
		near London
			from 1990 to
			  1992.
			since I was a child.
			last week.
			a year ago.
			once.
			outside.
			every week.

14 **Complete the sentences with the correct form of the verbs in brackets. (Use *will/won't* or present simple.)**

1 If you (*ring*) from the station I (*come*) and meet you.
2 What you (*do*) if (*it be*) late?
3 I'm sure you (*enjoy*) the film if you (*go*).
4 If I (*see*) her I (*not say*) anything.
5 If she (*phone*) tell her I (*be back*) at three.

Pronunciation: rising and falling intonation

15 **Listen to the pronunciation of sentence 3 in the grammar box. Listen and repeat. The tone of voice fell after *bars* and *tonight* and there was a pause before the rest of the sentence. These are hesitation pauses.**

41

Now listen to this sentence.
What will you do if he comes?

Listen and repeat.
In this sentence there was no noticeable fall in the tone of the voice and no distinct pause.

There is usually a pause and a fall in intonation where there is a comma separating two clauses.
Listen to this sentence.
If Tom goes, I'll go too.

Listen and repeat.

There is usually a pause and rise in intonation after commas separating a list of items.
Listen to this sentence.
I bought some oranges, apples, nuts and a litre of milk.

Listen and repeat.

Now read these sentences aloud and then listen to check your answers.

1 What will you do if it rains?
2 If it rains, I'll go to the cinema.
3 You can see him when he comes.
4 We'll go to the cinema, out for a meal, or just stay at home: whatever you like.

Practice

Honesty

16 **Here are the answers to a questionnaire about honesty. In pairs work out the original questions.**

1 Yes, I have. Once when the train was full and there was no room in the second class carriages.
2 Yes, I have. I once found £20. I shared it with my friend.
3 Yes, I have. I think most people use the phone at work for private conversations now and again.
4 No, I haven't. I always pay my taxes.
5 No, I haven't. Most of the stuff that you find in hotels isn't worth taking.
6 Yes, I have. When I lived in London. I don't think many people bought a ticket actually.
7 Yes, I have. I think the speed limit in some parts of town is ridiculously low.
8 Yes, I have. Once somebody gave me the wrong rate of exchange in a bank. They got one of the noughts wrong, so I kept the extra.

Now take it in turns to ask each other the questions. Give complete answers explaining the circumstances. Invent another three similar questions together. Try out your new questions on other students.

What will you do?

17 **In pairs. Student A: You are planning to go and live in Britain for a year.**
Student B: You are not sure this is wise. Ask about these things.

accommodation   work   home sickness
the language   the food

Example Student A: *What will you do if you can't find a flat?*
Student B: *I'll stay in a hostel.*
Then change over.

Writing development

Speaking

18 The social services committee went to their local Member of Parliament to talk about improving living conditions for old people in the town. Here are some of the answers the politician gave.
In pairs decide what questions they asked.

1 I don't think they have too many problems, really.
2 No there really isn't enough, I suppose.
3 Yes some of them must be quite lonely.
4 Well, there is a day centre.
5 In the centre of the High Street.
6 No, no transport.
7 Well, I suppose they have to rely on other people to take them.
8 There's a TV lounge, and a games room.
9 No. You see we don't have any space outside for that sort of thing.
10 Yes, that's true. We could use the park which isn't far away.
11 I think you should put your ideas into a letter and send it to me.

When you have finished, work with another student.
Student A: You are a member of the social services committee.
Student B: You are the Member of Parliament. Invent new answers to the questions.
Then change over.
As a class compile the best set of questions.

Writing

Formal letters (2)

19 Write a letter to James Barther MP at The City Hall, Blakeney Square, Newtown complaining about the present conditions and facilities for old people.

Write a paragraph for each of the following points.

a Refer to your previous meeting with the MP.
b Write down the points that you raised in exercise 18 and the MP's reaction to them.
c Say what you think the MP should do next.

You should be determined but polite in your letter.
Here are some expressions that are useful when you are writing a letter of complaint.

With reference to our meeting of ...
We talked about ...
We suggested ...
You stated that ...
At the moment there is no ....
We agreed ...
We sincerely hope that ...

Say the right thing

Hesitating

Most people hesitate when they are speaking. Hesitation gives you time to think about what you are saying and find the best way of expressing yourself.

"Er . . . mind if we swear?"

 1 **Listen to these people talking. Which hesitation devices do you hear?**

er
um
I mean...
What was it?
Let me see...
you know
you know what I mean
the thing is...
you see...
sort of...
well...

2 **Conversation pieces.**
In groups. Give each other topics to talk about unprepared. It is not important to give information but you must use as many hesitation devices as possible. The best speaker is the one who avoids silence. Here are some suggestions but you can choose anything!

Money
Happiness
Ambition
Free time
Education
Life in the year 2050

Vocabulary

Types of prejudice

1 **Read the statements and write the prejudice words.**

1 If you think people are inferior because of the colour of their skin.

2 If you think only women (or men) can do certain jobs.

3 If you are not happy about your son's long hair and strange clothes.

4 If you think people from one part of your country are inferior to those from another part of your country.

5 If you think people who have less money than you are inferior.

6 If you wouldn't feel happy with your bank manager if he wore jeans and had long hair.

Crime vocabulary

2 **Complete the paragraph using words from exercise 4 in Unit 8.**

Incidents of c____ involving young people have risen sharply over the last few years. There were three cases of b____ in our street last week, always when the family were out of the house. Fortunately the b____ were a____ and so people are a bit more relaxed now. Then there was a case of v____; going around smashing shop windows not, it seems, to s____ anything but just for the fun of it! It sometimes looks as if our young people are turning into a group of d____!

Grammar

Past passive

3 **When you checked into a hotel you found your bedroom in a real mess. You changed hotel immediately. Write a formal letter to the manager of Sea View Hotel, Main Street, Brighton, complaining about the service.**
These are some of the things that were wrong.

You asked for a quiet room overlooking garden: given room overlooking busy road

Bed not made

Towels in bathroom not changed

Ash trays not emptied

Window broken

Conditional clauses (1)

4 **What do you usually do in these situations? Use the beginnings of these sentences to write true statements about yourself.**

1 If I am very depressed, I...

2 If someone makes me angry, I...

3 If I want to go out and celebrate a special occasion, I...

4 If friends come and visit me unexpectedly, I...

5 If I have visitors from another country, I...

6 If I have a very hard day at work, in the evening I...

7 If I feel very happy, I...

8 If I'm under stress from work, I...

Irregular verb game

5 **In pairs. Choose five irregular verbs.**
Student A: Give Student B a verb in the infinitive.
Student B: Supply the past simple and the past participle of the verb. Now make a sentence about yourself with the past simple or past participle of the verb. When Student A has finished the list of five verbs, change roles.

Conditional clauses (2)

6 **Match the first and second halves of these sentences.**

1 I won't say that I saw you ...	a	leave a message on the answerphone.
2 If I see Mary ...		
3 Will the neighbours look after the cat ...	b	if you don't want me to.
	c	I'll tell her you rang.
4 If you speak more clearly ...	d	if you go to New York.
5 Will you start cooking dinner ...	e	I'll be able to understand.
6 If I'm not in ...	f	while you are away?
7 What will you do ...	g	if you get home before me?
8 You will certainly see the Statue of Liberty ...	h	if you miss the last bus?

Guide to better language learning: Part 4 - Reading

If you have difficulty knowing how to approach reading, or want to improve your technique look at page 119.

Love is 1 very strong feelings of affection towards someone who you are romantically or sexually attracted to. 2 the feeling that a person's happiness is very important to you, and the way you show this feeling in your behaviour towards them.

What do these pictures all have in common?
Make a list of different types of love.

Example   *love for a pet animal*

What types of love do the photos represent?
When you have finished compare and discuss your description of the photos with another student.

Reading

Before you read

1 Discuss. Is love always a positive experience? Give your reasons. What's the best 'cure for love' in your opinion?

While you read

2 Which mental disturbance does the writer compare love to? Which three methods of treatment does he suggest?

Vocabulary comprehension

3 Find the words in the text and choose the correct definition for the context.

1 *run-up*
  a the running approach made by an athlete before jumping, throwing etc.
  b the period of time and the events that happen before an event.

2 *palms*
  a trees which are usually very tall, have no branches and a mass of leaves that grow out of the top of them.
  b the inside of your hands between the fingers and wrist.

3 *breathlessness*
  a the state of being hardly able to breathe because you are afraid or excited.
  b difficulty in breathing because you have been running or because you are ill

4 *smitten*
  a if you are smitten you find someone so attractive that you are or seem to be in love with them.
  b if you are smitten by something you are very impressed and enthusiastic about it.

5 *failure*
  a an unsuccessful person, action or thing.
  b a lack of success in a particular area or activity.

6 *treatable*
  a curable by means of medical attention.
  b easily handled or dealt with.

7 *remedy*
  a a successful way of dealing with a problem or difficulty.
  b something that is intended to cure you when you are ill or in pain.

8 *underlying*
  a situated below something else.
  b not obvious; requiring effort to discover or reveal.

4 In pairs. Find these phrases in the text. Discuss their meaning and write an explanation for each of them.

1 make a fool of yourself
2 reared its head
3 works a treat
4 gets my vote as well
5 give up the fight
6 open an account

 17 ▶

Speaking

5 What type of love is the doctor describing in the article according to your definitions on page 63?
Discuss the doctor's view of love. Do you agree with him? Give reasons.

A CURE FOR LOVE  In the run-up to St Valentine's Day
5 the shops are full of greetings cards which display two naked children and some
10 platitude such as 'Love is - never having to say you're sorry.' That's not love - most people in love spend their whole time having to apologise to each other. Love is something else
15 entirely. Love is 'palpitations and breathlessness. It is dryness of the mouth, dampness of the palms, tremor, weakness and confusion.' I found this list of symptoms in a textbook of psychiatry under 'Anxiety'. The description continues for another
20 page or so and most of it seems to fit pretty well: 'feeling of apprehension ... obsessional thoughts' (yes), 'commoner in women than men' (debatable), 'some genetic predisposition' (probably), 'antecedents include ... prolonged drinking and lone-
25 liness' (certainly).

On this evidence you could make a pretty good case for the fact that love, or at least the feeling of being hopelessly smitten, is closely related to fear. Love is anxiety - anxiety about rejection, anxiety
30 about failure, anxiety that you are about to make a fool of yourself. Love is a panic attack. This may sound cynical but in fact it's very good news for lovers the world over because anxiety is eminently treatable.

35 There are three types of remedy for anxiety: environmental change, physical treatment and psychotherapy. In Victorian times, whenever love reared its head, environmental change was most commonly prescribed. Six months in Mauritius still
40 works a treat. Under 'Physical Treatment', modern textbooks include 'vigorous exercise ... and dance therapy', which gets my vote as well: jumping up and down at some awful disco usually leaves you too knackered for the 2 am detour past your loved one's
45 flat. Psychotherapy is a complex subject, but the basic idea here is that 'the patient should be encouraged to look at the underlying problems and take the necessary decisions'. Most of us lack such heroic resolve and give up the fight, book the
50 restaurant for Wednesday the 14th and open an account at Interflora. If you have chosen this route you are beyond medical help.

Vocabulary

Vocabulary development: feelings and emotions

6 Listen to the list of nouns. Write each word in the
43 appropriate column.

POSITIVE		NEGATIVE	
Noun *happiness*	Adjective	Noun *dislike*	Adjective

Now complete the second column with the equivalent
adjective for each noun.
Note: *dislike* and *well-being* have no equivalent
adjective.
Listen and check your answers.
Can you add any other words describing emotions and
feelings to the list above?

Vocabulary building: nouns ending in -ness

7 The suffix *-ness* combines with some adjectives to
form nouns that refer to the state or quality
described by the adjective.
A final *y* is replaced by *i* before adding *-ness*.
Make these adjectives into nouns.

bitter   friendly   happy   lonely
nervous   sad   tender

Practice

Love and friendship

9 Which emotions and feelings are characteristic of
loving or being in love and which are characteristic of
friendship?
In pairs. Look at the words in exercise 6 again and
make two lists. Compare your lists with another pair
of students. Have you got similar results?
Add up the number of negative words in each column.
Which column has the greater number of negative
words?
Discuss in groups of four. Which of the two states
(loving or being in love) is the healthier?

Edward Hopper

10 Look at these paintings by Edward Hopper. Discuss
these questions.

1 What is the relationship between the people in the pictures ?
2 What are the emotions and feelings of the people in the
paintings? Write down two or three words for each person.

Now compare your answers with a student from
another group. Did you agree?
45 Listen to these people doing the same activity. Did
they have the same answers as you?

Pronunciation: *ie* and *ei*

8 Listen to the pronunciation of 'ie' and 'ei' in these
44 words.
receive /iː/   anxiety /aɪ/   patient /ə/   tie / aɪ/
veil /eɪ /   earlier /ɪə/   height /aɪ /

Listen and repeat.

Which pronunciation do these words have?
Note: Some of the words have different spellings but
the same pronunciation.

cried   weight   perceive   piece   believe   alienate
supplier   sufficient   either (2 pronunciations)

Try to write more *ie* or *ei* words under the headings.
Note: *Friend* /e / and words based on it are exceptions.
There are no other *ie* or *ei* words with the same
pronunciation.

Listen and check your answers.

Speaking

11 **How would you define true friendship?**
In pairs. Ask the questions and fill in the chart for your partner.
Which of these things would you do for or to a friend?

a Lend him/her money?
b Lend him/her your car?
c Talk about him/her behind his/her back?
d Be prepared to listen to him/her talking about his/her problems?
e Feel able to trust him/her completely?
f Tell lies to protect him/her?
g Tell others something he/she told you in confidence?
h Steal for him/her?

Yes, definitely	Yes, maybe	Probably not	Definitely not

Discuss in pairs. Which answers do you think are necessary to say that a person is a true friend?

Listening

Before you listen

12 **You are going to hear Kathy talking about friendship. Nimue asked the question:**
If you had to choose the three most important qualities in a friend, what would those qualities be?
Can you predict what those qualities will be?

While you listen

13 **Make a note of the three qualities Kathy mentioned.**

46 **Listen again. Kathy talks about English people and Americans. How does she describe English people? How does she describe Americans?**

18 ▶

Speaking

14 **Ask as many people as possible the question from the listening. If you had to choose the three most important qualities in a friend, what would those qualities be?**
Do they expect the same qualities as you?

Grammar and pronunciation

1 If you had to choose the three most important qualities in a friend, what would those qualities be?
2 If I found out that somebody wasn't loyal to me, I'd leave them.
3 I've been living here for fifteen years.
4 She's been studying English since she was ten years old.

Grammar: conditional clauses (3) (*if* + past simple + *would*)
(Grammar reference, page 142)

15 **Look at sentences 1 and 2 in the grammar box. Are these statements true or false?**

1 These sentences describe a hypothetical situation which may exist in the future.
2 The *if* clause can come before or after the main clause.
3 You can use *would* in the *if* clause as well.
4 The *if* clause needs a main clause to make a complete sentence.
5 These sentences describe a situation which is generally true or happens often.

Grammar: present perfect continuous
(Grammar reference, page 142)

16 **Look at sentences 3 and 4 in the grammar box. In which three explanations do you use the present perfect continuous?**

1 To talk about actions which began in the past, have finished, but the results are visible?
2 To talk about the results of something which happened at a definite time in the past?
3 To talk about actions which began in the past and are still in progress at the time of speaking?

4 To talk about repeated actions up to the present?
5 To talk about specific moments in the past?

Grammar check

17 **Make sentences using the chart below.**

If I	(meet) someone famous (see) a burglar (have) the choice (find) a lot of money (need) help	I	travel round the world faint scream phone the police shout for joy

18 **Complete the sentences using the verbs in brackets in the present perfect continuous tense.**

1 Oh, look, the ground's all white: it (*snow*)
2 I (*think*) a lot about you recently.
3 She (*wait*) for an hour and she's still there.
4 Look how red he is! He (*lie*) in the sun too long.

Pronunciation: voiced and unvoiced consonants.

19 **When a consonant is voiced you feel your vocal chords vibrate as you say it. Listen to these words.**

[48]

<u>b</u>ark (*consonant 'b' voiced*) <u>p</u>ark (*consonant 'p' unvoiced*)

Look at these pairs of words. Tick the word in each pair which contains a voiced consonant. Then listen and check your answers.

zoo - Sue   service - surface   die - tie   glue - clue
    waiting - wading   fail - veil   price - prize

Listen to the groups of words and pick out the word which sounds different.

Example *a zoo* *b <u>Sue</u>* *c zoo* *d zoo*

Practice

Reactions

20 **Write the *if* clauses for these sentences.**

Example *If a friend told me lies, I'd feel angry.*

1 ... I'd feel angry.
2 ... I'd feel incredibly happy.
3 ... I'd feel very lonely.
4 ... I'd be very worried.
5 ... I'd be very disappointed.
6 ... I'd consider it a sign of great friendship.
7 ... I'd be very jealous.
8 ... I'd be very frightened.

Now invent questions based on your answers to see if your partner would feel the same as you.

Problems at work

21 **In pairs. Discuss what you would do in this situation.**

Someone at work has been annoying you with a 'nervous whistle'. They have been very tense and irritable recently. The whistle has been preventing you from concentrating.

Work together and invent some more difficult situations. Use the present perfect continuous in each of your situations at least once. Here are some possible starting points.

smoking   window open/closed   late   stealing

When you have written five situations, work with other students and try them out.

Writing development

Speaking

22 What have these films got in common?

Discuss in groups. What makes a good love story?

Write a list of ingredients which are common to nearly all love stories.

Think about the following points.

first meeting   obstacles   unforeseen events   conclusion

Look at the photographs on page 137. Work in pairs. Choose one of the people but don't tell your partner which one. (One of you must be a man and the other a woman).

Invent a 'life' for the person you have chosen. Invent a name, age, job, family situation, ambitions, disappointments etc.

Now imagine that you 'are' this person. You meet your partner's person on a train. You want to talk to him/her. What do you say? Act out the situation.

Writing

23 Good dialogue is also important in a love story. Look at this section from a telephone conversation in *Valediction*, a detective novel by Robert B Parker. Spenser, the detective, is based in Boston, while his girlfriend, Susan, has gone to live in California.

When you write dialogue it is important to use the correct punctuation.
How do you distinguish speech from other writing in English?
How is the comma used when writing dialogue?
How can you tell who is speaking in the dialogue?

What information do you get from the dialogue about the following?

1 The relationship between the narrator, Spenser and Susan.
2 Susan's other relationship
3 What has happened in the story up to this point.
4 What is going to happen next.

Write the dialogue for the scene at Boston airport when Susan comes back from Los Angeles and meets Spenser.

In pairs. Write the continuation of the love story between the two characters you invented in exercise 22. Include all the ingredients of good love stories that you listed. Use dialogue where necessary.

'He's gone,' Susan said.
It was like not drowning. I took a breath. *Steady*.
'He's gone back to his wife,' she said.
'He's got a wife?'
'Yes.' Susan's voice was tiny.

And then her voice wasn't small. 'I will not leave you,' she said.
'In a manner of speaking.'
I could hear the smile in her voice. 'In a manner of speaking.'
'He wanted to move in?' I said.
'He wanted to divorce his wife and marry me.'
'And you wouldn't.'
Again the strength. 'I will not leave you,' she said.
'Nor I you,' I said.

marriage /ˈmærɪdʒ/, **marriages**. 1 a **marriage** is
1.1 the relationship between a husband and wife
EG *It has been a happy marriage ...*

1.2 the act of marrying someone, or the ceremony
at which this is done. EG *I was one of her brides-
maids at the marriage ...*

2 **Marriage** is the state of being married

**What aspect of the marriage ceremony is taking place in these
photographs? What is the significance of these rituals?
In which countries are these marriages taking place?**

In which countries are the following statements about marriage true?

1 Two out of three marriages end in divorce.
2 It is not possible to get divorced.
3 It is common for the husband and wife to see each other for the first time at the
   marriage ceremony.
4 The couples exchange gold rings during the ceremony.
5 It is not unusual for the husband to have more than one wife.

Reading

Before you read

1 **In groups answer the questions.**

Who is Superman?
Who is Clark Kent?
Who is Lois Lane?

While you read

2 **Find out the following information.**

1 The year in which 'Superman' appeared for the first time.
2 The reason Lois accepted Clark Kent's proposal.
3 The reason Superman never asked her to marry him.

Superman comes down to earth with a proposal

From CHARLES BREMNER IN NEW YORK

AFTER half a century thinking about it, Clark Kent has finally put aside his mild manner, summoned his nerves of steel, and asked Lois Lane for her hand in marriage.
5 Faster than a speeding bullet, she accepted.

DC Comics, which has tracked Superman's exploits since he hit the drawing board in 1938, broke news of the betrothal ahead of the publication of the historic strip
10 on November 1. "End of an era" was the verdict of television news broadcasts yesterday.

Lois takes pity on her fellow reporter at the Daily Planet and consents to his bumbling
15 proposal. She remains unaware that the meek Kent is the alter ego of America's original superhero.

But in a move that shocked the faithful, the publishers said yesterday that Kent will
20 eventually reveal to his fiancée the secret that she should have guessed years ago. After years of barely tolerating her feeble colleague, she has come to realise that Kent is "always there when she needs him",
25 according to the DC Comics announcement.

The writing team originally envisaged having Lois say no because she still loves the man of steel but then relented because
30 "she may have been rough and mean on Clark Kent over the years but it was always work-related". For most of the past 50 years, Lois has burned with an unrequited passion for Superman.
35 Only in one of the films was the passion consummated. The usual brush-off went like this: "I'd like to be in your arms always, Superman, (sigh)!" she told the fighter for truth, justice and the American way, when
40 he rescued her from one scrape a couple of decades ago. "Uh, Sorry Lois, but you know the answer to that," Superman replied. "My life is a constant round of superaction and danger and only a super-
45 girl could keep up with me!"

Kent takes the fateful decision after losing his superpowers in a brush with the dreaded red Kryptonite. Reduced to the level of ordinary mortal, he opts for married life. At
50 least, it means he no longer needs to hunt for telephone booths in a country which long ago abandoned them. "It's not a gag, not a one-issue trick story," said the publishers. "This time, for the first time
55 since the characters were created, it's for real."

"Listen, I'd better go. That guy's still waiting to get his clothes."

Vocabulary comprehension

3 **Match the words from the text on the left to their equivalents on the right.**

1	half a century	a	agrees
2	exploits	b	second self
3	betrothal	c	changed their minds
4	consents	d	brave actions
5	bumbling	e	joke
6	unaware	f	not reciprocated
7	alter ego	g	fifty years
8	barely	h	clumsy
9	feeble	i	scarcely
10	envisaged	j	difficult situation
11	relented	k	engagement to be married
12	unrequited	l	imagined
13	brush-off	m	chooses
14	scrape	n	weak
15	opts for	o	rejection
16	gag	p	oblivious

19▶

Vocabulary

Vocabulary development 1: marriage

4 **In groups complete the marriage mind map. Use these words and any others you can think of. Check your answers with other students. Some words can go in more than one category.**

get married	reception	wedding	guests
in-laws	registry office	couple	honeymoon
proposal	bride/bridegroom		presents
church	ring	fiancé(e)	

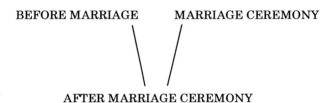

BEFORE MARRIAGE   MARRIAGE CEREMONY

AFTER MARRIAGE CEREMONY

Vocabulary development 2: family relationships

5 **Look at the family-tree.**

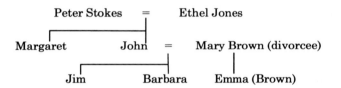

Peter Stokes = Ethel Jones

Margaret   John = Mary Brown (divorcee)

Jim   Barbara   Emma (Brown)

In-laws

The relatives of your husband/wife are your *in-laws*.
Peter Stokes is Mary's *father-in-law*.
Mary is Peter and Ethel Stokes' *daughter-in-law*.
Margaret Stokes is Mary's *sister-in-law*.

Remarriage

John is Emma's *stepfather*.
Emma is John's *stepdaughter*.
Emma is Jim and Barbara's *half-sister*.

Vocabulary building: compound adjectives

6 **Compound adjectives are made up of two or more nouns or adjectives and are frequently written with a hyphen between them.**

Lois's problems with Kent were mostly *work-related*.

Note:

1 A noun which is used as part of a compound adjective remains in the singular even if the meaning is plural.

Example *We went for a five-mile walk.*

2 Numbers can be written in words or figures.

Now look at these examples.

A woman with dark hair.   A dark-haired woman.
A child who behaves well.   A well-behaved child.
A person between fifty and sixty.   A middle-aged person.
A family which has two cars.   A two-car family.

Pronunciation 'ou'

7 **Listen to these five ways of pronouncing the vowels** **49** **'ou'. Listen and repeat.**

announcement /aʊ/   country /ʌ/   should /ʊ/
cough /ɒ/   bought /ɔː/

Which pronunciation do these words have?

could	couple	enough	loud	sound
bough	round	would		count
thought	rough	about	house	trough

Listen and check your answers.

Practice

Guess the word

8 **In pairs. Student A: Choose one of the words from exercises 4 and 5.**
1 Give an explanation for the word.
2 Give the number of letters.
3 Give the first letter.
4 Give the last letter.

Student B guess the word.
Then change over.
Example Student A   *This is the marriage ceremony*
It has seven letters.
It begins with 'w'.
It ends with 'g'.
Student B   *Wedding.*

Preparations

9 **In pairs. You are planning a family celebration.**
1 **Decide what celebration it is (e.g. birthday, welcome home, wedding).**
2 **Discuss the things you have to do beforehand. Make a list. These ideas will start you off.**

invitations (what sort of invitation?)
guest list (how many family/friends?)
food (buffet/sit down meal?)
shopping (food, drinks?)
entertainment (music, games?)

Speaking

10 **What factors are important for people to be compatible? Consider these things.**

the same kind of lifestyle
a similar education
the same interests
about the same age
the star sign they were born under
their personality (similar or very different?)

What other factors do you think contribute to compatibility?

Listening

11 **Listen to Kathy talking about her marriage. Are these statements true or false?**

1 Kathy was married in the States.
2 Kathy finished studying before she got married.
3 Her life didn't change much after she got married.
4 Her marriage consisted of good times and bad times.
5 She thinks friendship between husband and wife is very important.
6 She thinks there is pressure on people not to get married now.

Listen again. What three things does Kathy think help to make a successful marriage?

20 ▶

Grammar and pronunciation

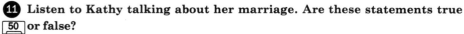

1 What had you achieved by the time you got married?
2 I'd finished college before I got married.
3 By the time I got married, I'd done a lot of travelling.
4 Would your life have been very different if you hadn't got married?
5 Of course it would have been different.
6 I wouldn't have any children.
7 I wouldn't be living in this country.

Grammar: past perfect tenses
(Grammar reference, page 142)

12 **Look at sentences 1-3 in the grammar box. Underline the past perfect tense in each sentence. What difference in form is there between this tense and the present perfect?**

You use the present perfect form to relate the past to the present. Which of the following explanations of the past perfect tense is more accurate?

a To talk about a situation that happened in the past.
b To talk about a situation which happened before a particular time in the past.

Grammar: conditional clauses (4): *if* + past perfect + *would have* + past participle
(Grammar reference, page 142)

13 **Look at sentences 5-7 in the grammar box. Which clause completes the answers?**

a if I didn't get married.
b if I hadn't got married.
c if I haven't got married.
d if I'm not married.

Which use does this conditional have?

a to talk about something which often happens or is generally true.
b to talk about something which may happen in the future.
c to talk about something unlikely to happen.
d to talk about something which could have happened in the past but didn't.

Grammar check

14 Complete the sentences using the expressions in the box.

would be	had finished	would have come
wouldn't be able	'd studied	had realised
would have been	arrived	came
hadn't lived	had known	'd travelled
wouldn't have started		

1 We ____ lunch by the time he ____.
2 She ____ if she ____ her sister ____ there.
3 I ____ to speak Japanese if I ____ in Japan.
4 It ____ different if I ____ harder at school.
5 Before he ____ to live here he ____ round the world.
6 If I ____ it was so difficult I ____.

Pronunciation: sentence stress

15 In spoken English some words or syllables are given
[52] **more stress than others depending on their importance in the sentence.**

Look at sentence 6 in the grammar box. Which is the most important word in that sentence? This word is given more stress. Listen to the sentence.

Now say the same sentence but stress the fact that you wouldn't have any children even if other people did. Underline the stressed word now.

Listen and check your answer.

Look at sentence 7 in the grammar box.

I wouldn't be living in this country.

The important word here is *country*.

What would the meaning of the sentence be if you put the stress on the word *living*?

Now look at this sentence.

Mary came to live here five years ago.

You will hear the sentence four times. Which meaning does it have each time?

a She didn't come six years ago.
b She didn't come five months ago.
c She didn't come on holiday.
d John didn't come.

Practice

Call my bluff

16 Write six sentences about yourself using the ages and the information below. Include some false information. In pairs guess the false sentences.

Example Student A: *By the age of eighteen my sister had finished studying.*
 Student B: *I don't think that's true.*
 Student A: *No, she finished studying when she was twenty-two.*

Age
six   ten   eighteen   twenty-two   twenty-five   thirty-five
Information
started school   fallen in love   finished studying
learnt to swim   got married   bought a car   moved house

A sad life

17 Jake Coles is in prison. Read the notes about his life.

met Sharon at university   -   fell in love   -   got married
honeymoon (2 months)   -   failed exams   -   left university
got a job   -   went abroad   -   bought expensive presents
short of money   -   stole from supermarket -   not caught
robbed a bank   -   arrested   -   put in prison

In groups of four. Take turns to make hypotheses about Jake's life. Each sentence must be linked to the previous one. You get a point for each correct sentence but no point if you repeat information. The winner is the one with most points.

Example Student A: *If Jake hadn't met Sharon he wouldn't have fallen in love.*
 Student B: *If he hadn't fallen in love he wouldn't have got married.*
 Student C: *If he hadn't got married ...*

Regrets

18 On three separate pieces of paper write three regrets. Disguise your handwriting!

Example   *I would be living in a wonderful house if I had married a rich man.*

Mix the pieces of paper together. Take turns to read the regrets and guess who wrote them. Choose from these topics.

education   relationships   happiness   family   friendship
ambitions   work

Writing development

Reading

19 Look at this advertisement from the travel section of *Time Out* magazine.

● **SAHARA,** explore the desert, small groups, landrover, 3½ weeks, September, October, November, £720 incl flights. 01-674 9793 for details.
● **EXPERIENCED MALE COMPANION** required by young lady, to organise and share adventure on uninhabited tropical island for one year. Box P454.
● **TRAVELLING COMPANION** for budget Sahara trip in 2CV via Portugal, Spain and Morocco for

Discuss in pairs. Do you think the ad was genuine?

What sort of a person would place such an ad?

What sort of difficulties would you expect to deal with in the course of the year on the island?

Make a list of the advantages and disadvantages of an adventure like this.

Writing

Letters (3)

20 In groups. Prepare to write a letter to the person who placed the ad. (If you are a woman imagine that a man placed the ad.) Consider these things.

Content: how to convince the advertiser that you are the right person
your relevant experience
your special skills
your personality (likes/dislikes)
your background

Layout
and style :   formal or informal?

Now write your letter. When you have finished, exchange letters with other students and discuss the content and any errors of grammar and spelling.

Speaking

21 In groups.

Group A: You are the advertiser in exercise 19. You are going to interview one of the candidates for the year on the island with you. Consider the sort of person you would want to spend a year on an island with.

Group B: You are the candidates for the year on the island. The advertiser is going to interview you. How are you going to 'sell yourself' for the job? What questions are you going to ask the advertiser?
In pairs. (One student from Group A and one from Group B.) You arrange a first meeting in a pub. Act out the interview.

Say the right thing!

Making suggestions and giving advice
There are different ways of making suggestions and giving advice in English depending on your relationship with the other person.

1 **Which of the following expressions would you use to:**
a   a senior colleague at work?
b   a junior colleague?
c   a friend?
d   a close relative?

1   I was wondering if you should....?
2   Have you ever thought of....?
3   I really think you should ...
4   Why don't you ...?
5   If I were you I'd ...
6   You'd better ...
7   Have you tried ...?

Here are some ways of responding to the suggestions or advice.

Yes, I know but it's easier said than done.
That's all very well, but ...
You don't seem to realise that ...
I see what you mean but ...

2 **In groups give and respond to suggestions or advice. Here are some situations.**

Your friend is drinking too much.
Your colleague finds her work boring.
Your boss is working too many hours and looking very tired.
Your son is not studying hard enough for his exams.
Your husband is smoking heavily and has a terrible cough.

3 **In groups. Roleplay one of these situations. One student takes the role and the others offer advice.**

1   You are a young man of thirty who has fallen desperately in love with a woman of forty-five. She is a widow and has three children. You love the children but have a very small house and cannot accommodate all of them. You don't have enough money to buy a larger house. The woman is very fond of you but is afraid of what people will say because of the age difference.

2   You are a middle-aged woman who is tired of her present situation. Your husband seems to be a workaholic. He often comes home late from work and even brings work home with him. You never seem to go out together any more, he is usually too busy to talk to you and never has time to play with the children. You are very worried both about your husband's health and what will happen to your family.

Vocabulary

Emotions and feelings

1 Complete the following sentences.

1 When I'm feeling sad I often ...
2 When I'm feeling lonely I sometimes ...
3 When I'm feeling anxious I often ...
4 When I'm jealous I ...
5 When I'm feeling tense I usually ...
6 When I'm feeling happy I often ...

Marriage

2 What are they?

1 A woman getting married.
2 The object you put on your finger during a wedding ceremony.
3 The names of two places where weddings are held.
4 The name of the 'party' you have after a wedding.
5 A word for the people who attend a wedding.
6 The name for the holiday you have after the wedding.
7 The wife's relationship to her husband's sister.
8 The husband's relationship to his wife's children by a previous marriage.

Grammar

Conditional clauses (3) (*if* + past + *would*)

3 *If* sentences of this kind are often used when giving people advice. Look at this series of problems. Give advice in each case.

Example 1 *If I were you, I'd take a taxi.*

1 I've been waiting for this bus for twenty minutes. If it doesn't come soon I'm going to be late for work.
2 I was walking down the street when this man walked up to me and snatched my handbag and ran away.
3 I haven't got any money and the bank's closed.
4 My boss is coming round to dinner and I've burnt the meat.
5 I've got a terrible sore throat and a headache.
6 I haven't got many friends and I'm a bit shy.

Present perfect continuous

4 Look at these time expressions. Make three sentences for each of them about your own experiences using the present perfect continuous.
... for one year now. ... since I was a child.
... since this morning.
Example *I've been studying in this class for one year now.*

Past perfect

5 Write a paragraph describing all the things you'd done before you started learning English.

Conditional clauses (4) (*if* + past + *would have/ would*)

6 Finish these sentences.
1 If I had not studied English I ...
2 I might have worked in France if ...
3 I would have liked to ... if ...
4 If I hadn't been born in my country I ...
5 I wouldn't have bought this ... if ...
6 If I had been able to ... I ...

7 If I hadn't gone on holiday to ... I ...
8 If I had known when I was younger, what I know now I ...

Conditional clauses revision

7 Choose the correct alternative in each sentence.
1 If she (*will fail/fails*) her exam she (*takes/will take*) it again.
2 If he (*was going to/is at*) the party I (*tell /'ll tell*) him you were trying to get in touch.
3 We have an appointment at twelve o'clock so if you (*are arriving/arrive*) late we (*wouldn't/won't*) be able to wait for you.
4 If she (*hasn't/hadn't*) married a Frenchman she probably wouldn't (*be/is being*) in France now.
5 If you (*visited/visit*) us next summer I (*take/'ll take*) you to see the National Park.
6 If you (*mix/will mix*) black and white you (*will get/get*) grey.
7 I (*wouldn't/won't*) eat too many sweets if I (*am/were*) you.
8 If they (*caught/had caught*) the train they (*have been/ would be*) in Scotland by now.

Guide to better language learning
Part 5 - Writing

If you have difficulty knowing how to approach writing, or want to improve your technique look at pages 119 -120.

personality /pɜːsənælɪtɪ/ **personalities** Your
personality is your whole character and nature.
EG *He has a wonderful personality... ...the*
belief that the environment shapes personality.

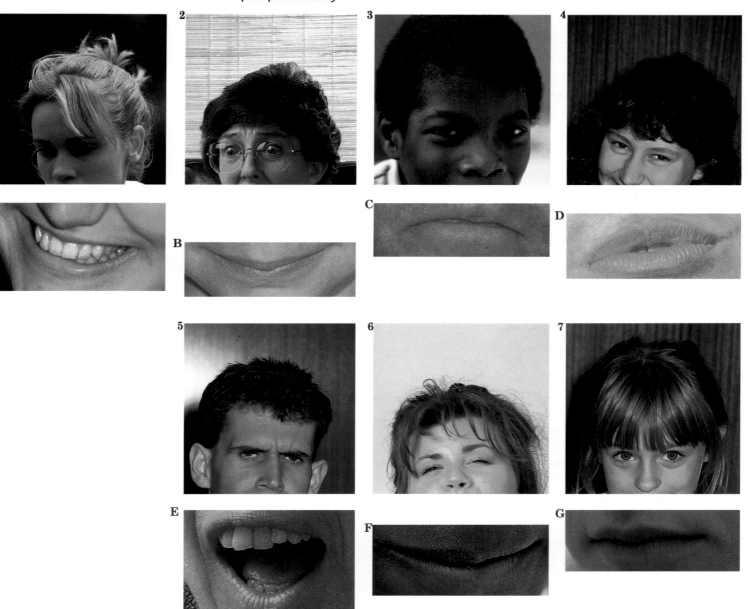

Look at the photos. Which mouths go with which faces?
Check your answers with another student and then look at the completed
photos on page 137.

What can you tell about these people from their photos?
In pairs. Student A: Describe the facial characteristics and
personality of one of the people.
        Student B: Guess which person it is.
Then change over.

Discuss and decide if you agree with each other's interpretation.

Reading

Before you read

1 What are the things you notice in people when you meet them for the first time?

How important are first impressions?

Some people say they can tell what a person is like just by looking at them. Do you think this is possible?

This extract is from the novel *Cry Freedom* and describes the first meeting between the newspaper editor, Donald Woods, and Steve Biko.

While you read

2 Which phrases from the text confirm these statements?
Find information in the text to support these statements.

1 Woods had already heard of Steve Biko.
2 Woods had expected Biko to be very different from what he was.
3 Woods was a wealthy man.
4 There was a definite moment in the interview when both men relaxed and showed they liked each other.

Vocabulary comprehension

3 The following are synonyms of words in the text. Find the words. The synonyms appear in the same order as the words in the text.

a wickedly
b amusedly
c didn't say it
d derision, disdain

e embarrassed
f ironic
g areas in South Africa where black or coloured people are allowed to live

h judgement
i proud way of walking
j rapid

21▶

But now that they were face to face, it was Woods' turn to stare. He could see that the man looked both younger and more handsome than his pictures because his face was unlined, and his deep, dark eyes were alive and clearly windows to a complex and sensitive mind. Biko smiled suddenly, devilishly, and Woods could also see the 'rascal' in those eyes that Ntsiki had hinted at.

'But of course,' Biko continued wryly, 'you would approve of my banning.'

Woods' temptation was to say 'you're damned right!', but he hedged. He had after all been talked into coming to hear what the man had to say. 'I think your ideas are dangerous,' he said, 'but no, I don't approve of banning.'

'A true "liberal",' Biko declared with a hint of mockery.

'It's not a title I'm ashamed of,' Woods responded sharply, 'though I understand you regard it with some contempt.'

Biko grinned. From the moment they began speaking he had had a dry, amused air and it deepened as Woods grew more and more belligerently unamused. 'Oh, that's too strong,' Biko protested. 'I just think that a "white liberal" who clings to all the advantages of his white world - jobs, education, housing, Mercedes' - Woods blinked involuntarily at the thrust - 'is perhaps not the person "best qualified" to tell blacks how they should react to apartheid.'

Woods nodded coolly. 'I wonder what kind of "liberal" you would make, Mr Biko, if you were the one who possessed the house, the job, and the Mercedes - and the whites lived in the townships.'

This produced a burst of laughter from Biko - at the inversion and the assessment of his own character, because there was no denying that a certain swagger and masculine display were fundamental parts of his personality. 'Now that is a charming idea,' he said, 'whites in the townships and me in a Mercedes.' And then, with a smile that was as warm and genuine as his wife's, he stuck out his hand. 'It was good of you to come, Mr Woods. I've wanted to meet you for a long time.'

Woods hesitated for a moment, absorbing the swift change in mood, the intelligence, the unexpected sincerity in the eyes and the smile. Then he took the proffered hand.

It was the beginning.

Vocabulary

Vocabulary development: physical features and personality

4 **In pairs complete the mind map. Use these words and any others you can think of. Check your answers with other students.**

bald	handsome	unlined	sensitive
cool	sincere lazy	genuine	high
brown	fair tidy	curly	bright
bad-tempered	bushy deep		aggressive
forehead	eyebrows thick		wrinkles
outgoing	hazel low	freckles	sociable
impatient	selfish eyelashes	shy	
extrovert	large		

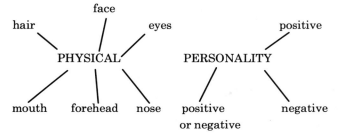

Add any other words you know to do with physical features or personality to the mind map.

Vocabulary building: negative prefixes

5 **The prefixes *un-*, *in-*, *im-* before adjectives have the meaning *not*. The most common of these prefixes is *un-*.**
Here is a list of adjectives from exercise 4 with their prefixes.

lined	unlined
sensitive	insensitive
secure	insecure
tidy	untidy
sociable	unsociable
patient	impatient
selfish	unselfish

Look at these descriptions of people and complete the adjectives.

1 You know exactly how he'll react.   p _ e _ i _ t _ b _ e
2 She can no longer look after herself.   d _ p _ n _ e _ t
3 He seems older than his years.   m _ t _ r _
4 She was always loyal and supporting.   f _ i _ h _ u _
5 She learns quickly.   i _ t _ l _ i _ e _ t
6 She is always honest.   s _ n _ e _ e

Put the correct prefix in front of each adjective to give the opposite meaning.

Pronunciation - *ow* /aʊ/ or /əʊ/

6 **Listen to the pronunciation of the letters 'ow' in these words from the text.**
`53`

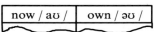

now / aʊ /	own / əʊ /

Listen to these words and put them in the correct column.

low	brown	crown	crow	know
tomorrow	snow	blow	down	cow
window	how			

Listen and repeat.
Now practise saying this sentence.
How now brown cow.

Practice

Sketches

7 **In pairs. Each student prepare a description of your own physical appearance and personality. Do the same for your partner. Read and compare your descriptions. How similar or how different are they? Why is this?**

Who is it?

8 **In groups take turns to describe the personality and facial characteristics of someone in the class. The person to guess describes the next person.**

Speaking

Personality questionnaire

9 **Tick the questions which are true for you. Then work through the questionnaire with another student and discuss your answers. What do they show you about your personality?**

1 When you go to a party do you
a enjoy meeting new people?
b feel uncomfortable for most of the time?
c find an excuse to leave early?
d react in a different way? What way?

2 When someone compliments you on something you have made do you
a accept the compliment with pleasure?
b feel very embarrassed and deny that it is any good?
c say you think it's very nice too?
d react in a different way? What way?

3 If friends arrive unexpectedly and your house is in a terrible mess do you
a feel embarrassed?
b forget the mess and enjoy their company?
c tell them you have to finish cleaning the house and can they come back later?
d react in a different way? What way?

4 Do any of these things make you laugh?
a Comedy shows?
b Seeing other people laughing?
c Something you are reading?
d Anything else? What?

5 When do you cry?
a When you are saying goodbye at the airport or train station?
b At weddings?
c When you are watching a sad film?
d At any other time? When?

6 When you relax do you usually
a sit on the floor with your legs under you?
b sit on a comfortable chair with your legs under you?
c sit with your legs crossed?
d sit in a different position? Which position?

7 Would you say anything if
a someone said something nasty about your best friend?
b the food you had in a restaurant tasted strange?
c someone insulted you?
d You saw your husband/wife with another woman/man?

8 Do you prefer
a being with a crowd of people?
b being on your own?
c being with one other person?
d being with people you know very well?

Listening

10 **Listen to Clare describing herself.**
54 Listen and tick the person you think is Clare.

These are some of the words Clare uses when describing her personality. Listen again. Use the words to make notes about her personality.

... shy ... difficult talking ... close friends ... worried ...

She goes on to talk about her regrets. What did she regret most?

1 That she didn't spend more time in the States?
2 That she worked as a waitress?
3 That she didn't travel more?

Grammar and pronunciation

1 I find it difficult talking to new people.
  I wish I didn't find it difficult talking to new people.
2 I would sometimes like to be more outgoing.
  I wish I were sometimes more outgoing.
3 I wish I had done an awful lot more.
4 She wishes she hadn't wasted her time.
5 She wishes she was going too.
6 She wishes people would do more to help each other.
7 She wishes she could spend more time talking to people.

Grammar: wishes and regrets

(Grammar reference, page 142)

11 **Look at the sentences in the grammar box.**
In which sentences is the speaker expressing regret about something which is generally true?
In which sentences is she regretting past actions?
In which sentence is she expressing a constructive attitude to the resolution of a problem?
Are these statements true or false?

1 To express regret about the present we use *wish* + the present tense.
2 To express regret about past events, we use *wish* + past perfect.
3 To focus on a situation we would like to improve we use *wish* + *would*.
4 We can use *wish* + *would* for the first person singular + plural.
5 To express regret that we or someone else is unable to do something, we use *wish* + *could*.

Grammar check

12 **Put the verbs in brackets in the correct tense to complete the sentences.**

1 I wish I (*go*) to see them while they were here.
2 I wish the children (*try*) to be a bit tidier.
3 She wishes she (*play*) the piano.
4 I wish he (*stop*) smoking.
5 They wish they (*live*) in the country.

Pronunciation: unstressed words

13 **Some words in English are usually unstressed. They**
56 **are only stressed when they appear in isolation or when we need to stress a particular meaning.**

Look at sentences 3 and 5 in the grammar box. Underline the weak words in the sentences.

Listen and check your answers. Listen and repeat.

Listen to this sentence. Each time you hear it it has a different meaning. Which meaning does the sentence have each time?

Peter and Mary are coming.
a Both people are coming.
b We are surprised that Mary is coming too.
c We didn't think they were going to come.

Look at this list of words. Which words do you think are usually unstressed? Check your answers with another student.

and	when	as	that	with	plan
from	for	are	two	send	
them	her	happy			

Which of these do you think are usually unstressed?
nouns   main verbs   prepositions   adjectives
articles   adverbs   auxiliaries

Practice

Mistakes

14 **Look at these results of mistaken actions. Can you guess what the people would have said in each case? Write the regrets then compare your answers in pairs.**
Example *I got completely soaked.*
        I wish I hadn't left my umbrella at home.
1 I crashed into the car in front.
2 I'll have to borrow some money from my sister until the end of the month.
3 I fell thirty metres down the mountain.
4 I couldn't get to sleep for hours.
5 I failed the exam.
6 I had to walk all the way home.

Who said it?

15 **Complete these sentences on separate pieces of paper. The sentences you make should be true for you.**

I wish I hadn't ... when I was a child.
I wish I had ... when I was a child.
I wish I was ...
I wish I wasn't ...
I wish people would ...

Work in groups. Fold your pieces of paper and mix them all up on a table. Take five pieces of paper each. In turns read the wishes on your papers. The others guess who made those wishes.

Writing development

Speaking

The perfect man and woman

16 **Look at the two faces. Match the names to the facial features.**

Man
Charlie Chaplin
Robert Redford
Michael Jackson
Kirk Douglas
Prince Charles

Woman
Fanny Ardant
Martina Navratilova
Margaret Thatcher
Princess Diana
Julia Roberts

17 **In pairs. Discuss the characteristics of the perfect man and woman using elements of people who are famous in your country or the rest of the world.**

Example   *Nelson Mandela's courage and Tom Cruise's teeth and mouth.*

Use these characteristics.

Voice
Smile
Facial features: eyes   nose   teeth and mouth   ears   hair
Personality: sense of humour intelligence   courage   skill   determination
Life-style: money   job   place of residence   dress sense

Writing

Describing people

18 **You are going to write a description of a person you are either very close to or who you don't like at all. (150 - 180 words) Include the information listed in the categories in exercise 17.**

paragraph 1:   Introduction - name of the person, how long you have known him/ her, where you met.

paragraph 2:   Physical description - facial features, height, build.

paragraph 3:   Character description - things you like/don't like, incidents which show what sort of person she/he is.

paragraph 4:   Summary - what you feel about the person and why.

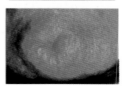

freedom /fri:dəm/ , **freedoms**. 1 **Freedom** is 1.1 the right to express any political or religious opinion and live or act without the government or another country interfering.
1.2 the state of being able or allowed to do what you want to do without being restricted by anything or anyone.

In pairs. Look at the photos and decide what freedom is represented in each one. Write a sentence for each one.

Compare your sentences with another student.

Choose the three types of freedom which you think are absolutely essential.
In groups. Compare and discuss the choice you have made. Which types of freedom do you disagree with? Give your reasons.

Reading

Tracy Chapman was born and raised in Cleveland, Ohio. She began writing poetry, prose, and songs in her adolescence and says that 'music was so much a part of my life when I was growing up, I didn't even think about it.' Tracy's mother was and is a singer of popular and gospel music, and also played the electric guitar.

Tracy was awarded scholarships to her private high school in Danbury, Connecticut, and to Tufts University in Medford, Massachusetts. Even before graduating in 1986, Tracy was appearing regularly in the area's coffee houses and clubs, and at special events such as the Folktree Women's Festival.

The song below is from her debut album 'Tracy Chapman' on Elektra Records.

Before you read

1 *Why?* **is the title of the song by Tracy Chapman which you are going to read. The song consists of a series of questions. What sort of questions do you think Tracy is going to ask? Make a list of possible questions.**

While you read

2 **Look at this list of issues. Which of them are discussed in the song?**

War   Unemployment   Euthanasia

Women's rights   Environment   Famine

Freedom of speech   Loneliness   Housing

> *Why do the babies starve*
> *When there's enough food to feed the world*
> *Why when there's so many of us*
> *Are there people still alone*
>
> *Why are the missiles called peace keepers*
> *When they're aimed to kill*
> *Why is a women still not safe*
> *When she's in her home*
>
> *Love is hate*
> *War is peace*
> *No is Yes*
> *And we're all free*
>
> *But somebody's gonna have to answer*
> *The time is coming soon*
> *Amidst all these questions and contradictions*
> *There're some who seek the truth*
>
> *But somebody's gonna have to answer*
> *The time is coming soon*
> *When the blind remove their blinders*
> *And the speechless speak the truth*

Vocabulary comprehension

3 **Make a list of three words you do not know and that you think are necessary in order to understand the song.**
In groups compare lists and help each other to work out the meanings of the words.
Check the meaning of the words on your list with your teacher or in a dictionary.

Vocabulary

Vocabulary development: world problems

4 Listen and list the words that you hear under one of
57 the headings. (There are four words in each list)

human rights	famine / poverty	violence	environment
economy			

Now work together to find more words to extend the
lists.

Vocabulary building: nouns ending in -ence and -ance

5 The suffixes *-ence* or *-ance* combine with adjectives
ending in *-ent* and *-ant* to form nouns. These nouns
refer to the state or quality described by the original
adjectives. For example, *violence* is the state of being
violent.

Convert these adjectives into nouns.
independent   intelligent   reluctant   innocent
indifferent   affluent   patient
Can you find any other adjectives which behave in the
same way?

Pronunciation: '-ough'

6 Listen to this sentence from the song on page 84.
58 'Why do babies starve
When there's enough food to feed the world?'

-ough is pronounced /ʌf/ in the word '*enough*'.
Listen to the list of words in A below. How many
different pronunciations of *-ough* are there?

A Although   bought   bough   rough   through
trough   thorough

For each word in list A there is a word in list B with the
same pronunciation of *-ough*. Can you find the pairs?

B cough   thought   tough   borough
throughout   plough   dough

Listen and check your answers.
Listen and repeat.

Practice

Spot the difference!

7 Find the word or phrase which is different from the others in the lists.
Explain why the word is different.

A	B	C
greenhouse effect	starvation	disarmament
recycling	poverty	chemical weapons
acid rain	foreign aid	nuclear weapons

In pairs. Prepare similar sets of words containing one word different from
the other two. Use the words that you listed in exercises 4 and 5. Then try
out your exercise on other students.

The speech game

8 In two teams of three to four people. Each team makes a list of topics
from the words that you have studied in this lesson.
Take turns to choose a topic for the other team to speak about.
Team A: Choose the topic.
Team B: One person has to talk about the topic for one minute.
If he or she hesitates for more than five seconds then a member of Team A
takes over for the remainder of the time. The person who is talking when
the minute ends wins a point.

Listening

Before you listen

9 You are going to hear Dr Roy Gardner of the Institute of Education, University of London, talking about the major problems facing developing countries. Look at the list. Which things do you think Dr Gardner will mention as being problematic for developing countries?

money   personnel   food   energy
communications   water   building materials   climate

While you listen

10 | **59** Listen and check your answers to exercise 9. Now complete the sentences with the words provided.

lower   countries   dependent   responsibility
problems   jobs   initiative   developing   university
people   instruction   senior   education   industry

1 Not all ____ countries have the same ____ to the same degree of intensity.
2 There are plenty of ____ at the ____ level who would be able to carry through the routine ____.
3 There's been a great demand for ____ of high quality in lots of ____ over the last two or three decades.
4 ... anyone who can get into school or ____ hopes to get into a job in government or in big ____.
5 Along with that goes another question of people accepting ____.
6 ... the whole society has been geared to receiving ____ and not taking ____.
7 ... therefore there's very much a ____ culture, dependent very much on the ____ telling you what to do.

Listen again and check your answers.

Speaking

11 In groups. You are politicians of a small developing country. You have received a large sum of money from another country which you have to decide how to spend. What percentages of the money will you spend on these things?

education   food and water supply   energy production   transport and roads
army and police   health service   agriculture   industry

When you have finished, compare answers with other groups.

Grammar and pronunciation

1 'One common characteristic ... is that they lack technicians.'
Dr Gardner said that one common characteristic is that they lack technicians.
2 'There has been a great demand for education over the last twenty or thirty years.'
He said there had been a great demand for education over the last twenty or thirty years.
3 'I'm in Belgium,' Richard wrote.
When he wrote, Richard said he was in Belgium.
4 'The government has tried to reduce inflation.'
The minister said the government had tried to reduce inflation.
5 'I'll try to phone some time today.'
She told me she would try to phone some time today.
6 'I'm ill and I'm not coming into the office today.'
Geoff says he's ill and that he isn't coming into the office today.

Grammar: reporting (1)
(Grammar reference, page 142)

12 Look at the sentences in the grammar box. Which sentences demonstrate the following rules?

a You use a present tense for the reporting verb when you are reporting what someone says or thinks at the time you are speaking.
b You normally use past tenses in reports about the past.
c You can use a present tense in the reported clause if what you are saying is important or still true in the present.
d You use a conditional tense in the reported clause if the future was used in the original sentence.
e You can introduce the reported clause after *say* and *tell* with *that* but it is optional.

Look at the sentences again and answer these questions.

1 How do the tenses change between the original words of the speaker and when they are reported?
2 Do you always report the exact words that people say when reporting?

Grammar check.

13 Put the sentences into reported speech.

1 'I'm going home,' she said.
2 'They came at six,' he said.
3 'I'll see you next week,' he said.
4 'There are still a lot of things to do,' she said.
5 'I'm really tired,' she said.

Pronunciation: using stress to change meaning

14 Listen to the two ways of saying this sentence.

61 When he wrote Richard said he was in Belgium.

In one of them the speaker doesn't believe that Richard was in Belgium. Which one?

How does the stress change in the sentence when you want to show that you don't believe what the other person says?

Listen and repeat, paying attention to the stress and intonation of the two sentences.

In pairs. Take it in turns to say these sentences in one of the two ways above. Your partner has to say whether he/she believes what you said or not.

She said she was ill and that's why she didn't come to the party.
They said they were moving away because of his job.
He said he had to go home because he had a headache.
He said he hadn't taken the money.

Listen and repeat.

Practice

What did they say?

15 Listen to the statements on the cassette and match
62 **them to the reported statements.**

a The woman said that she thought that people needed to think more carefully about what they did with waste products.
b The man said that developing countries sometimes don't like to accept foreign aid because there are often strings attached.
c The man said that the right to vote was the most important thing in the fight for democracy in his country.
d The man said there had been a lot of progress towards nuclear disarmament.
e The woman said that people would have to work together if they wanted to change their government's policy on human rights.

Now look at these statements, and convert them into reported speech.

1 'More developed countries will have to give more money to less developed countries, if we want to avoid more deaths from starvation.'
2 'One important threat to world peace is the continuing existence of vast stocks of chemical weapons.'
3 'Acid rain was a fashionable environmental issues in the 80s, while global warming has now taken over.'
4 'Some countries in the West which criticise others for their human rights record have a very poor record themselves.'

Example *One person said that if we ...*

Now listen and check your answers.

Newspaper article

16 Reported speech is often used in newspaper articles.
63 **In groups, listen to what Dr Gardner said about aid to developing countries and make notes using the key words for your group.**

Group A:
bad press - political tag - political commitment - coercion - equipment - donor country - lack of willingness

Group B:
1% gross national product - guideline - Britain - no better - 0.6% - countries - follow guideline - national income - international support

Group C:
recipient countries - handle the money - personnel - viable outcomes

In groups, write your part of a short newspaper article reporting what Dr Gardner said.

When you have finished your section of the article, read other students' work and produce a complete article.

Writing development

Speaking

Balloon debate

17 Three famous people, living or dead, are in a balloon which is gradually deflating. One by one they have to be thrown out to keep the balloon in the air. Only one person will be able to stay in the balloon and survive. Each of the famous people thinks they should be the one to stay in the balloon.

In groups of six. Each student decides who he/she is.
You have five minutes to prepare your speech. Work out all the points in favour of you staying in the balloon.
The first three students give their speeches.
The other three students can ask further questions.
They then vote and the one who stays in the balloon is the winner.
Then change over.

Writing

Preparing a speech

Greetings

18 **Here are three ways of beginning a speech. Number them from the most formal (1) to the least formal (3).**

a   Good evening everybody and thank you so much for coming today ...

b   Ladies and gentleman, I should like to say how pleased I am to ...

c   Hi, everyone. It's great to see so many of you here today ...

Do the same with the other groups.

Linking words

d   The first thing I would like to say is ...

e   To begin with I ...

f   First of all let me say ...

Continuing the speech

g   Well now let's go on to the next thing on my list ...

h   The next thing I would like to say is ...

i   To go on to my next point ...

Concluding the speech

j   To sum up I would like to say ...

k   So on the whole I think ...

l   Now I think I've talked long enough so to finish I'll just say ...

"Today's topic is 'public awareness.'"

In pairs. Make notes for a speech (150 - 180 words) for the following occasion.
A colleague is leaving his job and you are having a dinner party to say goodbye. After dinner you have to say a few words and then present your colleague with the present you have bought.

Greet everybody. Talk about the good qualities your colleague possesses.
Say how you are going to miss him/her.
Wish him/her good luck for the future and present him/her with the gift.
Write your speech.

Say the right thing!

Asking permission to do something

1 **How you ask permission to do something will depend on**

a   who you are talking to   - Is the person more important than you?

                                - Is it someone you know well?

b   what you are asking   - Is it a reasonable request or not?

The more unreasonable the request and the more important the person, the more polite the language you use will have to be. (When the request is unreasonable you also usually give your reasons for making it).

Write down seven phrases you can use to ask permission using the words in the box. (Use each word once only)

Example   *Could I* (open the window)?

I	if	was	Could	Is	you	I
Would	I	it	Do	if	I	
alright	wondering		it	Can	you	
be	I	could	if	I		
if	Do	alright	I			
could	mind	I	think			

64 **Listen and check your answers. Then listen and repeat.**

2 **How do you reply to requests for permission to do something?**
In pairs make two lists, one for giving and the other for refusing permission. Put the phrases you write in order of formality/politeness.

Giving permission	Refusing permission

Now listen to Part 3 on the cassette. Tick the phrases you already have and add the others to your lists.

Which requests require a negative reply to give permission?

3 **Read this series of situations and prepare what you would say in each. Then work in pairs and take turns to make and reply to the requests.**

1   You work in an office. There's a lot of work to do at the moment. You want to leave early today because you are going to a concert this evening. Ask the office manager for permission to leave early.

2   You are staying with an English family who seem very friendly. You want to borrow one of their cars (they have two) to visit some friends in Scotland this weekend.

3   You are doing some maths homework in a library and you have left your calculator at home. The person next to you has a calculator and isn't using it. Ask for permission to borrow it.

4   You have seen a jacket that you like in a shop on the way to your English lesson but you haven't got enough money with you to buy it. Ask another student in the class to lend you some money to buy it after the lesson.

5   You're going on holiday next week and you want to take some photographs while you are away but your camera is broken. Ask a member of your family if you can borrow their camera.

"Mind if we join you?"

Vocabulary

Physical features and personality
Caricatures

1 **Choose three of the following and write a description.**

Example *Ski instructor.*
When I think of a ski instuctor he's always tall, dark, handsome, very sun-tanned. He's also charming, unfaithful, brainless with a very inflated opinion of himself!

ski instructor	television presenter	postman
teacher	lawyer	bank robber
scientist	rock musician	
bank clerk	soap opera character	

World problems

2 **Read the definitions and write the word or words.**
1 Death or extreme suffering caused by lack of food.
2 A political system in which people of different races are kept apart by law.
3 Basic rights that most nations believe all people should have.
4 Behaviour which is meant to hurt or kill people, for example hitting, or kicking or using guns.
5 Great pain which is deliberately caused to someone especially to punish them or get information from them.
6 The problem of the gradual rise in temperature in the Earth's atmosphere.
7 Weapons which explode by the energy released by atoms.
8 The right to express any political or religious opinion without the government or another country interfering.

Now add another word associated with each of the words listed and write a sentence with it to show you understand the meaning.

Grammar

Wishes and regrets

3 **Write three sentences with *wish* for each of the following situations.**

Example *You're feeling sick.*
1 I wish I hadn't eaten so much.
2 I wish I felt better.
3 I wish I could eat as much as I liked without suffering afterwards.

1 You've lost your job.
2 You're on top of a mountain and it's getting dark.
3 Your car has run out of petrol on a quiet country road.
4 The people next door are always having parties late at night.
5 You are in a foreign country and can't speak the language.
6 You've failed your driving test.

Reporting

4 **In pairs. Ask your partner's opinion on these subjects. Make notes when they reply. Report what they said.**

1 Football supporters
2 Vegetarianism
3 Video machines
4 Keeping pets in the home

Example Student A: *What do you think of Michael Jackson?*
Student B: *I think he's all right but he's silly to spend so much time and money on his appearance.*
Student A: *Rita said that she liked Michael Jackson but that he was silly to spend so much time and money on his appearance.*

Guide to better language learning
Part 6 - Vocabulary

If you have problems with vocabulary, or want to improve your technique look at pages 120 - 121.

commitment /kəmɪtmənt/ **Commitment**
is a strong belief in an idea or system,
especially when it is shown by your actions or
behaviour. EG T*here is no doubting his enthusiasm
or his commitment ... ... your long commitment
to feminism.*

**What type of commitment do the photos represent? Match the photos to
the commitment.**

a   a particular job
b   a particular religious belief
c   not conforming
d   a particular cause
e   a political party
f   a particular food
g   a sport

**Choose one of the photos above which you can identify with.
In groups. Compare and discuss the choice you have made.**

Speaking

1 In groups.

Group A: You are in favour of vegetarianism.

Group B: You are against vegetarianism.

**In your groups prepare your arguments for and against vegetarianism.
Then hold a debate and discuss the following statement.**

'Vegetarianism is a middle class fashion, not to be taken seriously'

*'Nothing can be more obvious than that all animals were created solely and
exclusively for the use of man'* Thomas Love Peacock

Listening

2 **You are going to hear Tris talking about two things he feels strongly
committed to.**

**Write down the things that Tris is committed to.
Listen again and find this information.**

Two reasons for becoming vegetarian.

His reason for wearing leather shoes.

Things he eats.

Things he doesn't eat.

His feelings on persuading people to become vegetarian too.

What he does about plastic bags.

How he saves on fuel.

His feelings about persuading people to be 'greener'.

25 ▶

Vocabulary

Vocabulary development: commitment

3 Complete the mind map on commitment. Add examples to each category.
Put these words under the appropriate headings. Add more words to each category.

jogging   Green party   Nursing   vegetarianism
punk   racialism   Jehova's Witness   bottle banks

Moral and environmental issues

Unusual dress and habits

Religion

Sport

COMMITMENT

Vocations

Human and animal rights

Diet

Political beliefs

Vocabulary building: *anti-*

4 The prefix *anti-* combines with some nouns and adjectives to show opposition.

Example *anti-racist = opposed to racial discrimination.*

Anti- can also combine with nouns and adjectives to show prevention or destruction.

Example *Anti-depressants are drugs which prevent people becoming depressed.*

Look at the list of words and put them under the appropriate heading.

anti-freeze   anti-apartheid   anti-religious
anti-rust   anti-British   anti-burglar
anti-pollution   anti-nuclear

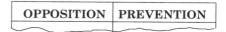

OPPOSITION	PREVENTION

Add any more words you can think of to the two lists.

Pronunciation: silent letters

5 In pairs write down as many words as you can think
67 of which begin with 'kn' and 'ps'.
Check your list against the words you hear. Add any words you didn't have to your list.
What is the pronunciation of 'kn' and 'ps' when they come at the beginning of words? What is the pronunciation of 'ps' when it comes at the end of a word?
Listen and repeat.

Practice

Guess the word

6 In pairs.
Student A: Give definitions of a word listed in exercise 3.
Student B: Guess the word.
Then change over.

Example   Student A: *This person doesn't eat meat.*
Student B: *Vegetarian.*
Student A: *No, because this person doesn't eat cheese either.*
Student B: *Then it's a vegan.*

For or against

7 In teams. Choose three topics from exercise 3 and write three arguments for and against each one.
Give the topic headings to the other team. They have to guess three of your arguments. They can be for or against.
As a team choose the topic you are most interested in, take sides and discuss it.

93

Speaking

8 In groups decide what foods are necessary for a
healthy diet.
Is a healthy diet still possible if you do not eat these
foods?
Make a list of alternative diets.
Would you consider changing your eating habits?

Reading

Before you read

9 Look at the headline. What do you think the article
will be about?

Saved from the turkey by a passion for fruit

While you read

10 Read the article quickly and see if you were right.
Then read the article again and list all the foods that
David Shelley eats.

Vocabulary comprehension

11 Find these words in the text. Try to work out their
meaning from the context.

mashing   sprinkling   encompasses   sinewy   current
delicacies   extolling   vast   starchy   boasts

**Look at these sentences. Replace the underlined word
with its synonym from the box.**

1 Many people believe that by cutting out <u>carbohydrate</u>
foods from their diet they will lose weight.
2 Artichokes and asparagus are considered <u>delicious but
expensive foods</u> in Britain.
3 The Green Party has a policy which <u>includes</u> all aspects
of conservation.
4 Our <u>present</u> methods of production are far too expensive.
5 She was always <u>praising</u> the virtues of her children.
6 He <u>declares strongly</u> that he is the best player in the
team.
7 When children are very small parents spend a lot of time
<u>crushing</u> their food so that they are able to eat it.
8 When she finished the cake she put a <u>small number</u> of
nuts on top to decorate it.
9 He has a broad <u>muscular</u> body.
10 He was responsible for running a <u>huge</u> organisation.

Sean O'Neill meets a man with a diet out of the Garden of Eden

David Shelley will have had a
light Christmas dinner. Perhaps a mango and an orange,
maybe a handful of nuts on
5 the side. Certainly he will have
stuffed no turkeys nor
steamed any sprouts, definitely no more extensive pre-
paration than the mashing
10 together of an avocado and a
banana and the sprinkling on
top of a few dates. For David
Shelley eats only fruit (his
definition encompasses nuts).
15 Aged 23, born, bred and
living in Leicester, Mr Shelley
has been a fruitarian for
almost three years. He is 9st
10lbs, stands 5ft 9ins and has a
20 26-inch waistline. He is thin,
but sinewy, has a clear com-
plexion and shiny, healthy
hair. His current diet is high in
oily nuts and avocados to
25 provide the extra fat he needs
to resist the cold of a British
winter, which he feels bitterly.
There are very few fruitarians
in Britain, but Leicester is a
30 good place to be one. The
city's huge fruit market allows
Mr Shelley to buy more than
enough food for a fiver a
week. His weekly shopping list
35 might comprise 3lb of bana-
nas, 2lb of apples, 10 oranges,
a bag of satsumas and delicacies such as mangos or avocados when they offer good
40 value. In Australia, with a
climate better suited to growing fruit, the Fruitarian Network has 250 subscribers.
Britain has no fruitarian so-
45 ciety, but callers to the vegetarian and vegan societies are
passed on to 81-year-old
Wilfred Crone from Dorset, a
fruitarian for 10 years. He
50 claims to answer 500 inquiries
a year with leaflets extolling
the virtues of his "Edenic"
diet.
Mr Shelley displays the same
55 missionary zeal. He has written his own pamphlet, "Food
of Truth: the Key to Perfect
Health", hailing, in 60 pages
of densely typed, preaching
60 prose, "the greatest of health
foods, fresh, unfried fruit".
In conversation he rattles off
endorsements from a vast
array of authorities, each
65 reinforced with the same,
unquestioned conclusion:
"Fruit is the true food for
man!"
"The apes are all fruitarians.
70 If they can get fruit they'll eat
nothing else. Our closest relatives are fruitarians, our
whole bodies are designed to
eat fruit. It's a fact."
75 But while the diet may be
cleansing, nutritionists say it is
unlikely to provide all the
body needs. In particular, by
not eating starchy foods or
80 dairy products, a fruitarian
may suffer calcium and iron
deficiencies. "It would be very
difficult to get all the nutrients
you need just from fruit," says
85 Caroline Hurren, a nutrition-
ist at the Health Education
Authority. "Certainly eat
plenty of fruit and vegetables,
but not to the exclusion of
90 other foods."
Mr Shelley dismisses those
views as "a myth". He claims
the healthiest and fittest he has
ever felt was during a 17-day
95 period when he ate only
grapes. Although he feels the
cold, he boasts that he will
never catch a cold or any other
disease: "For me to be ill now
100 is impossible. I know for a fact
that I will never be ill again as
long as I live."

26 ▶

94

Grammar and pronunciation

1 David Shelley will have had a light Christmas dinner.
2 He'll be eating a diet of fruit for the rest of his life.
3 By the time he's thirty he'll have been following his fruit diet for ten years.
4 He claims to answer 500 inquiries a year ....
5 He claims the healthiest he has ever felt was during a 17-day period when he ate only grapes.
6 He boasts that he will never catch a cold.
7 He told me he would never eat meat again.
8 He dreams of going to live in Australia one day.

Grammar: future perfect, future continuous, future perfect continuous
(Grammar reference, page 143)

12 Look at sentences 1-3 in the grammar box. Which tense do you use for the following?

1 To say something will be completed by a specific time in the future.
2 To guess that an action will be completed by the time of speaking.
3 To say what we will be in the process of doing at a time in the future.
4 To talk about things we have decided to do at a time in the future.
5 To indicate the duration of an action at a time in the future.

Grammar: reporting (2) - reporting verbs.
(Grammar reference, page 143)

13 A reporting verb shows that you are quoting or reporting what somebody said or thought. *Say* and *think* are examples of reporting verbs.
Look at sentences 4 - 8 in the grammar box.

agree   complain   shout   promise   believe   decide
think   invite   persuade

a *Claim* can be followed by a *to* or *that* clause. Find three more words in the list above which follow the same rule.

b Reporting verbs can report people's thoughts, beliefs or hopes. *Dreams* in sentence 8 is one. Find two more.
c Some reporting verbs must be followed by an object indicating who the hearer is. *Told* in sentence 7 is one. Find two more.
d Sometimes the reporting verb describes the way the speaker made the original statements. *Boasts* in sentence 6 is one. Find two more.

Grammar check

14 Use this information to help you complete a paragraph about Jane's plans for tomorrow.

8.00 catch train	10.30 - 11.30 visit museum
9.30 arrive London	12.30 - 1.30 lunch

15 Rewrite these sentences using the verb in brackets.
1 I'll finish it by tomorrow afternoon. (*promise*)
2 You always come late. (*complain*)
3 OK, I'll come. (*agree*)
4 I'm going away, Dave. (*tell*)
5 Please come to my party. (*invite*)

Pronunciation: the letter 'l'

16 Listen to the pronunciation of the letter 'l'.

[68] He'll be eating a diet of fruit for the rest of his life.

Listen again and repeat.

When 'l' appears before a vowel it is called a clear 'l'. e.g. life
Before consonants and in final positions it is called a dark 'l'. e.g he'll

Will in sentence 1 in the grammar box and *he'll* in sentence 3 do not seem to follow the rule. Why not? What do you notice about *l* in the word *would*?

Look at these sentences. Listen and repeat.
I'll be living in London soon.
They'll laugh when they look at the slides.
While you're lying in bed I'll tell you a story.

Practice

Matching up

17 In pairs write statements for each of these introductory verbs.
agree complain promise believe decide invite dream boast
Exchange sentences with another pair and convert the sentences to reported speech. Then check your answers in groups of four.
Example *'OK, if you really want me to do it I will.'*
      She persuaded me to do it.

Things will change

18 Complete the sentence heads or tails for yourself and another student. Compare and discuss your statements.

Example   *By 1998 I'll have finished buying my house.*
By this time next week ...   ... for more than a month.
By tomorrow night ...   ... for ten years.
By the time I retire ...   ... for a very long time.
By this time next year ...
In two months' time ...
At the beginning of the next decade ...

Writing development

Speaking

Commitment to unlikely causes

19 In groups. Your teacher will give you each a subject.
You have ten minutes to prepare a speech on that subject.
Take turns to give your speech. You can talk for one minute only.
The rest of the group ask questions and finally vote on the most convincing
speech.

Writing

Formal letters (3)

20 Read this letter to a newspaper from a member of the 'Save the Mouse'
group.
The writer uses certain expressions to add weight to her argument. Here
are three. Find three more.

I feel I must write ...   In my opinion ...   Who are we to say ...

Now give a title to each of the paragraphs in the letter.

Example   *Paragraph 1 - Introduction of topic / Reason for writing*

21 Write a similar letter to *The Daily Times* drawing the public's attention
to your cause. Make sure you set your letter in the correct way for a
formal letter and make your argument as convincing as possible.

64 Heseltine Road
Avon
Somerset
10 / 10 / 1993

The Editor
The Daily Times
77 Fleet Street
London EC1

Dear Sir,
        As a member of the Save the Mouse group I feel I must write to you to draw your
attention to the very real danger our poor house mice are facing.

        Every day people continue to try to poison the poor creatures, or worse still, try to
kill them by catching them in a trap. I ask you, do you think this is humane?

        What harm does the poor little mouse do to people? It simply wants to live a quiet
life, find enough food to live on, a place to bring up its young, just like the rest of us. Why
should we decide to deny it these things?

        Some people say that mice are dirty, carry disease, and must be eliminated at all
costs. In my opinion the people who make these remarks are probably making the world
a dirtier place than mice will ever do.

        I suggest that we should all try to see to it that these pretty little creatures are left to
live their own lives. Who are we to say they shouldn't?

        I remain,

        Yours faithfully,

        Betsy Batwood
        Betsy Batwood

persuasion /pəsweɪʒən/ , **persuasions Per-suasion** is the act of persuading someone to do something or persuading them to believe that something is the case. EG *I had to adopt other methods of persuasion... You could, with a little persuasion, get some of these people to help.*

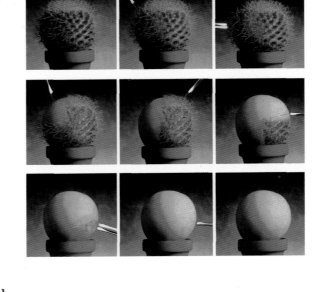

Look at these advertisements. Match them to their captions.

A 'With an Epilady you don't end up with a prickly pair'
B 'You can tell it's a Sony Trinitron from here'
C 'Of all the bars in the world'
D 'Pre-shrunk hifi'
E 'Dannimac. A true, trusted friend'

What products are the advertisements promoting? Discuss in groups.
How successful are these advertisements?
What makes them successful or not?
What are the three most important ingredients for a successful advertisement?
Compare answers with other groups.

Reading

Note: Michael Fish is well-known to the British public who see him giving the weather forecast on BBC television. A few years ago, on the evening before a devastating hurricane hit Britain, he committed the classic weather forecaster's gaffe by announcing that there was no truth in the rumours that strong gales were on their way.

Before you read

1 **The British Advertising Standards Association says that 'all advertisements should be ...'. Which four of the adjectives below do you think are included?**

funny	fair	legal
decent	honest	unbiased
truthful	eye-catching	non-sexist

While you read

2 **Find out the following information.**

1 What particular area of restriction the text deals with.
2 How regulations differ between television and printed advertisements in Britain.
3 How regulations differ between British and American practice in this field.

Vocabulary comprehension

3 **Find the words in this list which come from the text and then match each with another word from the list which has a similar meaning.**

distressed	sought	give	complied
appearing suddenly	shrugs off		removal
chagrined	compensation	donate	redress
similarity	given	granted	agreed
likeness	ignores	sprouting	looked for
withdrawal			

A name in vain?

Michael Fish, The BBC weatherman, felt somewhat overcast recently when he drove past a poster advertisement for International Ranch Paint. The advertisement showed weather symbols and a tin of paint at the foot of a white front door. The copy read: 'One coat shrugs off anything Michael Fish can throw at it.'

Mr Fish was annoyed that neither International Paint, a division of Courtaulds, nor MWP, its advertising agency, had sought his permission to use his name.

He sent a letter to the agency pointing out that as a civil servant - Mr Fish is employed by the meteorological department - he is forbidden to appear in advertisements, and asking MWP to donate a £1,000 'usage fee' to charity. MWP promptly complied. 'How could we not?' says Paul Wilmot, the agency's creative director.

Quite easily, in fact, because what MWP did was quite legal. It would not have been allowed to use Mr Fish's name in a television commercial, as the Independent Broadcasting Authority prohibits references in television advertising to any living person without his or her permission. But the code of practice for press and poster advertisements allows references to people with 'a high degree of public exposure', unless the references are defamatory, suggest commercial involvement with the product, or constitute an 'unreasonable' invasion of privacy. The more famous you are, the less redress you're likely to have, the code suggests.

'Looked at in this context, the Fish reference seems perfectly in order,' says Stephen Groom, a lawyer specialising in intellectual property. Mr Groom says that in the United States, celebrities often sue over the use of their name or photograph.

Here the advertiser can get away with a good deal more.'

Should chagrined celebrities feel they have cause for complaint, they can always, like Mr Fish, appeal to the advertiser or agency. Failing that, they can complain to the Advertising Standards Authority (ASA), which can insist on the withdrawal of advertisements that contravene its code of practice.

Members of the royal family regularly complain about appearing in ads against their wishes. Special, clear-cut rules apply to them.

'Without specific written approval, which has been granted only twice in the past decade on the occasion of the two royal weddings, the royal family cannot be used in advertising,' says David Williamson, the deputy director of the ASA.

But they often are, and they do complain. A likeness of the Prince of Wales recently appeared on a poster above the new British Library, the building he likened to the Soviet politburo. He was shown, head in hands, in an advertisement for a drainage company which claimed that the reason new buildings were sprouting everywhere was its quick service. The agency was, again, MWP, which removed the poster after Buckingham Palace complained to it and the ASA.

Why bother running it in the first place? 'An advertisement that is controversially withdrawn attracts far more attention than a regular campaign. That single poster received media coverage worth millions,' Mr Wilmot says.

'If you ring in advance to ask permission when you want to use a celebrity, they only say no, or ask for a large fee. So usually you just stick it up and hope for the best. It generally pays off either way.'

Vocabulary

Vocabulary development: advertising and marketing

4 Look at the text on page 98 again and make a list of all the words which have to do with advertising and marketing in the text.

In pairs. Help each other to understand the meaning of the words.

Using your dictionaries add any other words connected with advertising and marketing that you can think of.

Vocabulary building: -al

5 The suffix *-al* combines with some nouns to form adjectives.
Example ... *to promote a herbal tea.*
Note: A final '*y*' is replaced by '*ical*', not '*al*'.
Example   *meteorology   meteorological*

-ial is sometimes used after nouns ending in *-er, -or*, and *-ent*.
Example   *president   presidential.*
-al also combines with some verbs to form nouns.
Example   *renew   renewal*
Write the *-al* form of these words and say if it is a noun or adjective.

music	profession	deny	dismiss
classic	resident	portray	history

Pronunciation: pronouncing initials

6 Some names of companies, organisations, countries etc. are difficult to pronounce when speaking English because they probably exist in your own language with a different pronunciation.

69 Listen to the pronunciation of these initials.

BMW   CD   UFO

Now listen and write down the other initials.

A British radio and television company
A tax on goods sold
A French car
Great Britain and Northern Ireland
A German car company
A large and important nation
An international political organisation
Abbreviation for 'for example'
The most common piece of electrical equipment in people's homes
Abbreviation for 'that is'

Now listen and repeat.
Write a logical sentence containing as many of the initials above as possible! Now read your sentences to the rest of the class.

Practice

The link game

7 In groups. Student A: Say a word linked to advertising and marketing then give a sentence containing that word.
Student B: Say another word linked to A's word and incorporate both words in a new sentence.
Student C: Say another word associated with B's word and includes B's word and your own in a new sentence.

You can only use words linked to advertising. You have a time limit of one minute to find your word and make your sentence or you are out.

Write a TV ad

8 In pairs or groups. You are going to create and produce a one minute advertisement for television in which you can use a famous person for one of the products illustrated.

Discuss the best way of advertising the new product then prepare your ad and present it to the rest of the class.

Listen to other groups' ideas and give them a mark from 1 - 10 for originality and effectiveness.
(1 = not at all original and effective, 10 = excellent from point of view of originality and effectiveness.)
Find out which is the best ad in your class.

Speaking

9 People often complain about the quality of television in their country and more especially about the interference caused by TV commercials. Make a note of the best and the worst TV commercials that you have seen recently.

In groups. Tell the other people in your group about the two commercials you have chosen and explain why you like or dislike them.
What do the people in your group think about television advertising?

Listening

10 Listen to Carolyn talking to Dave about this advertisement. The first
[70] time you listen put the questions in the order you hear them.

a What do you think of television advertising?
b What do you think of that?
c Do you feel you are influenced by advertising?
d What's the thinking behind it?
e What do you think of advertising in general?
f Do you think it achieves its aim?
g Are there any types of advertising you don't like?

11 Here are some of Carolyn's answers. Match them to the appropriate question.

1 I probably am.	5 Anything which is too obvious.
2 I think it's a clever idea.	6 I suppose it's necessary.
3 I think on the whole it's quite clever.	7 It's comparing the rough with
4 Yes.	the smooth.

In pairs ask each other the questions Dave asked Carolyn and give your own answers.

 28 ▶

Grammar and pronunciation

1 This ad is being used to sell fabric softener.
2 What do you think of it?
   He asked her what she thought of the ad.
3 Do you think it achieves its aim?
   He asked her if she thought it achieved its aim.
4 Have you ever bought anything because you liked an advertisement?
   He asked her if she had ever bought anything because of an ad.
5 What's your favourite advertisement?
   He asked her what her favourite advertisement was.

Grammar: passives (2) (present continuous, present perfect and future)
(Grammar reference, page 143)

12 Look at sentence 1 in the grammar box again.
The same sentence in the past tense looks like this.

This ad *has been used* to sell fabric softener.

When speaking about the future it looks like this.

This ad *will be used* to sell fabric softener.

Now underline the correct word in this explanation of the use of the passive. Then add one of the sentences above where an example is required.

1 When you want to focus on the person or thing that is affected by an action, rather than the person or thing that performs the action, you use the *passive/indicative* voice.

100

2 The passive is formed with a form of the auxiliary *be/ have* followed by the *present/past* participle of a main verb. e.g. _____

3 Continuous passive tenses are formed with a form of the auxiliary verb *have/be* followed by *was/being* and the *present/past* participle of a main verb. e.g. _____

4 After modals you use the base form *have/be* followed by the *past/present* participle of a main verb. e.g. _____

Grammar: reporting (3) questions

(Grammar reference, page 144)

13 Look at the questions in 2 - 5 in the grammar box and the way in which they are reported.

1 In reported questions which comes first, the subject or the verb?

2 Question 2 needs the auxiliary *do*. What about the reported question?

3 When there is no question word in the question (4) how can you introduce the reported question?

4 Look at question 5. Where is the verb *be*? What about the reported question?

Compare your answers in pairs.

Grammar check

14 Put these sentences into the passive voice.

1 Someone has invited my sister to the party.

2 They will finish the work on the house by the end of the month.

3 Someone is feeding the cats.

15 Report the questions.

1 'Do you want a drink?'

2 'Where did you go?'

3 ' What time is it?'

4 'Have you ever been to Spain?'

5 'Is there anything you don't understand?'

Pronunciation: polite intonation in questions

16 The intonation in questions changes when you want [72] to be particularly polite.

Listen to this sentence being spoken in two different ways.

What do you think of it?

Which of the two intonations sounds more polite? Is there a rise or fall at the end of the more polite question?

Now listen and repeat.
In pairs. Practise reading these questions in the two ways illustrated above. Your partner has to tell you if you are being polite or not.

1 What's the time?

2 Where have you been?

3 What do you think of my new dress?

4 Why are you late?

5 When's your birthday?

Practice

Memory game

17 Prepare a series of six factual questions to ask other students.

Example *What's the capital of Scotland?* or
What's the boiling point of water?

In groups.
Student A: Ask Student B your questions.
Student B: Answer. (No writing allowed.) Try to remember A's questions. Now ask Student C your question and so on until everyone has asked their questions.
Everyone writes down from memory the questions they were asked. When everyone has finished each student reports the questions to the rest of the group.

Personal questions

18 Write down eight questions to ask other students in your class. Use different tenses of the passive in the questions.

Example *Have you ever been caught for speeding?*

Now try out your questions on as many people as possible. (You have the right to refuse to answer but you must remember those questions)
In groups. Report two of the questions you were asked to the rest of the group.

Writing development

Speaking

19 What is the aim of the first advertisement?

a To point out that 37% of adults risk death from smoking?

b To point out that smokers resent the high taxes they have
to pay on tobacco?

c To remind people that smokers make huge contributions
to public services through the taxes they pay?

**How does the second advertisement use ideas of disgust,
fear and common sense to discourage smokers?**

How persuasive do you find the two advertisements?

Debate

20 Group A:
You are members of an anti-smoking organisation.
You want smoking banned in all public places. You
think that all cigarette advertising is immoral because
smoking is bad for your health.

Group B:
You are members of a Smokers' Rights Association. You
believe in the complete freedom of the individual. You
think that cigarette manufacturers should have the
right to advertise.

**Discuss in your groups and make a list of points to
support your argument.**

**Now hold the debate. You must be very convincing but
give the other side a chance to state their point of view.
Make notes of the main arguments put forward in the debate.**

Did you know

that over 37% of the
adult population smoke
and they pay £22,500,000 a day
in taxes on tobacco?

Issued by the Tobacco Advisory Council, speaking for smokers.
Glen House, Stag Place, London SW1E 5AC

No wonder
smokers cough.

The tar and discharge th
of an a

Writing

Composition (3)

**21 Use the notes that you made for exercise 20 as a
basis for a composition entitled:**

**'Cigarette advertising should be banned completely.
What do you think of this statement?' (150 - 180 words)**
**Before you begin make a plan of the composition.
Here are some expressions to help you with each
phase of your composition.**

Paragraph 1	**a general introduction to the topic** There is a lot of talk these days about ... Cigarette advertising is ...
Paragraph 2	**arguments in favour of cigarette advertising** Many people think ... It is obvious that ... People should be allowed ...
Paragraph 3	**arguments against cigarette advertising** We must, however , take into consideration ... We cannot ignore the fact that ... Then, of course, there is also the question of ...
Paragraph 4	**conclusion** Having considered both sides of the argument I must say ... In my opinion ... I don't think it's right to ...

Hand in your plan with the finished work.

Say the right thing!

Agreeing and disagreeing

73 When you are giving an opinion, especially when expressing disagreement, you need to know a range of expressions if you do not want to offend people.

1 In pairs. Make a list of ways of agreeing and disagreeing.

Agree	Disagree

Now listen to the cassette. Add any phrases that you hear which you have not included in your list.

It is important to use the phrases that you have written with the correct intonation. Listen and repeat paying particular attention to your intonation.

74 Listen to the cassette again. You will hear a series of controversial statements. Agree or disagree with them.

2 In pairs. Choose one of the topics below. Discuss the topic together. Use the language you have practised in exercise 1 to agree and disagree with each other. Try to use a different phrase each time.

1 Capital punishment.
2 The introduction of pedestrian areas in all towns.
3 The raising of the school leaving age to eighteen.
4 A minimum of six weeks annual holiday for all workers.
5 The abolition of marriage.

Vocabulary

Commitment

1 Write eight words which you studied in exercise 3 on page 93 and write a sentence giving your opinion about each.

Example: *jogging - I think it's important that people exercise but some people who go jogging don't understand how they should go about it and so do more harm than good.*

Advertising and marketing

2 Write a list of six words which have to do with advertising and marketing.
Now give definitions of these words to another student. Your partner has to tell you what the words are.

Grammar

Future perfect, future continuous, future perfect continuous

3 Answer the questions using the appropriate form of the future.

1 What will you be doing at this time tomorrow?
2 In two months' time how many English lessons will you have had since you started the course?
3 At the end of this year how long will you have been studying English?
4 By the end of this year how long will the leader of your country have been in office?
5 Where will you be working next year?
6 How many years will you have been working by the time you retire?
7 What sort of car will you be buying next?
8 How many hours will you have spent watching television by the end of the week?

Reporting (2)

4 In groups of three take turns to give a reporting word, make a statement, and report the statement. Write the reported statements.

Example Student A: *Complain*
Student B: *What a mess in this room!*
Student C: *She complained about the way I'd left the room.*

1	boast	4	claim	7	agree
2	invite	5	persuade	8	promise
3	say	6	believe		

Passives (2): present continuous / future / present perfect

5 Look at the pictures and say what *has been done*, *is being done* and *will be done* soon in each case.

wheels   Engine   Bonnet

Pinkerton   Smallsville   Acresville

Last year   this year   next year

Reporting (3): questions

6 Rewrite the sentences in the correct order.

1 me where . I been She had asked
2 office her man time . The opened the asked what
3 where asked They us were . from we
4 a before wanted if car to She . I driven know had
5 travellers cheques . when the I The me bank clerk asked wanted
6 whether corner minded waiter I asked sitting in The . me the
7 Stallone George seen latest film had . asked the if me I
8 day . going would be next I them the asked they where

Guide to better language learning
Part 7 - Grammar

= My name's Brian

If you have problems with grammar study, or want to improve your technique look at pages 121 - 122.

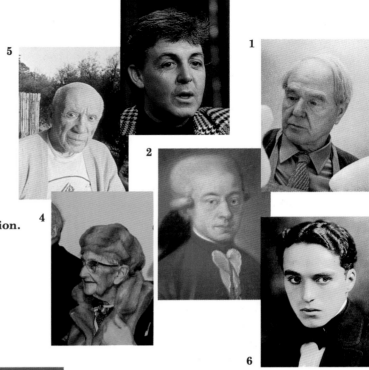

imagination /ɪmædʒɪneɪʃən /, **imaginations**. 1
Your **imagination** is 1.1 the ability that you have to
think of and form pictures or ideas in your mind of
things that are different, interesting, or exciting.
EG *He has very good taste and a marvellous
imagination... These plans reveal a complete
failure of imagination.*

Match the names of these people and their photographs.

Mozart
Agatha Christie
Henry Moore
Paul McCartney
Pablo Picasso
Charlie Chaplin

Now match the people and the products of their imagination.

Test your imagination
**The River Ganges, one of the most Holy and important rivers in India, has
108 names. These are some of them.**

The Pure   The Eternal   The Light Amid the Darkness
The Cow Which Gives Much Milk   The Liberator
The Destroyer Of Poverty And Sorrow   The Creator of Happiness

**In groups. You have ten minutes to invent alternative and poetic names
for the television!**
**When you have finished, compare your names with other groups. Find the
most imaginative name.**

Reading

Ruth Rendell is one of the most popular British crime fiction writers of the moment. Her first novel, *From Doon with Death*, appeared in 1964, and since then her reputation and readership has grown steadily with each new book. She has now received five major awards for her work: two Edgars from the Mystery Writers of America; the Crime Writers' Gold Dagger Award for 1976's best crime novel for *A Demon in my View*; the Arts Council National Book Award for Genre Fiction in 1981 for *Lake of Darkness*; and in 1985 the Crime Writers' Silver Dagger Award for *The Tree of Hands*.

Before you read

1 **The text is from one of her Inspector Wexford mysteries *The Best Man to Die*. In pairs. What can you deduce about the book from the title? What is a 'Best Man'?**

While you read

2 **Look at the list of descriptions of characters from the novel. Read the extract and match the names in A to the descriptions in B. Some characters can be described in more than one way.**

A Mrs Fanshawe   Hatton   Vigo   Wexford
B blackmailer   blackmailer's victim   murder victim
  murderer   detective   victim of an accident

Vocabulary comprehension

3 **Look at the words in context and choose the correct definition for the context.**

1 *reckon*   a   think that something is true.
  (l. 5)   b   calculate an amount.
    c   expect to do something.

2 *witness*   a   a person who sees an event e.g. an accident.
  (l. 21)   b   a person who appears in a court of law to tell what he or she knows about a crime or other event.
    c   a person who writes his / her name on a document to confirm that the person who was meant to sign has actually signed it.

3 *back up*   a   supply evidence to prove that a claim or story is true.
  (l. 21)   b   give someone help and support when they are in a difficult situation.
    c   drive a vehicle moving backwards a little way.

4 *nonsense*   a   words, speech or text that do not mean anything and do not make sense.
  (l. 32)   b   something spoken or written that you disagree with because you consider it untrue, stupid or meaningless.
    c   foolish behaviour that makes a particular situation very difficult.

5 *snort*   a   the noise that animals make when they breathe noisily through their noses.
  (l. 34)   b   breathe air noisily through the nose to express anger, disapproval, contempt or amusement.
    c   a glass of an alcoholic drink.

Choose three other words or expressions from the text that you don't understand.
Discuss the words on your list with another student. In pairs. Try to write an explanation.

 29 ▶

'On the following day, May 22nd, we know Hatton paid five hundred pounds into his own account, keeping two hundred for the Pertwees' key money and the remaining three hundred for incidental expenses, furniture, clothes and other frivolity. The
5 weekly payments of fifty pounds a time followed at once. I reckon Hatton got Vigo to leave the money in some prearranged hiding place down by the river on Friday nights somewhere along the route Hatton took on his way home from the darts club. And one Friday night ...'
10   'Yes, why that particular Friday?'
'Who can say at what point the victim of blackmail reaches the end of his tether?'
'Mrs Fanshawe,' put in Burden unexpectedly. 'You see, that wasn't quite right, what you said about the Fanshawes' intervention having
15 come to an end. Mrs Fanshawe regained consciousness the day before Hatton was killed. It was in the morning papers, just a paragraph, but it was there.'
'You've got something there, Mike. Nora was still missing, but once Mrs Fanshawe could talk, Vigo might believe she'd tell us the
20 girl's body couldn't be that of her daughter. Hatton was an

important witness with someone else now to back up his story. Once he'd had all he wanted out of Vigo...'
The doctor got up, stood for a moment staring at Wexford's flowers and then said, 'It's a good story, but it's impossible. It
25 couldn't have happened that way.' Wexford smiled at him. Crocker said irritably, 'What are you grinning like that for? I tell you there's an obvious flaw. If anyone throws a body out of a car, even feet first, it's going to fall well over to the left. Vigo would have had to be driving right on the grass section itself for the girl's head to have
30 been in the fast lane. And as to the theory of yours about the head being on his lap to stop the bloodstains getting on the passenger seat, it's nonsense. That way her feet would have been in the fast lane and Fanshawe would have swerved to the left to avoid her head.'
He stopped and gave a defiant snort as the nurse came back with a
35 sleeping pill.
'I don't want that,' said Wexford. He slid down in the bed and pulled up the covers. 'I'll sleep, I'm tired.' Over the top of the sheet he said, 'Nice of you two to come. Oh, and by the way, it's a foreign car. Left-hand drive. Good night.'

Vocabulary

Vocabulary development: the arts

4 Listen to this description of the arts and make lists of
75 words using these headings.

Visual   Written   Music

Compare and complete your lists in pairs.

Vocabulary building: names of professions

5 The names of professions in English often end in *-er*,
-or, *-ist* and *-ian*.

76 Write the profession for each of these definitions.

-er   1   A person who writes books.

       2   A person who writes music.

-ist   3   A person who plays the piano.

-or   4   A person who makes statues from stone etc.

       5   A person who makes films.

-ian   6   A person who makes people laugh.

       7   A person who is an expert in history.

Listen and check your answers.

Now find another profession for each category.

Note: Exceptions. What do we call a person who writes plays? And poems?

Pronunciation: silent consonants

6 Look at this group of words. Find the pairs of words in
77 which the same consonant is silent. Write the 'silent' letter next to the pairs you find.

writer   fasten   science

       pneumatic   listen

what   wrong   where

       scene   pneumonia

Now listen and check your answers.

Listen and repeat.

In pairs find more words for each silent letter.

Practice

Categories

7 Individually. Complete the chart using words from exercises 4 and 5.

Work of art	Artist	Subdivisions within the work	Other words
book	writer	chapter	edit

In groups of four. Student A: Give the name of the work of art. The other students give a word for each category in turn. One point for each word. Anyone who gives extra words for any of the categories gets extra points.

Great works

8 Which of your favourite paintings or other works of art would you like to have painted or written?

Write the name of a work for at least two of these categories.

books   plays   poems   films

sculptures   pieces of music   paintings

In groups. Tell the other students in your group what you have chosen and why.

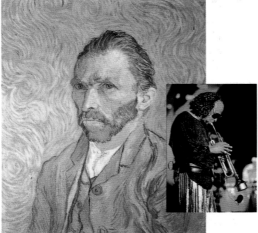

Speaking

9 **Look at the cartoon. Reorder the words to make the caption.**

handle - Scotland sergeant , where the found body Yard'll ,
OK ? was exactly . Now it

What are the essential ingredients in a good thriller? Work in groups and make a list.

(A thriller is a book, film or play which tells an exciting story about dangerous, frightening or mysterious events such as murder or kidnapping. Ruth Rendell is a writer of thrillers.)

Listening

10 **Read the text on page 106 again quickly.**

78 **Listen to these people discussing the text. Tick the things on this list that they mention.**

the blackmailer	Mrs Fanshawe
the person being blackmailed	Nora
the murderer	Crocker
the witness	Burden
the Pertwees	Wexford
the relationship between	Vigo
Pertwee and Hatton	the motorway
Hatton	

Listen again and make more detailed notes about the things that you have ticked.

Inspector Wexford

Grammar and pronunciation

1 I think Vigo must have killed Hatton.
2 He might have killed someone.
3 Mrs Fanshawe may have been involved in a car accident.
4 Nora can't have been in the car at the time of the accident.
5 Nora could have been killed as well.
6 It couldn't have happened like that.

Grammar: present perfect of modal verbs
(Grammar reference, page 144)

11 **Look at the sentences in the grammar box.**
Match the sentences to the explanations below. (In some cases the explanation describes more than one sentence.)

a When you want to say that you are almost certain that something has happened.
b When you want to say that you do not think that something has happened.
c When you want to say that there is a possibility that something happened in the past.
d When you want to say that it is not possible that something happened.

Grammar check

12 **Underline the correct alternative.**
1 Simon (*mightn't/can't*) have been at the party: he was away on holiday.

Practice

Guessing

14 **In groups. Look at the photo. Make hypotheses about what may/might/could (not) have happened just before the picture was taken.**
Now read your conclusions to the class.

Murder in Maidstone

15 **There has been a murder in the town of Maidstone, Kent. Student A: Look at page 134. Student B: Look at page 135. Student C: Look at page 136.**

Now work together and make hypotheses about the following details of the crime, using *must/might/may/ can't/could* have.

the motive for the murder
the means by which the murder was committed
the identity of the murderer

2 You (*must/may*) have seen her: she was sitting next to you.
3 He (*might/can't*) have missed the train: he's usually here by now.
4 She (*can't/must*) have been sitting in the sun all day: she's very red.
5 He (*couldn't/could*) have been there: he said he was going to be.
6 She (*couldn't/might*) have meant what she said: it would be out of character.

Pronunciation: juncture

13 **It is sometimes important to put the stress on the right words if you want to make your meaning clear.**

80 **Listen to these words – which do you hear first?**

blackmail   black male

Listen again and identify the phrases.

A		B	
1	a man eating fish	a	a man-eating fish
2	an English teacher (a teacher from England)	b	an English teacher (a teacher of English)
3	a crossword	c	a cross word
4	a hothouse	d	a hot house

Listen and check your answers.
Listen and repeat.

Writing development

Reading

16 Read this extract from *Red Wind*, a story by
Raymond Chandler.

Note: There are some idiomatic American phrases in
the extract which you may not understand.

souse	drunken person
straight rye	whisky without ice or water
you sure ...	you certainly ...
cut the clouds off	serve beer without foam
buddy	informal way of speaking to someone
	whose name you don't know
dimes	ten cent coins

Now look at the painting *Nighthawks* by Edward
Hopper. Make a note of the differences between the
scene in the Chandler story and the scene in the
painting.

The kid behind the bar was in his early twenties and looked as if
he had never had a drink in his life.

There was only one other customer, a souse on a bar stool with
his back to the door. He had a pile of dimes stacked neatly in
front of him, about two dollars' worth. He was drinking straight
rye in small glasses and he was all by himself in a world of his
own.

I sat further along the bar and got my glass of beer and said:
'You sure cut the clouds off them, buddy. I will say that for you.'

'We just opened up,' the kid said. 'We got to build up trade.
Been in before, haven't you, mister?'

'Uh-huh.'

'Live around here?'

'In the Berglund Apartments across the street,' I said. 'And
the name is John Dalmas.'

Speaking

17 Look at the painting and discuss the answers to these questions.

1 What time of day or night is this?
2 What is the relationship between the man and the woman in the painting?
3 What do they do?
4 Does the barman know the man or the woman?
5 Why do you think the man at the end of the bar is on his own?
6 Does this man know any of the other people in the bar?
7 What do you think the barman is saying to the man with the woman?
8 What do you think happened to the people before the scene in the painting?
9 What do you think happened after this scene?

Writing

Narration (2)

18 Here is a possible beginning to a story based on the scene in the
painting. Write the rest of the story. (If you want to you can change the
beginning.)

It was three o'clock in the morning in Phillie's Bar. It was empty but for three people, a
man and a woman who came in just after two thirty and a sad-looking character who
appeared about ten minutes after them.

When you have finished, exchange stories with other students and read
them. In pencil, underline any mistakes of grammar or vocabulary that
you notice and write the correct version above.

When you get your own story back, look at the mistakes. Check them by
using your dictionary and grammar book or by asking your teacher.

Vocabulary

The arts

1 Make a list of ten words from memory from the ones you studied in Unit 15.
In pairs. Student A: Choose one of the words from the list.

1 Give a synonym for the word.
2 Give the number of letters.
3 Give the first letter.
4 Give the last letter.

Student B: Guess the word.
Then change over.

Grammar

Present perfect of modal verbs

2 This a true story published in a British newspaper in the 1960s.

An elephant was washed ashore in Widemouth Bay, Cornwall. The police believe it was thrown overboard from a passing ship.

Make sentences hypothesising about how the elephant got there. Make a sentence for each of the following verbs.

can't have   must have   could have   couldn't have
might have   may have

Guide to better language learning
Part 8 - The FCE exam

If you have want to find out more about the FCE exam, or want to improve your exam technique look at pages 122 - 123.

Speaking

Discussion: learning from manuals

1 **On page 10 you read about Bert Weedon's guitar-learning manual. In groups, discuss the value of 'teach yourself' learning.**

1 What, if any, subjects can be successfully learnt in this way?
2 What is the particular attraction of these methods?
3 Is failure due mainly to the learner or to the method? Why?
4 Have you ever tried to learn to do something using a manual? What happened?

Roleplay: job interview

2 **Student A:**
You are Sally Griffiths from the article on page 14, attending an interview to join the pilot training course. You want to become a pilot more than anything else. You realise you are over the age limit but it's not by very much.

Student B:
You are interviewing Ms Griffiths. Show that you are very impressed with her but point out that rules are rules and you can do nothing about it. Try to offer other suggestions to Sally, including the private flying college in Oxford.

Discussion: excitement and fear are linked

3 **In groups. Discuss the following.**

1 Discuss times when you felt very excited. Was there also an element of fear in your excitement?
2 Think of times when you felt very frightened. Were you also excited?
3 On which occasions do you think the two things are connected?
4 When is there no connection at all?

Interview: fears and anxieties

4 **Write down five questions you are prepared to answer about your own fears and anxieties. Choose another student and exchange lists of questions. Ask and answer the questions.**

Example **Student A:** *If you are in the house on your own do you usually lock all the doors?*

Student B: *Yes, I'm not really afraid of burglars, but I like to know that if I'm upstairs there's no chance of someone coming in.*

Roleplay: second homes

5 **Student A:**
You intend to buy a cottage in the mountains. Make a list of the things you love about the cottage and your reasons for buying it (e.g. peace, garden, clear air). Include all the things you can do there which you can't do in your present house (e.g. long walks, skiing, wine making). Tell Student B about your plans.

Student B:
You think there are a lot of disadvantages about having a second home. Make a list of the disadvantages (e.g. distance from your first house, burglaries, difficulty of maintenance). Try to dissuade Student A from buying the house.

Interviews: happiness

6 **Write down five situations in which you have felt really happy. Talk to other students and try to find people who have felt happy for similar reasons. In groups, find out if there is a reason for happiness which you have in common.**

Discussion: ordering photos

7 **In groups, look at the photos and discuss the logical sequence.**

Giving instructions: descriptions

8 **Choose one of the photos on page 69. Describe it in detail for your partner to draw. When you are satisfied with the result show your partner the photo you chose.**

Roleplay: Third world problems

9 **Student A:**

You have just come back from visiting a third world country. (Decide which one.)
You have been into schools. (Describe what you saw.)
You have visited families in their homes. (Describe conditions there.)
You want more to be done to help these countries. (Decide what.)

Student B:

You are interviewing Student A.
Ask where he/she has been.
Ask what places he/she went to and what conditions he/she saw.
Ask what he/she thinks should be done.
Discuss whatever ideas he/she suggests.

Interview: food freak

10 **Student A:**

You are a fruitarian and believe more people should join you. Point out to Student B that fruit is:
good for you; cheap; a complete food; healthy.
Try to get Student B to change his/her habits.

Student B:

You really enjoy a variety of food, particularly meat. You think Student A is mad. Point out that:
fruit alone is not enough; we need a balanced diet; fruit will not protect us from the cold in winter; eating fruit is boring.
Try to get Student A to change his/her habits.

Discussion: advertising

11 **In pairs look at the advertisement. Benetton chose it to publicise their products.**

UNITED COLORS OF BENETTON.

Photograph by Oliviero Toscani for United Colours of Benetton. Campaign 1991.

1 Why did the advertisers decide to use this photo?
2 In what ways do you think it is successful or unsuccessful?
3 Some people have objected to this advertisement. Why do you think this is?
4 What do you think of advertisements like this which use strong images to attract the public's attention?

Reading

Mr Guitar's simple rule of strum

1 **Read the information in the chart on page 10 and write a paragraph of not more than sixty words about Bert Weedon.**

Stewardess sells home to win her wings

2 **Read the article on page 14 again. Make notes and summarise the main points of the article in not more than fifty words. Mention these things.**

her ambition   the problems
her previous job   how she overcame them

Road Runners

3 **Using the information in the article on page 24 continue each of these paragraphs. Use no more than thirty words for each paragraph.**

1 The writer says that bob sleigh racing is kid's stuff by comparison with land luging because ...
2 Bob Pereyra and Ron Amos very much hope that land luging will catch on because ...
3 Bob and Ron believe that ...

Don't panic!

4 **Write a summary of the text on page 30 in not more than 120 words.**

My favourite place

5 **Without referring to the text on page 36 again, complete the extract below using these words.**

middle aged   pleasant   olive oil   between   hoteliers
school teachers   roses   farm   joy   vegetables
steep   fashionable   restaurant   mystery

The Swallow's Nest is a ____, four-hectare ____ where we make our own ____ and wine. I grow all my own ____ and ____ too. If I eat out, the best ____ is Zaccharia ____ Amalfi and Atrani. The tourists here are mostly sedate, ____ English ____ and so on, rather ____ people. The town would prefer swingers but it is a ____ and ____ to me, if not to the ____ and restaurateurs of this so called Divine coast that it has never been ____.

Living with my own legend

6 **Using the information in the article on page 44 continue each of these paragraphs. Use no more than thirty words for each paragraph.**

1 Boris Becker felt he was unhappy because ...
2 After losing the tournament at Flushing Meadow he decided ...
3 Things finally began to go better for Boris when ...

Dressed to cure

7 **Without referring to the text on page 52 again complete the extract using these words.**

female	conservative	consulting	older
half	skirt	higher	suit	jeans
doctor	male	coat	concerned

People generally prefer to see their ____ dressed in a ____ fashion: ____ doctors in a ____ and tie, and ____ doctors a ____ and jumper and white ____. It is mostly ____ people and people in ____ social classes who are most ____. More than ____ the people said they wouldn't be very happy about ____ a doctor who was wearing ____.

James Galway

8 **Read the extract on page 56 again and decide which drawing best illustrates the text.**

A cure for love

9 **The writer of the article on page 64 believes that love is entirely different from what people commonly believe. Read the article again, make notes of the main points and then write a summary in about sixty words.**

Superman comes down to earth with a proposal

10 **Read the article on page 70 again. Write one sentence for each paragraph summarising the content of the paragraph.**

Cry Freedom

11 **Read the extract on page 78 again. Write a paragraph (about 60 words) describing Steve Biko, using the information from the text and any other information you can include from looking at the photo on page 78.**

'Why?'

12 **Here are some sentences taken from the Tracy Chapman song on page 84. Use these words to complete the sentences.**

starve	hate	safe	yes	starve	home	peace
free	peacekeepers	world				

Why do the babies ...
When there's enough ... to feed the ...
Why are the missiles called ...
Why is a women still not ...
When she's in her ...
Love is ...
War is ...
No is ...
And we're all ...

Saved from the turkey by a passion for fruit

13 **Read the article on page 94 again. Write one sentence for each paragraph summarising the content of the paragraph.**

A name in vain?

14 **Read the article on page 98 again. Summarise the article using these sentence heads. Your completed summary should not exceed 60 words.**

Michael Fish was annoyed....
The MWP donated....
Members of the royal family....
If advertisements are withdrawn....

The best man to die

15 **Without referring to the text on page 106 again complete the extract. You should use one word only in each space.**

____ the following day, May 22nd, we know Hatton paid five hundred ____ into his own account, keeping two ____ for the Pertwees' key money and the ____ three hundred for incidental expenses, furniture, clothes and ____ frivolity. The weekly ____ of fifty pounds a time followed ____ once. I reckon Hatton got Vigo to ____ the money in some pre-arranged hiding place ____ by the river ____ Friday nights somewhere along the ____ Hatton ____ on his way home ____ the darts club.

Writing

In each of the writing exercises your work should contain 150 - 200 words.

Formal letters

1 **In pairs. You are both going to attend a language school in Britain during July. Prepare a letter to the school. Include this information.**

- Confirmation that you have received final details of your course.
- Confirmation that you have received the address of your host family.
- Details of your flight.
- Any other information you think is necessary.

Discuss the way you will set out your letter.
When you have planned your letter together, write it separately.
When you have finished exchange letters and try to improve on them.

Informal letters

2 **Read the letter from Margaret to her sister Sally. The style is unsuitable for an informal letter. Rewrite the letter in a more suitable way.**

25 Smith Street
Coventry
22 March 1993

Sally Stokes
31 Hanover Lane
Bristol

Dear Ms Stokes,

I would like to take this opportunity to thank you most sincerely for the kind invitation to spend the weekend with you and your husband Mike.

It is with regret that I have to refuse the invitation. I have a previous appointment on that day with my parents. We have arranged for them to be present at our house on that weekend. It would give us very great pleasure to see you here before too long, however. We can then spend time together discussing what we have been achieving recently.

Once again a very sincere thank you for your kind invitation. We very much look forward to meeting you again.

Yours sincerely

Margaret Thomas

Margaret Thomas

Narration

3 **Look at the pictures. Put them in order and then write a story linking them.**

Biographical description

4 **Write a biography of yourself using this outline.**

Date of birth	Education	Family situation
Place of birth	Work experience	Hobbies

Dialogue writing

5 **You borrowed your sister's car to go for a drive in the country for the day. She was anxious for you to be back by 7.30 pm as she needed the car later. The pictures describe what happened. Write the conversation you had with your sister when you eventually got back.**

Reporting

6 **Look at Unit 10 exercise 19 again. Imagine that you have just returned from spending a year on the uninhabited tropical island. Describe your experience. Include the following in your report.**

- A brief description of the island.
- The things you liked about it.
- The things you hated about it.
- The reasons why you would or wouldn't repeat the experience.

Preparing a speech

7 **A motorway has been planned near your town, but nobody wants it to be built. Look at the notice for a public meeting about the motorway. You are one of the people to deliver a speech. Expand the notes below to make your speech.**

- enormous expense
- destroy the beauty of the countryside
- noise of traffic disturb local residents
- not necessary as main roads are good, fast, and direct
- money be better spent on other things

Begin your speech by addressing the audience and end it by making a counter suggestion.

Functional revision

In pairs do the following roleplays. You can develop the conversations as much as you wish.

Roleplay 1: At the airport

Student A: You are meeting a business contact at the airport. You have never met him/her before but you know he/she is about fifty. Check you have the right person, greet him/her, ask about the journey, say you are taking him/her on a tour of the town and then out to dinner.

Student B: You are the business contact, you are very tired, and so ask Student A if he/she minds taking you straight to the hotel. You definitely do not want to go out to dinner. Refuse the invitation politely.

Roleplay 2: Weekend plans

Student A: You and Student B have been invited to go climbing this weekend. You are very keen to go, although you don't want to if Simon is going. Student B will know if he is. Try to persuade Student B to go.

Student B: You don't want to go at all. You remember the last time a similar trip was organised and you were stuck in the snow for three hours waiting for help to arrive! Simon is definitely not going.

Roleplay 3: Good advice

Student A: You have been offered a new job which involves a higher salary than you had. It involves moving to a new town and you don't want to take the children away from their school where they are doing very well. Also houses cost much more in the new town. Ask Student B for advice.

Student B: You hesitate about giving advice as you are not sure what is the best thing for Student A to do. Ask him/her to explain more about the job, conditions, prospects, etc. Decide what advice to give finally.

Roleplay 4: Arguing

Student A: You and Student B seem to disagree about everything! Discuss the facilities in your town which you think are very inadequate.

Student B: It's almost impossible to have a reasonable conversation with Student A! Try to defend your local authority and point out what good work is being done providing more facilities for young and old.

Part 1 - The right approach

Have you got the right approach to language learning?

1 Why are you studying English?

a For your job.

b As a hobby.

c For use on holiday.

d As an academic subject at school or university.

e Other. Please specify.

2 Which of the following do you have greatest difficulty with?

a Speaking English.

b Understanding spoken English.

c Reading English.

d Writing English.

e Learning vocabulary.

f English grammar.

g Pronunciation.

3 How much contact do you have with English outside your English lessons?

a None.

b Almost none.

c Some.

d Frequent.

e Every day.

4 Which of the following are the most important qualities for the language learning student?

a A good 'ear'.

b A good memory.

c Good reflexes.

d Lack of inhibition.

e A logical mind.

Key and comment

1 Why are you studying English?

- It's not very important *why* you are studying English as long as you are really serious about wanting to learn the language. If you are motivated you will find it easier to learn.

2 Which of the following do you have greatest difficulty with?

- Most students at intermediate level say that they have greatest difficulty speaking the language and understanding English spoken by native speakers at normal speeds.
- *Workout Upper Intermediate* gives you many opportunities to work at your speaking and listening skills but develops the other skills as well.

- One of the reasons why students have difficulty speaking is that they don't have the necessary vocabulary. Through reading texts and specific vocabulary development work you will be able to 'reactivate' your passive vocabulary and learn many new words.
- At regular intervals you will have the chance to work on your study skills so that you become a more efficient language learner. These sections have the heading *Guide to better language learning*.

3 How much contact do you have with English outside your English lessons?

- The more contact you have with English outside the classroom the faster your progress will be.
- If you answered 'None' or 'Almost none' to this question there are many ways in which you can change the situation. Read the various *Guide to better language learning* sections to find out more.

4 Which of the following are the most important qualities for the language learning student?

- All of the qualities listed will help you learn a language more effectively.
- Many students are convinced that they have few of the qualities listed but don't despair! It's possible to develop all of these qualities if you are prepared to do the necessary work.

Part 2 - Speaking

1 Here is a list of what students say are their common difficulties when they are speaking English.

'I'm afraid of making mistakes and so I often end up saying nothing.'

'When I speak English I can make myself understood but I know that I'm making a lot of grammar mistakes all the time.'

'My English accent is terrible. People in my class understand me but they're students too. I'm sure English people would never understand me.'

'I often get half way through a sentence and find that I'm lost because the grammar has become too complicated.'

'I have a lot of difficulty speaking because I don't know the words. I get stuck all the time because of vocabulary.'

Which of these problems do *you* have? Make a note of any other difficulties you have when you are speaking.

Improving your speaking strategies

Vocabulary

Not being able to find the right words *is* a problem but there are ways round it.

- Try to explain your way round an unknown word by giving a definition, or using gestures. You can even point if it's an object!

- Try to spend a regular amount of time every day or at least every week increasing your vocabulary using the method that suits you best. Reading will increase your vocabulary.

Pronunciation

Students often worry too much about their 'accent'. There is a wide variety of English accents and it is unlikely that your accent is so non-standard that people will not understand.

There are pronunciation exercises in the Student's Book and Workbook which focus specifically on pronunciation problems. If you are worried about your pronunciation, spend extra time on these.

Fluency or accuracy?

Making yourself understood is more important than being accurate. At first, aim for fluency more than accuracy. Many mistakes that people make while speaking are just 'slips' and will disappear with time. Your main aim when speaking English should be to speak with sufficient accuracy for people to understand you without too much difficulty.

The key to developing your speaking ability is *CONFIDENCE*!
How do you develop confidence? By *PRACTISING* speaking as often as you can!

There are two places where you can practise speaking: inside and outside the classroom.

In the classroom.
- If there are people of different nationalities in your class avoid working with people of your nationality.

- If you are all of the same nationality make sure you use English not just to 'do' the activities but all the time you are in the classroom. If you are studying English in your own country your only chance to speak English may well be only during English lessons. Make the most of them!

Outside the classroom.
- Join an English language club.

- Try to practise English as much as possible, for example when you are on holiday or with English-speaking tourists in your area.

Part 3 - Listening

1 **What are the main difficulties with listening to English? Make a list.**

2 **What strategies do you have for dealing with these difficulties?**

3 **Where can you get listening practice in English?**

Compare your answers with the suggestions.

1 **Here is a list of difficulties which students often experience when listening to English.**

Speed Students often have the impression that English speakers speak faster than they do their own language. This is largely mistaken.

Accent Students are often used to hearing only one English accent and have difficulties adapting to any variations.

Sentence rhythm and elision
The accent falls on the important words in English sentences and others tend to disappear.

Background noise
This can interfere with what you are listening to.

More than one voice
People rarely wait for each other to stop speaking in conversation - this overlapping can increase difficulties in understanding.

2 **Things to help you.**

Hesitation
Most people hesitate when they are speaking any language; they hesitate more when the topic is more abstract. This is an advantage for you as it gives you time to absorb what is being said.

Repetition
Another advantage of spoken language is that people often repeat themselves which gives you more than one chance to understand what people are saying.

Listening technique.
- Most difficulties listed in point 1 will disappear in time if you *listen to English often*. Like training for a sport or playing a musical instrument you will only get better if you practise regularly.

- *Relax*! Many students are so worried about understanding that they are too tense to have any chance of success.

- *But* don't expect to understand much if you are unable to *concentrate*. In class, when listening to cassettes, make sure you shut off your mind to anything other than what you are listening to.

- *Don't expect or try to understand every word.* The main thing is to get the general idea of what the person is saying.
- When listening to cassettes in class or at home, decide what you are going to listen for each time and just *listen for those specific things*.

3 These are the main sources of listening material available to people in most countries.

Radio There are many international broadcasting services in English. You can usually find them on the short waveband.

Cassettes In many countries there are magazines with accompanying cassettes for learners of English. You can also buy cassettes of people reading stories and novels.

TV/video/satellite TV

In some countries films are shown on TV in the original language.
You can sometimes hire videos in English.
If you have access to satellite TV many programmes are broadcast in English.

Songs If you choose the singers carefully and buy cassettes, CDs or records which also supply the words of the songs, you may get valuable extra listening practice.

People If there is an English language club in your town, join it! Take every opportunity to speak and listen to English speakers.

Part 4 - Reading

Which of the following statements about reading do you agree or disagree with?

1 It's a waste of time to practise reading during English lessons.
2 People read newspapers, novels, instruction manuals and magazines in the same way.
3 Texts are easier to read if you are interested in the subject.
4 Reading helps you to learn new vocabulary.
5 Reading helps you to learn grammar.
6 You should try to understand as much of a text in another language as a text in your language.
7 When you read you have to understand every word.
8 It's a good idea to use a dictionary every time you find a word that you don't understand.
9 It's better to use a monolingual dictionary than a bilingual one.
10 You can guess the meanings of most unknown words if you see them in context.

Now read the notes and see if your answers correspond.

1 No! In your English lessons you will do exercises under the supervision of the teacher which will help you become a more efficient reader.
2 No, they don't. People employ a different reading technique according to the type of text they are reading. For example: if you are reading an instruction manual for a new hifi you will read very carefully and be looking at specific information in detail but if you pick up and read a newspaper you read headlines and small pieces of articles until you find something that interests you and even then you don't necessarily read in great detail.
3 Yes, they are. If you find a text interesting or need to get some information from it you will be more motivated to read efficiently and will worry less about things you can't understand.
4 Yes. If you see new words in context you are more likely to remember them.
5 Yes. When you read correct grammatical sentences the patterns will become more familiar to you and you will be more likely to remember them.
6 No. It doesn't usually matter if you don't understand a text in English as well as you would a text in your language. Don't be too ambitious about how much you expect to understand especially on a first reading.
7 No, this isn't necessary. You will usually find that there is the odd word which you don't understand. This is quite normal - you must learn to accept this and above all, don't panic!
8 No. It's better to use a dictionary only as a last resort. It's much better to work out the meaning of the word from the context.
9 Yes. Often bilingual dictionaries have only enough space to give you a word for word translation. Monolingual dictionaries will give you a more comprehensive explanation of a word.
10 Yes. You should be able to guess between 60% and 80% of unknown words if you look carefully at the context.

Part 5 - Writing

Answer these questions.

1 When do you write in your own language?
2 Why is it a good idea to learn to write while you are studying English?
3 What are your biggest difficulties when you are writing English?
4 What should you always do before you hand written work in to your teacher?

5 What should you do when you get written work back from your teacher?

6 How do you go about starting a piece of written work?

7 What are the writing targets in this book?

Now check your answers.

1 Many students of English have difficulty with writing because they rarely have to write in their own language, apart from the odd letter or postcard.

2 It may be useful for you to be able to write accurately in English for your work either now or in the future, but there are also other advantages. You will find that regular writing activities will consolidate and reinforce your knowledge of the vocabulary and grammar which you learn. If you are preparing for an exam like the Cambridge FCE you will also need to be able to write accurately.

3 Most students say that there are two main difficulties when writing: finding things to say and being able to write them accurately using the correct words. You will have all the help you need from the teacher and this book to solve both these problems.

4 You should always check your work thoroughly for spelling mistakes and small grammatical errors.

5 Always have a good look at the mistakes you have made. If you don't, you will have wasted your and your teacher's time.

6 Before you write anything, you should always check that you have understood the instructions and know what is expected of you. You should also make a plan of what you are going to write before you start so that you have time to organise your thoughts.

7 The writing targets include: formal and informal letters, composition, preparing a speech, writing dialogue, telling a story, describing an accident, and describing a person or a place. This range of tasks covers all the targets for the FCE exam.

Part 6 - Vocabulary

How effective are your vocabulary learning strategies?
Choose an answer to the questions. When you have finished check your score.

1 **Which of the following best describes your vocabulary learning strategy?**
   A I don't make any particular effort to learn vocabulary; I just pick up new words as I go along.
   B I have a methodical approach to vocabulary learning. I try to learn fifty new words a week and check that I know them regularly.

C I make a note of new words with my lesson notes but I often lose the list and never seem to find the time to look at them again.

2 **You decide you want to increase your vocabulary in English. What do you do?**
   A Learn a list of ten new words at regular intervals, say, every week.
   B Read more books and newspapers in English and note down the new words.
   C Buy a new dictionary and keep it with you all the time.

3 **You come across new vocabulary during an English lesson. What do you do?**
   A Write it down then transfer it to a special note-book or card index later.
   B Write it down then check you know it at regular intervals.
   C Nothing.

4 **You're talking to an English native-speaker who uses a word that you don't understand. What do you do?**
   A Bluff and pretend that you understand.
   B Stop the person and ask him or her to explain what the word means.
   C Carry on but make a mental note to look it up in a dictionary later.

5 **You're reading a text and you don't know the meaning of a word. What do you do?**
   A Look it up straight away in a dictionary.
   B Try to work out the meaning from the context.
   C Ignore it and carry on.

SCORE

		C 1	
		B 2	
		A 3	3
C 1		C 1	
B 3		B 3	
A 2	5	A 2	2
C 3		C 1	
B 2		B 3	
A 1	4	A 2	1

5 - 8   You need to think more carefully about your approach to vocabulary learning and be more systematic.

9 - 12   You're on the right track, but there are areas of your technique which you could improve.

13 - 15   Very good! Your approach to vocabulary learning is methodical and sound.

120

Notes on technique

Question 1

- Try to develop a methodical approach to vocabulary learning. Not all people learn languages in the same way. Experiment and find the right approach for you.

Question 2

- Reading is the best way to increase your vocabulary because you are learning the words in a context and you are more likely to remember them as a result.

Question 3

- Develop an efficient means of storing vocabulary which you can easily refer to later. Experiment with the following.
  - Alphabetical card indexes with definitions or translations of words.
  - A special note-book with new words listed by topic area.
  - An alphabetical note-book (e.g. an address book) which you can keep with you at all times.
  - An alphabetical list on your home computer. (This has the advantage over the others as it will be easier to update.)

Question 4

- When you are talking to someone you will not want to keep interrupting them as they might get irritated by you. Only interrupt when not knowing the word really does interfere with communication. Bluffing is theoretically all right but can get you into trouble sometimes.

Question 5

- You are more likely to remember the meanings of words which you have worked out from the context (see 2). Constant use of a dictionary will eventually spoil your enjoyment of the text you are reading. Use your dictionary to check the meanings of words which you really have no idea of or when you have seen a word many times in context and still don't understand it

Part 7 - Grammar

How effective are your grammar study strategies? Choose the statement which best expresses your point of view in each case. When you have finished check your score on the next page.

1 A I looked at a number of grammar books and chose the right one for my level.

   B I have no specific grammar book as I find that the grammar section at the back of my English course book is adequate.

   C I have no grammar book and rarely consult one as I find them confusing and unclear.

2 A When I am speaking English I am careful not to make any grammar mistakes although I realise that this makes my English a little slow and unspontaneous.

   B I don't care about grammar mistakes at all. My aim is to communicate efficiently and a few mistakes won't make much difference.

   C I occasionally make grammar mistakes when I'm speaking but usually they are things that I know already - when I have a real grammar problem I always go and check it in my grammar book.

3 A When I am writing compositions I write them then check the grammar afterwards.

   B When I write in English, I stop after every sentence and check the grammar.

   C I never worry too much about grammar when I'm writing; I haven't got a grammar book so I can't really check the grammar properly anyway.

4 A When my teacher gives me back my written work I just have a quick look at the corrections.

   B I ask my teacher to underline the mistakes in my written work without correcting them, then I correct them myself.

   C I work through all the mistakes in my written work using a grammar book even when I am almost sure of the answer.

5 A I have never bothered to learn grammatical terminology in English. I think it's a waste of time.

   B I know most of the grammatical terms in English; I find it easier to refer to a grammar book now that I know them.

   C I try to learn at least one new grammatical term in English every day.

6 A It's a waste of time to study grammar in the classroom when you can study it on your own at home.

   B I think it's a good idea to study grammar in the classroom; at least part of a lesson every week is necessary.

   C I think that grammar is the most interesting part of our lessons; I would like to do grammar in more than half our lessons.

6 - 9   You need to think more carefully about your approach to grammar study and be more systematic.

10 - 12   You're on the right track, but you should rethink your approach in certain areas.

13 - 16   Very good! Your approach to grammar study is methodical and sound.

Notes on technique

Statement 1

- Choosing a grammar book is very important and is a very personal matter. You must look for the right one for you - it must be clear and comprehensible for students of your level. By now you should be using a grammar book with the explanations in English rather than your own language.

Statement 2

- Although the ability to make yourself understood is important, as you continue with your study of English you should be aiming to get more accurate otherwise you will make the same mistakes for ever. So aim to be accurate but not to the point where your fluency suffers.

Statement 3

- Although it is a personal matter, it is a good idea to have a systematic approach to checking written work for grammar mistakes. But it is better to do the checking after you have written the composition, so that your writing becomes more fluent.

Statement 4

- You will learn more if your teacher just underlines your mistakes and you have to find them, although this may not always be possible. Don't forget that you will be wasting your own and your teacher's time if you don't bother to look at your mistakes.

Statement 5

- Now that you are at a more advanced level in your study of English, it is worth taking the time to learn the English grammatical terminology, especially if you intend to carry on with your English studies. Again, don't overdo it and spend too much time learning grammatical terms when you could be expanding your everyday vocabulary but make sure you know sufficient words to be able to understand grammar explanations in a grammar book or the grammar reference section of this book.

Statement 6

- A certain amount of time studying grammar in the classroom can be beneficial although you will be able to do a lot of grammar work on your own at home. Use the lesson time to clear up anything that you haven't fully understood.

Part 8 - The FCE exam

How much do you know about the First Certificate exam? Choose the correct answers.

1 **In the Reading Comprehension exam Section A there are:**
   a 25 multiple choice questions.
   b 10 multiple choice questions.
   c 15 true/false questions.

2 **In the Reading Comprehension exam Section B there are:**
   a two reading texts with ten questions on each.
   b three reading texts with fifteen questions altogether.
   c five questions and one reading text.

3 **In the Composition exam you have to write:**
   a two compositions of 120 - 180 words each.
   b three compositions of 100 words each.
   c one composition of 250 - 350 words.

4 **In the Use of English paper the first thing that you have to do in Section A is:**
   a write a letter.
   b sentence transformation.
   c complete a passage with blanks in it.

5 **In the Listening exam there are:**
   a three listening texts of similar type.
   b three very different listening exercises.
   c four quite similar listening exercises.

6 In the Oral exam you will have to:

a read a passage out loud and talk about some pictures.

b talk about one or two pictures, comment on a passage and take part in a role play or discussion.

c take part in a discussion and a role play based on one or two pictures.

Now check your answers below.

If you got more than two answers wrong and you are taking the examination soon, it's time you got down to some work! Now read the notes on the questions to see how to improve your technique.

Answers.

1 a 2 b 3 a 4 c 5 b 6 b

Paper 1 Reading Comprehension
1 hour (40 Marks)

Suggested techniques

Section A - 25 multiple choice questions.

- Look carefully at the questions - arrive at the correct answer by elimination if you don't know the answer.
- Answer all the questions even if you don't know the answer. Choose the most likely looking answer.
- Don't spend more than 15 minutes on this section.

Section B - three reading passages - 15 multiple choice questions.

- Spend about 15 minutes on each passage.
- Read the questions very carefully.
- There will often be two similar answers. Look at the relevant section of the text very carefully and choose the one that corresponds most closely to what is written there.
- Never leave a question unanswered - always make an intelligent guess - there are two marks for each answer.

Paper 2 Composition
1 ¹/₂ hours (40 Marks)

- Two compositions which might be:
  an informal letter   a speech
  a formal letter   a composition
  a story   a description
- The compositions are usually between 120 and 180 words but read the instructions carefully.
- Pay attention to:
  organisation and content
  grammatical accuracy
  use of vocabulary
  natural and fluent style

- Plan your composition for 5-10 minutes, allow 30 minutes to write it, and 5 minutes for checking it.
- Don't waste time doing a complete rough version and rewriting. You will not have time!
- Write neatly and in pen. You will get no marks if the examiner can't read what you have written.

Paper 3 Use of English
2 hours (40 Marks)
Section A

- Allow a total of 75 minutes for this section.

Cloze test

- Read the whole passage once or twice before filling in the gaps.
- Leave difficult blanks to the end and come back to them.

Sentence transformation

- Be careful that the sentences have exactly the same meaning when they have been 'transformed'.
- Pay particular attention to verb tenses.

Word-building/Phrasal verbs/Letter-writing/Dialogue completion

- Revise for these sections by looking back at specific work you have done on them in the course of the year shortly before the exam.

Section B

- Allow about 45 minutes for this section.

Reading Comprehension/Composition

- Pay particular attention to grammatical accuracy.
- Do not leave out any important information.

Paper 4 Listening
30 minutes (approx) (20 Marks)

- Expect the unexpected! Listening activities vary a great deal.
- You will hear each recording twice.
- Read the exercise carefully before you listen.
- Make notes the first time you listen and complete your definitive answers on the second listening.

Paper 5 Oral interview
15 minutes (approx) (40 Marks)

- Three parts: discussion of pictures; comment on a text; discussion in the form of role play, problem-solving.
- Pay attention to fluency, grammatical accuracy, pronunciation and stress, vocabulary and above all, communicating effectively.
- Be confident and speak clearly! The examiner will not be impressed if he or she can't hear you or has to push you to speak.
- Smile, relax and be positive! You will perform better if you are not tense or hostile.

Extra exercises

Unit 1

 page 8

 Listen to the conversation between Jean and Carolyn. Are these statements true or false? Give reasons.

1 Carolyn really enjoys the journey to work.
2 She made a definite decision to move to London.
3 She moved there because of her job.
4 She likes living in London.
5 She thinks experience is more important than qualifications.
6 She believes she has no control over her life.
7 She does not believe in any force which will determine the future.

2 ▶ page 10

1 **Read the text again. Are these statements true or false? Give reasons.**

1 The writer succeeded in learning to play the guitar using Bert Weedon's method.
2 Weedon has now retired from playing music.
3 Many young British rock singers and musicians were exploited.
4 Weedon considers himself the second greatest influence on young rock musicians.
5 Weedon took a long time to plan and write the guitar tutor.
6 *Play in a Day* has sold more than 2 million copies in English.
7 Weedon has had success as a performer.
8 Weedon has never drunk excessively or taken drugs.

2 **FCE type exercise**
Choose the correct answer.

1 **The surname of the writer of the guitar tutor is**
a Wilde.   b Weedon.   c Richard.   d Chappells.
2 **Who is 69 years old?**
a Marty Wilde.   c The writer of the article.
b Bert Weedon.   d Sinatra.
3 **Many young people had**
a short unsuccessful   c short but successful
b long and successful   d long but unsuccessful
careers as pop stars.
4 **Weedon had**
a seen how young people were exploited.
b exploited young people himself.
c disapproved of the way Elvis exploited young people.
d had changed the conditions of work for young people.

5 **Weedon claims that he**
a influenced many people to take up the guitar.
b created many pop stars.
c influenced Elvis Presley.
d got more people to play the guitar than Elvis.
6 **Weedon was**
a not sure   c unaware
b confident   d excited
that he would be able to write a good guitar method.
7 **Lennon and McCartney**
a used the Weedon method.
b had guitar lessons from Weedon.
c sold copies of Weedon's method.
d helped Weedon to write the guitar method.
8 **Weedon was always**
a a well-known rock sex-symbol.
b more interested in music than his image.
c mainly interested in presenting a dignified image.
d interested in his image and his music.

Unit 2

 page 14

1 **Write five comprehension questions about the text. Exchange questions with another student and write the answers to the questions you now have.**

Example *What did Sally Griffiths use to do?*

2 **FCE type exercise**
Choose the correct answer.

1 **The maximum age to join the pilot training course was**
a 26 years.   b 27 years.   c 24 years.   d 28 years.
2 **The course lasted**
a two years.   b one year.   c twelve years.   d one month.
3 **Sally Griffiths sold her flat**
a to pay for a private flying course.
b because she didn't need it any more.
c because the British Airways course was very expensive.
d to pay for the aeroplane.
4 a It was an advantage being a stewardess before joining the course.
b It was a disadvantage being a stewardess before joining the course.
c It made no difference that Sally was a stewardess before joining the course.
d You had to be a stewardess before joining the course.
5 **Sally's course was**
a held at Heathrow.   c held in Oxfordshire.
b not a very expensive one.   d run by British Airways.

124

6 Sally

a did extremely well in her exams.

b just managed to pass her exams.

c didn't pass her exams.

d didn't have to sit any exams.

7 Sally

a always wanted to be a stewardess.

b didn't enjoy being a stewardess.

c was always envious of pilots.

d preferred being a stewardess.

8 Sally's future husband

a doesn't work for an airline.

b was Sally's teacher.

c was on the same course as Sally.

d is a steward.

4 ▶ page 16

 Listen to Jean asking Colm about his work and
ambitions. Use information from A and B to write
sentences about Colm.

A	B
1 Colm writes	a best sellers.
2 He writes	b 10 or 11 short stories.
3 He doesn't want to talk about	c short stories and novels.
4 His first story was	d from home.
5 He does most of his writing	e to improve his writing.
6 He has written	f at night.
7 He doesn't have any ambitions except	g his other job.
8 He hopes all his books will be	h accepted by a newspaper.

Unit 3

5 ▶ page 22

 Listen to Dave talking about excitement and answer
the questions.

1 When did Dave go cycling across China?

2 How did they get into Tibet?

3 How old was he when he had his second exciting experience?

4 What time of year was it?

5 What did he do?

6 What do most of his exciting experiences have in common?

6 ▶ page 24

**1 Find these numbers in the article and write a short
sentence explaining what they refer to.**

1	eight	5	60
2	90	6	five
3	two-and-a-half	7	Nineties
4	50		

2 FCE type exercise

Choose the correct answer.

**1 According to the writer the main attraction of land
luging is that**

a it keeps you very fit.

b it's more exciting than skate-boarding.

c it's very dangerous.

d it's like a kids' game.

2 The land luges reach high speeds because

a they are smaller than cars.

b they have a small motor.

c they are pulled along by cars.

d they are powered by gravity.

**3 Pereyra and Amos have spent a lot of money on the
sport because**

a they think it will be very popular.

b they want to make a lot of money.

c they want to make the sport safer.

d they don't enjoy skate-boarding.

4 The writer of the article met Pereyra, Amos and Levy

a in the mountains.   c at the writer's house.

b at a party.   d at Pereyra's house.

5 The main danger of land luging is caused by

a lorries stopping suddenly.   c poor brakes.

b thunder and lightning.   d lorries and cars driving
next to the land lugers.

6 Pereyra stopped racing cars and bikes because

a he found it too expensive.   c he wasn't very successful at it.

b he discovered land luging.   d it was too dangerous.

7 Amos believes that within five years

a there will be races in other countries.

b he will be world champion.

c all the bugs will be worked out.

d he will have started an International Luge Roadracing
Association.

8 You can practise land luge racing

a only where there are mountains.

b only on specially built tracks.

c on specially built tracks or mountains.

d anywhere.

Unit 4

 7 page 28

18 **Listen and make notes about what worries the speaker most in these categories.**

1 Problems facing the world.
2 Two problems facing the country she lives in.
3 Problems facing herself personally.
4 What does Nadia do to overcome her anxiety?

8 page 30

1 Time sequencing words introduce clauses which answer the question *When?*.

Example *Three weeks ago she went to her doctor.*

Three weeks ago **is the sequencing expression.**

Find the sequencing words which begin the paragraph containing the following information.

1 She went to the doctor.
2 She lost all her confidence.
3 She is still worried about shopping.
4 She was afraid to go out.
5 She suddenly had strange symptoms.
6 She made herself go out more.

2 FCE type exercise
Choose the correct answer.

1 (para. b) When the writer had her first symptoms
a she had a stressful job in London.
b she was a very active, positive person.
c she was not worried about her relationship going wrong.
d her parents had just got divorced.

2 (para. a) At the time of her first panic attack the writer was living
a in London. b with her boyfriend.
c with her parents. d with a girlfriend.

3 (para. c) The writer
a did what her doctor suggested.
b had therapy for her symptoms.
c didn't do what her doctor suggested.
d threw away the medicine her doctor gave her.

4 (para. d) Within a short time
a she was convinced she had a serious illness.
b she wanted to die.
c she talked to people about her anxiety.
d she went to her doctor again.

5 (para. e) The writer
a wanted to go for a drive in her car.
b was more worried about being imprisoned in the house than about going out.

c was more worried about going out than staying in the house.
d was not worried as long as she didn't have to go out.

6 (para. a) The writer often cried because she
a was impatient with herself for feeling the way she did.
b was not getting any better.
c didn't know what was happening to her.
d realised her anxiety came from herself and she couldn't do anything about it.

7 (para. a) The writer's condition started to improve as a result of
a going to her doctor.
b moving away from her parents.
c starting to go out more.
d buying a car.

8 (para. g) The writer
a is now completely cured.
b will never be cured.
c is determined to conquer her anxiety.
d is worried that she still feels alone in her predicament.

Unit 5

9 page 36

1 Read the text again and look for biographical information about Gore Vidal.

Year of birth	Places where he lives
Family history	Favourite place
Languages spoken	Reasons for liking it

2 FCE type exercise
Which words or phrases in the text suggest the following?

1 Gore Vidal doesn't like giving interviews.
2 He likes and is liked by the people of Ravello.
3 He enjoys reading.
4 He likes to lead a peaceful life when he is in Italy.
5 He has a sense of humour.
6 He says he is not particularly materialistic.
7 He is quite a famous person.

10 page 38

24 **Jean and Carolyn are talking about places they lived in and spent holidays in when they were children. Listen and complete the information about them. Use the words below.**

horse riding   swimming   Reading   Cheshire
walking   Devon   cathedral   London   camping
big   rained   market   Lake District   boring
Birmingham   North   parks

Carolyn was born in ____, moved to ____ and later to St Albans. She mostly remembers the ____ in St Albans. She says St Albans is a ____ town and also has a ____ . She used to go ____ on Saturdays when she lived there. She went on holiday in Wales, ____, Cornwall, and the ____ . They used to go ____ and ____ .

Jean comes from ____ . She describes it as being ____, ugly and ____ . She thinks the reason is that it's too near ____ . She used to go ____ in ____ Wales during the holidays. She remembers it _____ a lot.

Unit 6

11 ▶ page 42

28 **Listen to Colm talking about happiness. Answer the questions.**

1 Which quote on page 42 does he find most interesting? Why?
2 Which of these statements are true of Colm?
He's happy if he's satisfied with what he's doing.
He feels he could be happier.
He doesn't expect to be any happier than he is at the moment.
He thinks you can't define happiness.

12 ▶ page 44

1 Read the text again. Are these statements true or false? Give your reasons.

1 Becker was unhappy because he was rich.
2 1987 was a very successful year for Becker's tennis career.
3 Becker identifies with other famous people who have been unhappy.
4 Becker believes that career success can cause unhappiness.
5 Becker thinks it is important to do what people expect you to do.
6 Becker has changed a lot since 1987.
7 Becker changed his image in 1987 so that he could play better tennis.

2 FCE type exercise
Choose the correct answer.

1 *It* in the first line refers to
a Becker's period of crisis.
b Becker's tennis tournament.
c Becker's tennis career.
d Becker becoming rich.

2 Becker felt his problems were caused
a by his inability to play good tennis.　　c by being rich.
b by himself.　　　　　　　　　　　　　d by other people.

3 Becker
a admired　　　　　　　c was taught by
b identified with　　　　d was jealous of
people like Elvis Presley and Marilyn Monroe.

4 Becker's ambition when he started playing tennis was to
a win the Wimbledon title.　　c be a rich man.
b keep the Wimbledon title.　　d buy a big car.

5 Boris Becker is happier now because
a he is going to retire from tennis.
b he is starting to win matches again.
c he understands what his goals are.
d he understands that he has no goals.

6 In 1987 Becker decided.
a to take no notice of people.
b to behave as people wanted him to.
c to behave as he thought right.
d to behave better.

7 1987 was an important year for Becker because
a he had become very rich.
b he lost the Flushing Meadow tournament.
c he understood why he was unhappy.
d he knew he was a puppet.

8 Becker thinks he became
a a happier person　　c a more human person
b a better player　　　d a champion
after his 1987 defeat.

Unit 7

13 ▶ page 50

34 **Listen to Judy talking about prejudices. Are these statements true or false? Give your reasons.**

1 Judy lived in London as a child.
2 Her parents wanted her to become a Christian.
3 People used to know that Judy was Jewish because she looks Jewish.
4 Judy was brought up to hate Germans.
5 Judy had German friends.
6 A lot of Judy's family were killed in Germany.
7 Judy doesn't blame the little girl for what she said about Jews.

14 page 52

1 Read the text again. Are these statements true or false? Give your reasons.

1 Doctors are trendy but shouldn't be.

2 The Scottish doctor saw almost five hundred patients during his research.

3 Most people agree about the kind of clothes doctors should wear.

4 The research shows that women patients are more concerned than men about the way doctors dress.

5 People prefer doctors to wear formal clothes.

6 Elderly people and rich people feel the same way about the way doctors dress.

7 More than half the patients said they would refuse to see a doctor who was wearing jeans.

8 The researchers think doctors are wrong to dress as their patients want.

2 FCE type exercise
Choose the correct answer.

1 People consider doctors to be

a badly dressed professionals.

b trendy professionals.

c unimaginatively dressed professionals.

d conservatively dressed professionals.

2 Women doctors

a dress more casually than men.

b wear the same clothes as men.

c are considered in the same way as men on the question of dress.

d have fewer restrictions than men.

3 The research was carried out

a among Scottish doctors.

b by a Scottish doctor.

c in Scotland.

d by patients in Scotland.

4 As a result of the survey doctors

a will have to please their patients.

b will have to become more trendy.

c will have to remain conservative.

d will have to wear brighter clothes.

5 a People in the lower classes are less concerned about the way doctors dress.

b Young people like doctors to look trendy.

c Elderly patients are afraid of trendy doctors.

d People in the upper classes dislike trendy doctors.

6 More than half the patients said

a it was important for doctors to be suitably dressed.

b they liked the look of their doctor.

c they couldn't remember what their doctor looked like.

d doctors all looked the same.

7 Quite a lot of people admitted they

a preferred women doctors.

b wouldn't go to a woman doctor if she was wearing jeans.

c wouldn't go to a woman doctor.

d preferred women doctors not to wear trousers.

8 Doctors should try to inspire confidence in their patients by

a being efficient doctors.

b taking their patients' preferences into consideration when deciding what to wear.

c wearing jeans if they are happy in them.

d not wearing stylish clothes.

Unit 8

15 page 56

1 Without looking back at the text, complete the summary.

James Galway didn't really think he was a ____ because he never committed any ____ crimes. He and his ____ thought it was fun to steal ____ from Johnny Rankin's and cakes and ____ from the ____. They used to make a ____ afterwards and eat the things they took.

2 FCE type exercise
Choose the correct answer.

1 Johnny Rankin's was

a a shop that sold old clothes.

b a shop that sold rabbits.

c a shop that sold animal skins.

d a shop that sold rags.

2 Mercer's Bakery

a was in the same street as the writer's house.

b was not far from the writer's house.

c was back to back with the writer's house.

d had windows which looked onto the writer's house.

3 The writer and his friends

a hammered on the door of the bakery.

b broke the windows of the bakery.

c made a hole in the door of the bakery.

d hammered a hole in the wall of the bakery.

4 They broke into the bakery

a when it was dark enough for them not to be seen.

b in the middle of the night.

c early in the evening.

d at midnight.

5 a They didn't take cakes and buns from Mercer's.

b They only took cakes and buns from Mercer's.

c They didn't take any bread from Mercer's.

d They didn't like bread.

6 The vegetables were

a from their houses.

b in the same shop as the rabbit skins.

c in the bakery.

d from somewhere nearby.

7 The children

a sold the things they took.

b ate the things they took.

c burnt the things they took.

d gave away the things they took.

8 The children stopped taking things because

a they were caught.

b the police kept an eye on the bakery.

c the wall was repaired.

d they got bored with doing it.

16 ▶ page 58

40 **Listen to Louise talking about morality. Choose the correct alternative from the brackets in each sentence.**

1 Louise (*has/has never*) stolen apples from somebody's tree.

2 Louise (*feels/doesn't feel*) bad about not paying her fare on a bus or train because she (*thinks/doesn't think*) it is too expensive.

3 She has taken stationery from work (*accidentally/deliberately*).

4 She (*frequently/rarely*) makes phone calls from work.

5 She has (*often/never*) kept money she found in the street.

6 She (*has/has never*) driven the wrong way up a one way street in Britain but she (*has/hasn't*) done it abroad because it (*seemed/didn't seem*) important.

7 She (*has never/has occasionally*) stolen a toy from a shop.

8 She thinks (*several of the things mentioned are/ only stealing is*) immoral.

Unit 9

17 ▶ page 64

1 Read the article again and complete a chart with the symptoms of love and some suggested remedies.

SYMPTOMS	REMEDIES

2 FCE type exercise

Choose the correct answer.

1 The writer thinks that Valentine's Day cards are

a vulgar.　b inaccurate.　c boring.　d childish.

2 According to the writer people who are in love

a are never sorry.

b never have to say they are sorry.

c are always sorry.

d often have to apologise to each other.

3 The writer thinks that being in love

a is a form of psychological illness.

b is a form of physical illness.

c is a dangerous experience.

d is like living in a state of anxiety.

4 The writer says that

a more men than women fall in love.

b he is not sure which sex falls in love more often.

c the same number of men as women fall in love.

d more women fall in love than men.

5 He believes that

a it is a positive thing that love is like anxiety.

b love, like anxiety can make people cynical.

c people who suffer from anxiety are afraid of falling in love.

d love is a hopeless state.

6 Of the three types of remedy the writer seems to prefer

a environmental change.

b a combination of psychotherapy and physical treatment.

c a combination of environmental change and physical treatment.

d psychotherapy.

7 In his conclusion the writer

a accepts that you can't do much about being in love.

b says that the best solution to being in love is to go and have a nice meal in a restaurant.

c says we should buy a lot of flowers for our loved one.

d says we should continue to fight love.

18 ▶ page 66

47 **Listen to Louise talking about friendship.**

1 What three qualities does she say are important?

2 Louise talks about an incident she and her friend found very funny. Listen again and put the facts in order.

a They thought it was funny at the time.

b Her mother was coming to stay.

c They were going yellow.

d Before her mother came they had to hide them.

e Her mum had given her some vegetables.

f They were giggling hysterically.

g They were at the bottom of the fridge.

Unit 10

 page 70

1 In which paragraph or paragraphs do you find the following information?

a The name of the newspaper Clark Kent and Lois Lane work for.

b The news that Lois accepted Kent's proposal.

c Information about how Superman lost his super powers.

d Information about the first issue of the Superman comic.

e Superman's usual reaction to Lois's passion.

f The reasons why the writers decided to make Lois accept Kent.

g The news that Kent will reveal his true identity to Lois.

2 FCE type exercise
Choose the correct answer.

1 Clark Kent is
a a rather shy person.   c a calm person.
b a very difficult person.   d a strong person.

2 News of the betrothal came
a at the same time as the November issue came out.
b sometime in November.
c on November 1st.
d in October.

3 Lois
a thinks Kent is foolish.
b is sorry for Kent.
c believes that Kent is in fact Superman.
d is in love with Kent.

4 Kent
a will not tell anyone his secret.
b will tell Lois his secret.
c will tell the public his secret.
d will tell his publishers the secret.

5 Lois
a will refuse Kent because she still loves Superman.
b will accept Kent because they get on well except at work.
c will accept Kent because she is in love with him.
d will accept Kent because Superman doesn't love her.

6 Superman had always explained that there was no hope for Lois because
a she is too weak.   c he is already married.
b he is in danger.   d she is not a supergirl.

7 Kent loses his powers because
a he reveals his identity to Lois.
b he loses his job on the Daily Planet.
c he comes into contact with red Kryptonite.
d he falls in love with Lois.

20 ▶ page 72

51 Listen to Louise talking about her marriage. Complete the information about her wedding. You may need to use more than one word in each space.

Louise was married in ___ because her husband is ____ and she was living there at the time. She didn't have ____ and nobody from her ____ was present at the ____. The only people at the ____, apart from Louise and her ____, were ____. They received ____ as wedding presents. Her ____'s family were ____ and Louise told her parents after the wedding. Her father wanted to know if ____!

Unit 11

21 ▶ page 78

1 Read the text again. Are these statements true or false? Give your reasons.

1 It was Donald Woods' idea that he should visit Biko.

2 Woods met Ntsiki before he met Biko.

3 Woods wanted to ban Biko from South Africa.

4 The purpose of Woods' visit was to find out more about Biko's beliefs.

5 Biko enjoyed making Woods feel uncomfortable at first.

6 Biko appreciated the fact that Woods quickly summed up his personality.

7 Biko was not married.

2 FCE type exercise.
Choose the best answer.

1 At the beginning of the interview
a Biko seemed to enjoy himself more than Woods.
b Woods seemed to enjoy himself more than Biko.
c Both men were very uncomfortable.
d Both men were pleased to meet each other.

2 Woods
a didn't like Biko.
b couldn't understand Biko at all.
c only understood the kind of person Biko was towards the end of their talk.
d thought Biko was a dangerous man.

3 During the interview
a Biko showed that he didn't like Woods.
b Biko was very angry with Woods.
c Biko seemed to make fun of Woods.
d Biko showed how much he respected Woods.

4 Biko seemed to
a enjoy the interview.
b want to have a fight with Woods.
c think Woods was a bit silly.
d think Woods was a powerful man.

5 During the interview

a Biko admitted he would have liked to have all the things Woods had.

b Woods offered Biko his car.

c Biko showed that he didn't like Woods.

d Woods points out that Biko would have behaved like Woods if he had had the same opportunities.

6 At the end of the interview

a Biko thought Woods was offering him his Mercedes.

b Biko showed his approval of Woods.

c Biko wanted Woods to meet his wife.

d Biko thought Woods was going to live in the townships.

 22 ▶ page 80

55 Listen to Deborah describing herself and complete the diagram with vocabulary she uses.

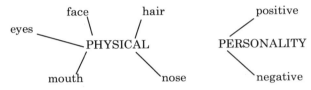

Unit 12

23 ▶ page 84

1 Read the song again and answer the questions.

1 Why is there no need for people to go hungry?

2 Why is there no need for people to be lonely?

3 Why does Tracy Chapman say that 'peace keepers' is not the right way to describe missiles?

4 Why is a woman not safe in her own home?

5 What comments does Tracy Chapman make about people's opinions of war and peace?

6 What makes her believe that things will change?

2 In pairs. What is Tracy Chapman trying to say in this song? Discuss and write a sixteen word summary of the song.

24 ▶ page 86

60 You will hear Tris talking about world problems. Listen and complete the information. Use only three or four words for each answer.

1 The main problem is dependency on ____.

2 The more developed countries are not doing ____.

3 People are getting tired of ____.

4 You keep giving money but you don't know ____.

5 Tris is interested in Vietnam and Cambodia because ____.

6 After the Vietnam War the Vietnamese managed to support ____.

7 In Cambodia they're starting to have a ____.

Unit 13

 25 ▶ page 92

66 Togo is talking to Tony about issues he feels committed to. Listen and write down three things he feels very strongly about.

Listen again and write two sentences about each issue summarising what he believes.

26 ▶ page 94

1 Read the text again and answer the questions.

1 Where did David Shelley spend his childhood?

2 What evidence is there in the text to believe that David Shelley is a healthy person?

3 Why does he feel the cold more than other people?

4 Why is Leicester a good place for David to live in?

5 What evidence is there in the text that a fruitarian diet is not expensive?

6 Why does Mr Shelley make the point that apes are fruitarians?

7 What reasons do nutritionists give for not believing that a fruit diet is a complete diet?

8 What grounds does Mr Shelley have for believing that what nutritionists say is rubbish?

2 FCE type exercise
Choose the correct answer.

1 a Mr Shelley will have turkey but no sprouts for his Christmas dinner.

b Mr Shelley will have turkey and sprouts for his Christmas dinner.

c Mr Shelley will have neither turkey not sprouts for his Christmas dinner.

d Mr Shelley will not be having a Christmas dinner.

2 a Mr Shelley has lived in Australia.

b Mr Shelley has always lived in Leicester.

c Mr Shelley was only born in Leicester.

d Mr Shelley has visited Leicester.

3 a Mr Shelley has to buy other things to supplement his diet.

b Mr Shelley has difficulty finding enough good fruit in England.

c Mr Shelley has plenty of choice of fruit in Leicester.

d Mr Shelley buys fruit and other foods at the market.

4 a There are probably more fruitarians in Australia than in Britain.

  b There are probably more fruitarians in Brtain than in Australia.

  c There are about the same number of fruitarians in Britain as in Australia.

  d There are certainly fruitarians in every country.

5 a Mr Shelley recommends the fruit diet for missionaries.

  b Mr Shelley thinks everyone would benefit from the fruit diet.

  c Mr Shelley has written a lot of books on the subject.

  d Mr Shelley thinks some people would be unwise to start a fruit diet.

6 a Nutritionists believe fruit is bad for you.

  b Nutritionists believe we should eat fruit.

  c Nutritionists believe Mr Shelley has the answer to diet problems.

  d Nutritionists believe we should not eat too much fruit.

7 a Mr Shelley doesn't feel the cold.

  b Mr Shelley often gets a cold.

  c Mr Shelley never gets a cold.

  d Mr Shelley doesn't like cold weather.

Unit 14

 page 98

1 Read the text again. Are these statements true or false? Give your reasons.

1 Michael Fish objected to his name being used in the advertisement because he disapproved of the paint.

2 He saw the advertisement in the street.

3 Mr Fish was right to think it was illegal to use his name without permission.

4 Famous people are often used in TV advertisements without their permission.

5 Mr Fish could have complained to the ASA and insisted they withdraw the advertisement.

6 Rules affecting members of the royal family are not the same as those affecting other famous people.

7 The Prince of Wales appeared in a poster advertising a new library.

8 Advertisers are often more than happy when they have to withdraw an advertisement.

2 FCE type exercise
Choose the correct answer.

1 Mr Fish is

  a a BBC producer.

  b a civil servant.

  c a meteorologist.

  d an advertising agent.

2 a Michael Fish was paid £1,000 by MWP so they could use his photo.

  b Paul Wilmot received £1,000 from Mr Fish.

  c MWP agreed to send £1,000 to charity.

  d MWP wanted Mr Fish to send £1,000 to charity.

3 The Independent Broadcasting Authority

  a uses famous people from the past in its TV ads.

  b never uses famous people in its ads.

  c uses members of the royal family in its ads.

  d only uses people who give permission in its ads.

4 Poster ads can use famous people

  a if the people agree.

  b if they are paid.

  c unless the poster invades their privacy too much.

  d unless the product is not good.

5 Advertisers can only use members of the royal family

  a if they have written permission.

  b when there is a royal wedding.

  c if the members of the royal family are interested in their product.

  d if they think the advertisement will sell their product.

6 The agency removed the poster advertising a drainage company because

  a the person in the advertisement was not really Prince Charles.

  b Prince Charles did not approve of the reference to the politburo.

  c the royal family complained about it.

  d it included a photo of a library.

7 a Effective advertisements are never withdrawn.

  b Advertisements must never be controversial.

  c Good posters are always withdrawn.

  d Posters which are withdrawn often receive more attention than others.

8 Advertising agencies

  a never use celebrities without ringing to ask for permission.

  b are afraid celebrities will charge too much.

  c think it's worthwhile not asking for permission.

  d don't want celebrities to refuse permission.

28 ▶ page 100

71 Colm is talking about the advertisement on page 100. Answer the questions.

1 Why does he say the advertisement is effective?
2 What are they trying to get you to do?
3 What does Colm say about the standard of advertising?
4 Has he ever bought anything because he liked an advertisement?
5 He ignores advertisements for which products?
6 Why?
7 What does he think of TV advertising?
8 What sort of advertising works best in his opinion?

Unit 15

29 ▶ page 106

1 Read the text again. Are these statements true or false? Give your reasons.

1 Wexford was in a hospital bed at the time of the extract.
2 Hatton was alive on May 22nd.
3 Vigo paid Hatton £500 a week.
4 Hatton usually stayed at home on Friday nights.
5 Hatton was killed by Mrs Fanshawe.
6 Nora was Mrs Fanshawe's daughter.
7 A girl's body was found on the road.
8 Wexford drove a left-hand drive car.

2 FCE type exercise.
Choose the correct answer.

1 On May 22nd Hatton had £1000 and put
   a half   b all   c a third   d none of it
   in the bank.

2 After he had deposited the money, Hatton got £50 a week from
   a the bank.   c Vigo.
   b the Pertwees.   d Mrs Fanshawe.

3 When he went to the darts club on Fridays Hatton
   a hid by the river.
   b met Vigo by the river.
   c picked up some money.
   d gave the money to the darts club.

4 Hatton was killed by
   a Mrs Fanshawe.
   b the person he was blackmailing.
   c a member of his darts team on a Friday night.
   d Nora

5 At the time Mrs Fanshawe regained consciousness her daughter
   a was at her hospital bedside.
   b was being looked for by the police.
   c was with Vigo.
   d was on her way to the hospital.

6 Crocker
   a thought Wexford had misunderstood the facts.
   b was angry with Wexford.
   c believed Wexford's story.
   d thought they needed more information.

7 When he threw the girl's body out of the car, Vigo was driving
   a on a small country road.
   b the wrong way down a motorway.
   c Crocker's car on a motorway.
   d on a motorway or dual carriage-way.

8 When he told his visitors that the car was left-hand drive, Wexford
   a wanted to annoy them.
   b proved that his version of what had happened was probably right.
   c proved that Crocker's version of the story was probably right.
   d introduced another complication to the story.

30 ▶ page 108

79 Tris and Simon are also discussing the Ruth Rendell extract. Listen and complete the information. Write no more than four words for each answer.

1 They say Hatton ____.
2 They say ____ was being blackmailed.
3 They presume Vigo ____.
4 They say ____ knew of another crime.
5 Tris says Nora ____.
6 Simon thinks Hatton knows ____.
7 Simon also says ____ when Mrs Fanshawe regains consciousness.

Unit 2 Exercise 9

Score:	1	a1	b2	c2		6	a1	b2	c3
	2	a2	b2	c1		7	a2	b1	c3
	3	a3	b2	c1		8	a2	b3	c1
	4	a1	b2	c1		9	a2	b3	c1
	5	a3	b2	c1		10	a3	b2	c3

10-15 You are not really ambitious enough. People tend to take advantage of you. You must try to be more assertive and take your job seriously.

16-20 You have found the right balance. You are probably happy at work and in your life outside work.

21-28 Be careful! You are over-ambitious. You may be quite happy with your life at the moment but you also need to relax. If you continue to disregard everybody and everything for your ambition you will end up by having no friends at all.

Unit 2 Exercise 15

Student A. Ask:

1 if it's more important to be flexible or determined. Why?
2 which qualities are necessary to be a good politician.
3 what Student B's family is doing at the moment.
4 what Student B has done since he/she left school.
5 what sort of thing adults say to children.
6 why Student B decided to learn English.

Unit 3 Exercise 18

Mayor of Brownsville: You have to control the meeting. Introduce yourself and the other people present at the meeting. Introduce the problem. Invite the participants to speak in turn. Ensure that one group does not dominate and that everyone has a chance to speak. When everyone has finished speaking you must decide whether to ban land-luging or not according to the strength of the arguments presented.

Unit 4 Exercise 8

Student A

Claustrophobia is a fear of being shut in a small place. (true)
Bellophobia is an unnatural fear of beautiful women. (false)
Hippophobia is a fear of hippos. (false)
Hydrophobia is a horror of drinking water. (true)
Testophobia is anxiety about tests. (false)
Scriptophobia is a fear of writing. (false)

Unit 4 Exercise 16

Student A: Ask Student B these questions to complete the paragraph.

When did Sarah have her first panic attack?
When did she feel her body freeze?
When did her parents decide this?
What was Sarah afraid was wrong with her?
How severe were the attacks?
Why did Sarah go into a state of depression?
Who did her friend put Sarah in touch with?
Why was this important?

_____ , Sarah had her first panic attack. She was having great difficulty in maths and _____ her body just froze. In just a week it was all she could do to sit through the lessons. _____ her parents realised her school phobia was becoming a serious problem and that Sarah needed professional help. Over the next month or two she was frequently staying awake all night thinking _____ . By this time she had got to the point when the attacks were really severe. _____ . She went into a period of deep depression after she had visited her doctor. _____ . Then one day she spoke to a friend who had suffered similar attacks. Her friend put her in touch with _____ . This doctor gradually helped her to conquer the problem. She taught her self confidence and self respect again _____ . Today she has fully recovered and is looking forward to going to university.

Unit 4 Exercise 18

Student A: Anthony and Cleopatra

One day Anthony came home and found Cleopatra lying dead on the carpet. Near her body was some broken glass and some water. He was heartbroken. How did Cleopatra die?

(Solution: Cleopatra was his goldfish and her glass bowl had been knocked on the floor and broken. She died of 'suffocation').

Unit 15 Exercise 15

Student A: Henry Fortescue, the owner of a jewellery shop in Maidstone was killed. He suspected William Hunt, his assistant, of having an affair with his wife (he was a very jealous man). He was robbed two years ago, so he used to keep a small gun in the shop. He has a son, called Martin, who was at home on the day of the murder. Martin says that his mother was out shopping between one and two on the day of the murder.

Unit 5 Exercise 9

Unit 5 Exercise 19
Student A

Unit 3 Exercise 18
Citizens of Brownsville: You are unanimous in your condemnation of the sport of land-luging. You make various predictions about what will happen if it is allowed. Think of these areas: accidents, traffic problems, the effect on tourism. Criticise the sport. (Use the adjectives you have studied in Unit 3 exercises 1 - 9.)

Unit 7 Exercise 16

Student A: Ask Student B these questions.
1 What do you do if someone gives you a present that you don't like?
2 What do you do if someone turns up for an appointment an hour late?
3 What do you do if a friend borrows money from you and forgets about it?
4 You are at a friend's house for dinner. What do you do if they serve you tripe, which is the one thing that you can't bear to eat?

Unit 15 Exercise 15
Student B: Maude Fortescue is Henry's wife. She has expensive tastes and spends a lot of money each month but doesn't work and refuses to have anything to do with her husband's work. Martin, her son, had argued with his father about money and had been disinherited.

Unit 7 Exercise 17
Student A: You are Brendan Clark. Describe what happened after you saw the advertisement for the house. Explain your comfortable financial status. You were not informed that a higher offer was made. Note particularly the comments made by your potential neighbour. Explain why you think this is a clear case of discrimination.

Student B: You are the estate agent. Explain what happened when you took Brendan Clark to see the house. Explain that he was very keen to buy and willingly paid the deposit. Explain that you took another family to see the house and were told by neighbours that they did not want 'undesirable people with loads of children' in the area. Explain that this made no difference to the situation. The only reason you let the second family have the house was that they made a higher offer.

Student C: You live in the area where Brendan Clark wants to buy his house. You have nothing against large families but are worried about the effect these new people, with their strange dress, will have on the neighbourhood. You had no idea what his profession was.

Student D: You are the magistrate in charge of this case. Listen to everybody's point of view and make a final decision about whether Brendan Clark's case is one of prejudice.

Unit 2 Exercise 15
Student B. Ask:

1 if it's more important to have qualifications or experience and why.
2 which qualities are necessary to be a good nurse.
3 what Student A's best friend is doing at the moment.
4 if Student A has ever wished he/she was somebody else and who.
5 what period of Student A's life was the happiest. Why?
6 what Student A did when he/she was angry as a child.

Unit 3 Exercise 18
The police: You are worried about the new sport but you don't want to stop it altogether. (One of your police officers has tried it and enjoyed it!) You have already come up with some measures as a result of previous complaints. You should go to a meeting with a list of your intentions. Think about these areas:
* limiting the number of participants
* patrolling the roads when the sport is in progress
* suggesting a timetable regulating the activity.

Unit 4 Exercise 8
Student B
Agoraphobia is a fear of open spaces. (true)
Anglophobia is a horror of English people. (true)
Paedophobia is the fear of children. (false)
Aquaphobia is a fear of water. (true)
Cascaphobia is a fear of hats. (false)
Leggophobia is anxiety about reading. (false)

Unit 8 Exercise 7

abandon	announce	develop	manage
accomplish	argue	discourage	move
achieve	arrange	employ	pay
acknowledge	assess	enjoy	punish
adjust	assign	entertain	puzzle
advertise	attach	excite	replace
agree	attain	improve	require
amaze	commit	invest	resent
amuse	deploy	involve	retire

Unit 4 Exercise 16
Student B: Ask Student A these questions to complete the paragraph.

What was wrong when Sarah started having the attacks?
Why did Sarah's parents decide she needed professional help?
What happened over the next month or two?
What had happened by this time?
When did she go into a period of severe depression?
What did her friend have in common with Sarah?
What did this doctor do?
How is she today?

Two years ago, Sarah had her first panic attack. ____ and as soon as she walked into the classroom her body just froze. In just a week ____ . After a short time her parents realised her school phobia was becoming a serious problem and that Sarah needed professional help. Over the next month or two ____ thinking she was going mad and would never get better. By this time ____ . They were so severe that she couldn't leave the house.
She went into a period of deep depression ____ . He could find nothing wrong with her. Then one day she spoke to a friend who ____ . Her friend put her in touch with a fantastic doctor. This doctor gradually ____ . She taught her self confidence and self respect again both of which Sarah had lost. Today ____ and is looking forward to going to university.

Unit 4 Exercise 18
Student B: The lift
Every morning, a man who lived on the tenth floor of a block of flats left his apartment at half past eight, got in the lift and went down to the ground floor, where he got out, went to his car and drove off to work. When he returned home in the evening, he parked his car, got in the lift and went up to the second floor, where he got out of the lift and walked up the remaining eight flights of stairs. Why?

(Solution: Because he was a dwarf and could only reach the lift button for the second floor. In the morning he could go the whole way down in the lift because the he could reach the ground floor button).

Unit 15 Exercise 15
Student C: William Hunt works for Henry Fortescue but doesn't like him because he's very bad-tempered. Henry was shot at lunchtime when the shop was closed. Martin, Henry's son, needed money, because he was a compulsive (and unsuccessful) gambler. Martin saw Maude and William together in a club late one night and he suspects them of having an affair.

Unit 5 Exercise 19
Student B

Unit 7 Exercise 16
Student B: Ask Student A these questions.

1 What do you if a friend comes to your house when you are half-way through dinner with some other people?
2 What do you do if someone borrows one of your records and you find that it's scratched when you get it back?
3 What do you do if someone starts smoking in a non-smoking compartment on the train?
4 A friend has come to stay for the weekend with her boyfriend. What do you do if you come home and find the boyfriend using the phone, speaking Spanish?

Unit 3 Exercise 18
The land-lugers: You must present your case strongly but not in an aggressive way. If you make the people at the meeting angry they will ban your sport. You must try to convince the others that your sport is not anti-social and dangerous to others. Say what you are going to do to make your sport safer. Make predictions about how the sport will bring money and more tourists to the area. Describe the sport and explain why you think it's so good. (Use the adjectives that you studied in Unit 3 exercises 1 - 9.)

Unit 9 Exercise 22

Unit 11 Introduction

Grammar reference

Unit 1

Here is a checklist for the use and formation of some common verb tenses.

Tense	Affirmative	Negative	Use
Present simple	3rd person singular adds 's' - otherwise use base form	3rd person singular - doesn't. All other persons don't + base form	For repeated actions or habits
Present continuous	Appropriate form of verb 'be' + base form + -ing	Negative of appropriate form of 'be' + base form + -ing	For temporary situations or something happening at the moment of speaking
Present perfect	Appropriate form of 'have' + past participle (base form + -ed of regular verb	Negative of appropriate form of 'have' + past participle	To describe a situation which began in the past and continued up to the present
Past simple	Base form + -ed Many irregular forms	Didn't or did not + base form of the verb	To describe completed events in the past

Unit 2

Question forms

1 Questions which can be answered 'yes' or 'no' are called 'yes/no'-questions.

'Are you ready?' - *'Yes.'*
'Have you read this magazine?' - *'No.'*

If the verb group has more than one word, the first word comes at the beginning of the sentence, before the subject. The rest of the verb group comes after the subject.

Is he coming?
Can John swim?
Will you have finished by lunchtime?
Couldn't you have been a bit quieter?
Has he been working?

2 If the verb group consists of only a main verb, you use the auxiliary 'do', 'does', or 'did' at the beginning of the sentence, before the subject. After the subject you use the base form of the verb.

Do the British take sport seriously?
Does that sound like anyone you know?
Did he go to the fair?

Note that when the main verb is 'do', you still have to add 'do', 'does', or 'did' before the subject.

Do they do the work themselves?
Did you do an 'O' Level in German?

3 If the main verb is 'have', you usually put 'do', 'does', or 'did' before the subject.

Does anyone have a question?
Did you have a good flight?

When 'have' means 'own' or 'possess', you can put it before the subject, without using 'do', 'does', or 'did', but this is less common.

Has he any idea what it's like?

4 If the main verb is the present simple or past simple of 'be', you put the verb at the beginning of the sentence, before the subject.

Are you ready?
Was it lonely without us?

5 When you want someone to give you more information than just 'yes' or 'no', you ask a 'wh'-question, which begins with a 'wh'-word:

what	where	who	whose	–
when	which	whom	why	how

Note that 'whom' is only used in formal English.

6 When a 'wh'-word is the subject of a question, the 'wh'-word comes first, then the verb group. You do not add 'do', 'does', or 'did' as an auxiliary.

What happened?
Which is the best restaurant?
Who could have done it?

7 When a 'wh'-word is the object of a verb or preposition, the 'wh'-word comes first, then you follow the rules for 'yes/no'-questions, adding 'do', 'does', or 'did' where necessary.

How many are there?
Which do you like best?

If there is a preposition, it comes at the end. However, you always put the preposition before 'whom'.

What's this for?
With whom were you talking?

Note that you follow the same rules as for 'wh'-words as objects when the question begins with 'when', 'where', 'why', or 'how'.

When would you be coming down?
Why did you do it?
Where did you get that from?

8 You can also use 'what', 'which', 'whose', 'how many', and 'how much' with a noun.

Whose idea was it?
How much money have we got in the bank?

You can use 'which', 'how many', and 'how much' with 'of' and a noun group.

Which of the suggested answers was the correct one?
How many of them bothered to come?

Unit 3

Future with 'will' and 'going to'

1 You cannot talk about the future with as much certainty as you can about the present or the past. You are usually talking about what you think might happen or what you intend to happen. This is why you often use modals. Although most modals can be used with future reference, you most often use the modal 'will' to talk about the future.

Nancy will arrange it.
When will I see them?

2 When you are making predictions about the future that are based on general beliefs, opinions, or attitudes, you use 'will'.

The weather tomorrow will be warm and sunny.
I'm sure you will enjoy your visit to the zoo.

When you are using facts or events in the present situation as evidence for a prediction, you can use 'going to'.

It's going to rain. (I can see black clouds)
I'm going to be late. (I have missed my train)

3 When you are talking about your own intentions, you use 'will' or 'going to'.

I'll ring you tonight.
I'm going to stay at home today.

When you are saying what someone else has decided to do, you use 'going to'.

They're going to have a party.

WARNING: You do not normally use 'going to' with the verb 'go'. You usually just say 'I'm going' rather than 'I'm going to go'.

'What are you going to do this weekend?' - 'I'm going to the cinema.'

When you are announcing a decision you have just made or are about to make, you use 'will'.

I'm tired. I think I'll go to bed.

4 In promises and offers relating to the future, you often use 'will' with the meaning 'be willing to'.

I'll do what I can.
I'll help with the washing-up.

Unit 4

Past continuous, past simple, past perfect

1 When you want to talk about an event that occurred at a particular time in the past, you use the past simple.

The Prime Minister flew into New York yesterday.
The new term started last week.

You also use the past simple to talk about a situation that existed over a period of time in the past.

We spent most of our time at home last winter.
They earned their money quickly that year.

2 When you want to talk about something which took place regularly in the past, you use the past simple.

They went for picnics most weekends.
We usually spent the winter at Aunt Meg's house.

WARNING: The past simple always refers to a time in the past. A time reference is necessary to say what time in the past you are referring to. The time reference can be established in an earlier sentence.

3 When you want to talk about something which continued to happen before and after a given time in the past, you use the past continuous.

I hurt myself when I was mending my bike.
It was midnight. She was driving home.

You also use the past continuous to talk about a temporary state of affairs in the past.

Our team were losing 2-1 at the time.
We were staying with friends in Italy.

4 When you are looking back from a point in past time, and you are concerned with the effects of something which happened at an earlier time in the past, you use the past perfect.

I apologized because I had left my wallet at home.
They would have come if we had invited them.

Unit 5

'Would' and 'used to'

When you want to talk about something which occurred regularly in the past, you can use 'would' or 'used to' instead of the past simple.

We would normally spend the winter in Miami.
People used to believe that the world was flat.

WARNING: You do not normally use 'would' with this meaning with verbs which are not used in the continuous tenses.

Unit 6

'Must' / 'have to' / 'need to'

1 When you want to say that someone has an obligation to do something, or that it is necessary for them to do it, you use 'must' or 'have to'.

You must come to the meeting tomorrow.
The plants must have plenty of sunshine.
I enjoy parties, unless I have to make a speech.
He has to travel to find work.

You can use 'need to' to talk about the necessity of doing something.

You might need to see a doctor.
A number of questions need to be asked.

2 There is sometimes a difference between 'must' and 'have to'. When you are stating your own opinion that something is an obligation or a necessity, you normally use 'must'.

I must be very careful not to upset him.
We must eat before we go.
He must stop working so hard.

When you are giving information about what someone sees as an obligation or a necessity, you normally use 'have to'.

They have to pay the bill by Thursday.
She has to go now.

Note that you normally use 'have to' for things that happen repeatedly, especially with adverbs of frequency such as 'often', 'always', and 'regularly'.

I always have to do the shopping.
You often have to wait a long time for a bus.

You use 'don't have to' when there is no obligation or necessity to do something.

Many women don't have to work.
You don't have to learn any new typing skills.

You can also use 'don't need to', 'haven't got to', or 'needn't' to say there is no obligation or necessity to do something.

You don't need to buy anything.
I haven't got to go to work today.
I can pick John up. You needn't bother.

3 You also use 'needn't' when you are giving someone permission not to do something.

You needn't say anything if you don't want to.
You needn't stay any longer tonight.

You use 'must not' or 'mustn't' to say that it is important that something is not done or does not happen.

You must not talk about politics.
They mustn't find out that I came here.

Note that 'must not' does not mean the same as 'not have to'. If you 'must not do' something, it is important that you do not do it. If you 'do not have to' do something, it is not necessary for you to do it, but you can do it if you want.

WARNING: You only use 'must' for obligation and necessity in the present and the future. When you want to talk about the past, you use 'had to' rather than 'must'.

She had to catch the six o'clock train.

4 You use 'do', 'does', or 'did' when you want to make a question using 'have to' and 'not have to'.

How often do you have to buy petrol for the car?
Does he have to take so long to get ready?
What did you have to do?
Don't you have to be there at one o'clock?

WARNING: You do not normally form questions like these by putting a form of 'have' before the subject. For example, you do not normally say 'How often have you to buy petrol?'.

5 Informally, you can use 'have got to' instead of 'have to'.

You've just got to make sure you tell him.
She's got to see the doctor.
Have you got to go so soon?

WARNING: You normally use 'had to', not 'had got to', for the past.

He had to know.
I had to lend him some money.

Unit 7

Past passive

1 When you want to talk about the person or thing that performs an action, you use the active voice.

Mr Smith locks the gate at 6 o'clock every night.
The storm destroyed dozens of trees.

When you want to focus on the person or thing that is affected by an action, rather than the person or thing that performs the action, you use the passive voice.

The gate is locked at 6 o'clock every night.
Dozens of trees were destroyed.

2 The passive is formed with a form of the auxiliary be, followed by the past participle of a main verb.

Two new stores were opened this year.

3 Informally, 'get' is sometimes used instead of 'be' to form the passive.

Our car gets cleaned every weekend.
He got killed in a plane crash.

4 When you use the passive, you often do not mention the person or thing that performs the action at all. This may be

because you do not know or do not want to say who it is, or because it does not matter.

Her boyfriend <u>was shot</u> in the chest.
Your application <u>was rejected</u>.
Such items should <u>be</u> carefully <u>packed</u> in tea chests.

5 If you are using the passive and you do want to mention the person or thing that performs the action, you use 'by'.

He had been poisoned <u>by</u> his girlfriend.
He was brought up <u>by</u> an aunt.

You use 'with' to talk about something that is used to perform the action.

A circle was drawn in the dirt <u>with</u> a stick.
He was killed <u>with</u> a knife.

6 Only verbs that usually have an object can have a passive form. You can say 'people spend money' or 'money is spent'.

An enormous amount of money <u>is spent</u> on beer.
The food <u>is sold</u> at local markets.

Unit 7

Conditional clauses (1)

1 You use conditional clauses to talk about a situation that might possibly happen and to say what its results might be. You use 'if' to mention events and situations that happen often, that may happen in the future, that could have happened in the past but did not happen, or that are unlikely to happen at all.

If the light comes on, the battery is OK.
I'll call you <u>if</u> I need you.
<u>If</u> I had known, I'd have told you.
<u>If</u> she asked me, I'd help her.

2 When you are talking about something that is generally true or happens often, you use a present or present perfect tense in the main clause and the conditional clause.

If they <u>lose</u> weight during an illness, they soon <u>regain</u> it .
If an advertisement <u>does not tell</u> the truth, the advertiser <u>is committing</u> an offence.
If the baby <u>is crying</u>, it <u>is</u> probably hungry.
If they <u>have lost</u> any money, they <u>report</u> it to me.

WARNING: You do not use the present continuous in both clauses. You do not say 'If they are losing money, they are getting angry'.

3 When you use a conditional clause with a present or present perfect tense, you often use an imperative in the main clause.

<u>Wake</u> me <u>up</u> if you're worried.
If he has finished, <u>ask</u> him to leave quietly.
If you are very early, <u>don't expect</u> them to be ready.

Unit 8

Present perfect and past simple

1 You use the present perfect tense when you are concerned with the present effects of something which happened at an indefinite time in the past.

I'm afraid I'<u>ve forgotten</u> my book.
<u>Have</u> you <u>heard</u> from Jill recently?

Sometimes, the present effects are very recent.

Karen <u>has</u> just <u>passed</u> her exams.

You also use the present perfect when you are thinking of a time which started in the past and is still continuing.

<u>Have</u> you really <u>lived</u> here for ten years?
He <u>has worked</u> here since 1987.

You also use the present perfect in time clauses, when you are talking about something which will be done at some time in the future.

Tell me when you <u>have finished</u>.
I'll write to you as soon as I <u>have heard</u> from Jenny.

2 When you want to talk about an event that occurred at a particular time in the past, you use the past simple.

The Prime Minister <u>flew</u> into New York yesterday.
The new term <u>started</u> last week.

You also use the past simple to talk about a situation that existed over a period of time in the past.

We <u>spent</u> most of our time at home last winter.
They <u>earned</u> their money quickly that year.

3 When you want to talk about something which took place regularly in the past, you use the past simple.

They <u>went</u> for picnics most weekends.
We usually <u>spent</u> the winter at Aunt Meg's house.

WARNING: The past simple always refers to a time in the past. A time reference is necessary to say what time in the past you are referring to. The time reference must be established in an earlier sentence or by another speaker.

Unit 8

Conditional clauses (2)

When you are talking about something which may possibly happen in the future, you use a present or present perfect in the conditional clause, and simple future in the main clause.

If I <u>marry</u> Celia, we <u>will need</u> the money.
If you <u>are going</u> to America, you <u>will need</u> a visa.
If he <u>has done</u> the windows, he <u>will want</u> his money.

WARNING: You do not normally use 'will' in conditional clauses. You do not say 'If I will see you tomorrow, I will give you the book'.

Unit 9

Conditional clauses (3)

1 When you are talking about something that you think is unlikely to happen, you use the past simple or past continuous in the conditional clause and 'would' in the main clause.

If I had enough money, I would buy the car.
If he was coming, he would ring.

WARNING: You do not normally use 'would' in conditional clauses. You do not say 'If I would do it, I would do it like this'.

2 'Were' is sometimes used instead of 'was' in the conditional clause, especially after 'I'.

If I were as big as you, I would kill you.
If I weren't so busy, I would do it for you.

You often say 'If I were you' when giving someone advice.

If I were you, I would take the money.
I should keep out of Bernadette's way if I were you.

Present perfect continuous

1 When you are concerned with the present effects or future effects of something which happened at an indefinite time in the past, you use the present perfect.

I'm afraid I've forgotten my book, so I don't know.
Have you heard from Jill recently? How is she?

You also use the present perfect when you are thinking of a time which started in the past and still continues.

Have you ever stolen anything? (= at any time up to the present)
He has been here since six o'clock. (= and he is still here)

2 When you want to emphasize the fact that a recent event continued to happen for some time, you use the present perfect continuous.

She's been crying.
I've been working hard all day.

Unit 10

Past perfect tenses

You use the past perfect tense when you are looking back from a point in past time, and you are concerned with the effects of something which happened at an earlier time in the past.

I apologized because I had forgotten my book.
He felt much happier once he had found a new job.
They would have come if we had invited them.

You also use the past perfect when you are thinking of a time which had started earlier in the past but was still continuing.

I was about twenty. I had been studying French for a couple of years.

Conditional clauses (4)

When you are talking about something which could have happened in the past but which did not actually happen, you use the past perfect in the conditional clause. In the main clause, you use 'would have' and a past participle.

If he had realized that, he would have run away.
I wouldn't have been so depressed if I had known how common this feeling is.

WARNING: You do not use 'would have' in the conditional clause. You do not say 'If I would have seen him, I would have told him'.

Unit 11

Wishes and regrets

You can also express what you want to happen now by using 'I wish' or 'If only' followed by a past simple verb.

I wish he wasn't here.
If only she had a car.

Note that in formal English, you sometimes use 'were' instead of 'was' in sentences like these.

I often wish that I were really wealthy.

When you want to express regret about past events, you use the past perfect.

I wish I hadn't married him.

When you want to say that you wish that someone was able to do something, you use 'could'.

If only they could come with us!

When you want to say that you wish that someone was willing to do something, you use 'would'.

If only they would realise how stupid they've been.

Unit 12

Reporting (1)

1 When you are reporting what someone said, you do not usually repeat their exact words, you use your own words in a report structure.

Jim said he wanted to go home.

Jim's actual words might have been 'It's time I went' or 'I must go'.

Report structures contain two clauses. The first clause is the reporting clause, which contains a reporting verb such as 'say', 'tell', or 'ask'.

She said that she'd been to Belgium.
The man in the shop told me how much it would cost.

You often use verbs that refer to peoples thoughts and feelings to report what people say. If someone says 'I am wrong', you might report this as 'He felt that he was wrong'.

2 The second clause in a report structure is the reported clause, which contains the information that you are reporting. The reporting clause can be a 'that'-clause, a 'to'-infinitive clause, an 'if'-clause, or a 'wh'-word clause.

She said that she didn't know.
He told me to do it.
Mary asked if she could stay with us.
She asked where he'd gone.

Unit 13

Future perfect, future continuous, future perfect continuous

1 You use the future perfect tense when you are looking back from a point in the future and you are talking about something which will have happened at a time between now and that future point.

In another two years, you will have left school.
Take these tablets, and in 24 hours the pain will have gone.

You also use the future perfect when you are looking back from the present and guessing that an action will be finished.

I'm sure they will have arrived home by now.
It's too late to ring Don. He will have left the house by now.

2 When you want to talk about something that has not happened yet but will happen before a particular time in the future, you use the future perfect tense.

By the time we phone he'll already have started.
By 1992, he will have worked for twelve years.

3 When you want to say that something will happen because arrangements have been made, you use the future continuous tense.

I'll be seeing them when I've finished with you.
I'll be waiting for you outside.
She'll be appearing at the Royal Festival Hall.

4 You use the present perfect continuous tense when you want to emphasize how long something will have been happening.

By 1992, he will have been working for ten years.

Reporting (2) Reporting verbs

1 If you want to report a statement, you use a 'that'-clause after a verb such as 'say'.

admit	argue	decide	insist	reply
agree	claim	deny	mention	say
answer	complain	explain	promise	warn

He said that he would go.
I replied that I had not read it yet.

You often omit 'that' from the 'that'-clause, but not after 'answer', 'argue', 'explain', or 'reply'.

They said I had to see a doctor first.
He answered that the price would be three pounds.

You often mention the hearer after the preposition 'to' with the following verbs.

admit	complain	mention	suggest
announce	explain	say	

He complained to me that you were rude.

2 'Tell' and some other reporting verbs are also used with a 'that'-clause, but with these verbs you have to mention the hearer as the object of the verb.

convince	notify	reassure	tell
inform	persuade	remind	

He told me that he was a farmer.
I informed her that I could not come.

The word 'that' is often omitted after 'tell'.

I told them you were at the dentist.

You can also mention the hearer as the object of the verb with 'promise' and 'warn'.

I promised her that I wouldn't be late.

3 Note the differences between 'say' and 'tell'. You cannot use 'say' with the hearer as the object of the verb. You cannot say 'I said them you had gone'. You cannot use 'tell' without the hearer, as the object of the verb. You cannot say 'I told that you had gone'. You cannot use 'tell' with 'to' and the hearer. You cannot say 'I told to them you had gone'.

Unit 14

Passives (2)

Continuous passive tenses are formed with a form of the auxiliary 'be' followed by 'being' and the past participle of a main verb.

Jobs are still being lost.
It is being done without his knowledge.

Other passive tenses are formed by using the appropriate tense of the auxiliary 'be' followed by the past participle. The present perfect passive is formed by using the present perfect of 'have' followed by the past participle.

The room has been cleaned recently.

The future passive is formed by using the future of the auxiliary 'be' followed by the past participle of the verb.

The books will be sent to you.

Reporting (3) Questions

1 When you are talking about a question that someone has asked, you use a reported question.

She asked me why I was so late.
He wanted to know where I was going.
I demanded to know what was going on.
I asked her if I could help her.
I asked her whether there was anything wrong.

In formal and written English, 'enquire' (also spelled 'inquire') is often used instead of 'ask'.

Wilkie had enquired if she did a lot of acting.
He inquired whether he could see her.

2 In indirect and reported questions, the subject of the question comes before the verb, just as it does in affirmative sentences.

Do you know where Jane is?
I wonder if you can help me.

3 You do not normally use the auxiliary 'do' in indirect or reported questions.

Can you remember when they open on Sundays?
I wonder what he feels about it.
She asked him if his parents spoke French.

The auxiliary 'do' can be used in indirect or reported questions, but only for emphasis, or to make a contrast with something that has already been said. It is not put before the subject as in direct questions.

She asked me whether I really did mean it.

4 You use 'if' or 'whether' to introduce indirect and reported 'yes/no'-questions.

I wonder if you'd give the children a bath?
I am writing to ask whether you would care to come and visit.

'Whether' is used especially when there is a choice of possibilities.

I was asked whether I wanted to stay at a hotel or at his home.

Note that you can put 'or not' immediately after 'whether', but not immediately after 'if'.

The police didn't ask whether or not they were in.

5 When you are reporting a question, the verb in the reported clause is often in a past tense. This is because you are often talking about the past when you are reporting someone else's words.

She asked me why I was so late.
Pat asked him if she had hurt him.

However, you can use a present or future tense if the question you are reporting relates to the present or future.

Mark was asking if you're enjoying your new job.
They asked if you'll be there tomorrow night.

Unit 15

Present perfect of modal verbs

1 When you want to say that you are almost certain that something has happened, you use 'must have', followed by a past participle.

This article must have been written by a woman.
We must have taken the wrong road.

To say that you do not think that something has happened, you use 'can't have', followed by a past participle.

You can't have forgotten me.
He can't have said that.

2 When there is a possibility that something happened in the past, but you are not certain if it actually happened, you use 'could have', 'may have', or 'might have', followed by a past participle.

It could have been tomato soup.
You may have noticed this advertisement.

You can also use 'might not have' or 'may not have' in this way.

He might not have seen me.
They may not have done it.

3 You use 'could not have' when you want to indicate that it is not possible that something happened.

He didn't have a boat, so he couldn't have rowed away.
It couldn't have been wrong.

You also use 'could have' to say that there was a possibility of something happening in the past, but it did not happen.

It could have been awful. (But it wasn't awful.)
You could have got a job last year. (But you didn't get a job.)

Excellence

in Scientific Enquiry

Year 6

By Graham Peacock

RISING ★ STARS

Rising Stars UK Ltd., 76 Farnaby Road, Bromley,
BR1 4BH

Website: **www.risingstars-uk.com**

Every effort has been made to trace copyright
holders and obtain their permission for the use
of copyright material. The authors and publishers
will gladly receive information enabling them to
rectify any error or omission in subsequent
editions.

All facts are correct at time of going to press.

First Published 2003. Reprinted 2003

Text, design and layout ©Rising Stars UK Ltd.

Editorial: Tanya Solomons

Concept design: Burville Riley

Design: Ken Vail Graphic Design

Illustration copyright ©Louisa Burville-Riley

Cover photo ©Inc. Archive Holdings/Getty Images

British Library Cataloguing in Publication Data

A CIP record for this book is available from the
British Library.

ISBN 1-904591-26-4

Printed in Grimsby, UK.

Contents

How to use this book

The *Excellence in Scientific Enquiry* series is designed to help you to master the investigative skills and to apply what you know about science to practical problems.

The introduction

This section introduces the topic that you will be studying and gives you a basic idea of the skills and content covered.

The investigation

Here the investigation is described and you are provided with all the data you need to answer the questions on the following page.

Approaching the investigation

This is the important bit! The flow chart can be used with any investigation and gives you a way of looking at all investigations in the future.
If you can answer these key questions, you have covered the skills you need to know. The same questions are important when you are doing investigations in class too!

More about dissolving – there is a limit

Class 6L have been studying the amounts of a solid they can dissolve in water.

The investigation

The class were dissolving sugar in water.

- Pat says that you can add more and more and it will dissolve so long as you stir.
- Lena says that water will only dissolve a certain number of spoons of salt and sugar.
- Jo says that there is no limit to the amount you add as the solid disappears.
- Kate says that twice as much water will dissolve twice as much solid.

The class decided to test the predictions.

Mrs Legg said it would be a good idea to use two solids in two different containers.
They decided to use salt and sugar.

They used 50 ml of water.
They made sure that the water was all the same temperature.

These are the results:

	number of spoons of salt that dissolved	number of spoons of sugar that dissolved
50 ml	1	3
100 ml	2	6
150 ml	3	9
200 ml	4	12

Approaching the investigatio

1. **What did the class want to find out?**
   They wanted to see if there was a limit to the amount of solid that w dissolve in water.

2. **What did they predict?**
   There were four different predictions.

3. **How did they test the ideas?**
   They decided to measure the number of spoons of sugar and sa that will dissolve in different amounts of water.

4. **What equipment did they use?**
   Spoons
   Measuring jugs
   Stopwatch

5. **What conclusion did they come to?**
   Water will dissolve a certain amount of each solid.
   Twice as much water dissolves twice as much solid.

Investigate! Hints and tips

- ★ When seeing if a material dissolves you should stir it well.
- ★ Wait a short time and stir again.
- ★ If there is less material each time you stir, it will dissolve in the end.
- ★ Once the powder has dissolved it should not settle on the bottom again.

Investigate! Hints and tips

The hints and tips section gives you useful ideas for completing the questions. They also give advice about completing the investigation in your class.

The questions

The questions get harder as you move down the page.

- Section 1 questions are often multiple choice and cover the basic elements of the investigation.
- Section 2 questions will often ask you for more information about the investigation.
- Section 3 questions usually relate to data handling and you will often have to complete a graph or chart to get full marks.

Activity

This activity will help you to remember the key points of the subject.

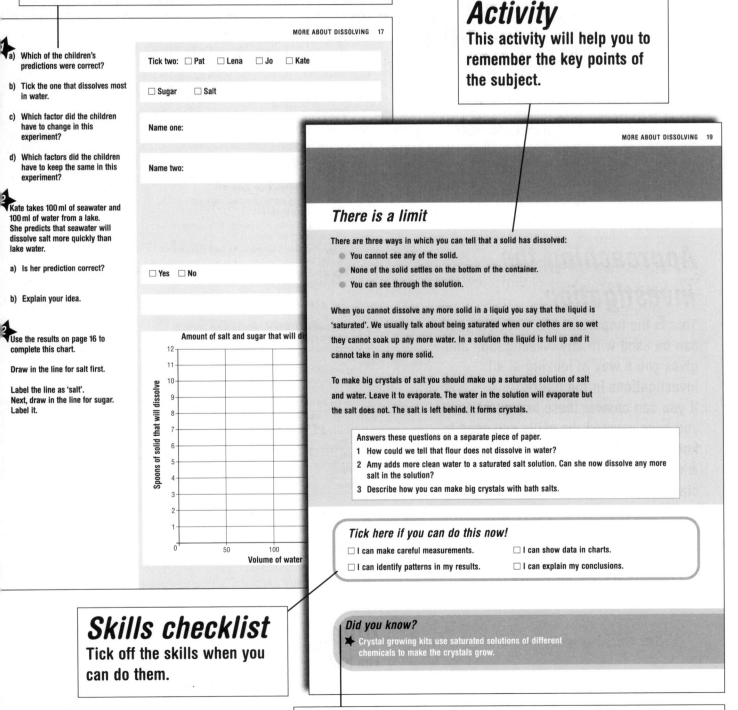

MORE ABOUT DISSOLVING 17

a) Which of the children's predictions were correct?

b) Tick the one that dissolves most in water.

c) Which factor did the children have to change in this experiment?

d) Which factors did the children have to keep the same in this experiment?

Kate takes 100 ml of seawater and 100 ml of water from a lake. She predicts that seawater will dissolve salt more quickly than lake water.

a) Is her prediction correct?

b) Explain your idea.

Use the results on page 16 to complete this chart.

Draw in the line for salt first.

Label the line as 'salt'.
Next, draw in the line for sugar. Label it.

Tick two: ☐ Pat   ☐ Lena   ☐ Jo   ☐ Kate

☐ Sugar   ☐ Salt

Name one:

Name two:

☐ Yes   ☐ No

Amount of salt and sugar that will dissolve

Spoons of solid that will dissolve — 0 to 12

Volume of water — 0, 50, 100

MORE ABOUT DISSOLVING 19

There is a limit

There are three ways in which you can tell that a solid has dissolved:

- You cannot see any of the solid.
- None of the solid settles on the bottom of the container.
- You can see through the solution.

When you cannot dissolve any more solid in a liquid you say that the liquid is 'saturated'. We usually talk about being saturated when our clothes are so wet they cannot soak up any more water. In a solution the liquid is full up and it cannot take in any more solid.

To make big crystals of salt you should make up a saturated solution of salt and water. Leave it to evaporate. The water in the solution will evaporate but the salt does not. The salt is left behind. It forms crystals.

Answers these questions on a separate piece of paper.
1 How could we tell that flour does not dissolve in water?
2 Amy adds more clean water to a saturated salt solution. Can she now dissolve any more salt in the solution?
3 Describe how you can make big crystals with bath salts.

Tick here if you can do this now!
☐ I can make careful measurements.
☐ I can identify patterns in my results.
☐ I can show data in charts.
☐ I can explain my conclusions.

Did you know?
★ Crystal growing kits use saturated solutions of different chemicals to make the crystals grow.

Skills checklist

Tick off the skills when you can do them.

Did you know?

This section gives you some interesting facts about the subject.

Scientific Enquiry – what you need to know

Top 10 Safety Hints

Remember these key rules when carrying out investigations:

1 Always listen to your teacher's instructions.

2 Follow written instructions carefully.

3 If you don't understand any instructions, ask your teacher for help.

4 Take care when CUTTING or HEATING materials.

5 Make sure your hands are dry and keep water away from electrical equipment.

6 Don't run near flames or sharp instruments.

7 Treat your classmates with care and consideration at all times.

8 Always clear up the equipment when you have finished with it.

9 Tell your teacher if anything goes wrong with the investigation or someone is hurt.

10 Tie back hair and loose clothing when working on investigations.

1 What do I want to find out?

2 What can I predict?

3 How can I make a fair test?

4 What do I need to change?

5 What do I need to keep the same?

6 How should I record my results?

7 What have I found out?

8 How should I present my findings?

9 What else could I test?

10 Can I explain my ideas?

Scientists you should know

Edward Jenner 1749–1823

He was a doctor from Gloucester who invented a vaccination for smallpox. This disease had previously killed thousands of people all over the world. By giving people a small dose of another illness (called cowpox) he stopped them getting smallpox.

Louis Pasteur 1822–1895

He invented modern biology and a cure for rabies. Pasteur realised that small organisms called germs carried diseases. Knowing this, he invented a way to keep milk fresh by destroying all the germs in the milk. This is called pasteurisation.

Isaac Newton 1642–1727

Newton was the first person to discover that our tides are affected by the Moon. He also wrote much of what we know today about gravity.

Marie Curie 1867–1934

Curie discovered radium and won the Nobel Prize twice. She invented X-ray vans in the First World War to help save soldiers' lives.

Interdependence and adaptation – green plants

Class 6L have been studying the way that green plants grow best in places where it is very bright. They notice that plants do not grow well in shady places.

The investigation

Class 6L and Mrs Legg put a mat of carpet in their nature area. It covered part of the grass, which contained weeds. They weighed it down with a brick.

Four days later they put down another mat next to the first one.

Four days after that they put down a third mat. They made sure that all three mats were the same.

The class predicted that all the grass would be killed very quickly.

They also predicted that it would be very dry under the mats.

One week later they looked under each mat.

These are the results:

Under the first mat the grass and weeds were long, thin and yellow.
Under the second mat the grass and weeds were going yellow but some were green.
Under the third mat the grass and weeds were mainly green but becoming yellow.
Under each mat the ground was still damp.

Approaching the investigation

❶ What did the class want to find out?
They wanted to know what effect covering grass would have on the plants.

❷ What did they predict?
They predicted all the grass would be killed very quickly. They also said it would be dry.

❸ Which variable did they try to keep the same?
The type of mat.

❹ Which variable did they alter?
The length of time the mat was down for.

❺ What did they observe?
The colour and appearance of the grass and other plants.

❻ What conclusion did they come to?
Plants need light to grow normally. The green is chlorophyll and it is destroyed if there is no light. The plants need chlorophyll to make food, so they die in the dark.

a) Were the predictions made by the class correct?

☐ Yes   ☐ No

b) Explain your answer.

They leave the mats for six weeks.

c) What will it look like under each mat after six weeks?

Tick one:
☐ The grass will grow back.
☐ There will be no green plants at all.
☐ The grass and other plants will still be yellow.

d) Explain your answer.

The children decide to try another investigation using clear plastic mats compared with carpet.

a) Suggest an investigation they could do with the clear mats and the carpet.

A gardener wanted to get rid of weeds on his plot. He did not want to use weed killers or dig the ground.

b) Suggest what he might do.

3

Class 6L try another investigation. They started to grow 20 cress seeds in pots.
They put each of the pots with 20 seedlings in different places.
They watered each pot.

Place plants kept	Number of seedlings at first	Number of seedlings after 14 days
on a bright windowsill	20	20
in a dark part of the room	20	15
in a dark cupboard	20	5

On a separate piece of paper, draw a bar chart showing these results.

Investigate! Hints and tips

Do this investigation yourself:
★ Make sure the mats are in a place where people cannot interfere.
★ Put the mats in a place where they will not look untidy.

★ Look carefully at the insects and other tiny animals that might gather under the mats.
★ Count the number under each mat and see if there is a trend.

Micro-organisms – growing yeast

Class 6L have been studying bread making. One of the main ingredients is yeast and the class wanted to know more about it. The baker told them that when yeast worked it produced bubbles of carbon dioxide gas.

The investigation

The class collected different kinds of yeast but their favourite was the block of yeast they got from the supermarket bakery. They decided to put the same amount of the supermarket bakery yeast in each tube. They kept the tubes in the same place.

In five small glass tubes they put:

1 yeast only
2 yeast and water only
3 yeast and salt and water
4 yeast and flour and water
5 yeast and sugar and water

The class predicted that the yeast would bubble in all the tubes apart from tube 1. They looked at each tube after one hour.

tube		
1	yeast only	no change
2	yeast and water only	no change
3	yeast and salt and water	no change
4	yeast and flour and water	bubbles
5	yeast and sugar and water	lots of bubbles

Then they tried different temperatures.
They put the yeast and sugar and water mix in different places.
They left the samples for an hour.
They used water at different temperatures to start the experiments off.

	Temperature of water at start	Number of bubbles
Tube surrounded by ice	4 °C	no bubbles
Tube surrounded with cold water	10 °C	few bubbles
Tube surrounded by warm water	20 °C	lots of bubbles

Approaching the investigation

1 **What did the class want to find out?**
What yeast feeds on.
What temperature it worked in best.

2 **What did they predict?**
They thought it would work in all conditions except when it was left by itself.

3 **Which variable did they try to keep the same in the feeding tests?**
In the feeding tests they tried to keep the amount of yeast the same.
They kept the tubes the same.
They kept all the tubes in the same place.

4 **Which variable did they try to keep the same in the temperature tests?**
In the temperature tests they kept the amount of yeast, sugar and water the same.

5 **Which variable did they alter?**
In the feeding tests they altered the food they put in the tube.
In the temperature test they changed the temperature of the water and the place where the container was kept.

6 **What did they measure?**
The number of bubbles.

7 **What equipment did they use?**
Glass tubes

8 **What conclusion did they come to?**
Yeast works best in warm places with sugar or flour.

1

a) Which of these do you think makes yeast work?

Tick one: ☐ raisins ☐ glass ☐ orange cordial ☐ water

b) Explain your idea.

2

Mrs Legg took two small bottles.
- In one bottle she put yeast and sugar.
- In the other container she put yeast and salt.
- She put a balloon over the neck of each bottle.

a) Predict what will happen.

Tick one: ☐ Both balloons will fill with gas.
☐ Only the balloon under yeast and salt will fill with gas.
☐ Only the balloon under yeast and sugar will fill with gas.
☐ Neither of the balloons will fill with gas.

b) Explain your idea.

c) Why do bakers keep their bread dough warm?

d) What do you think causes the holes in a loaf of bread?

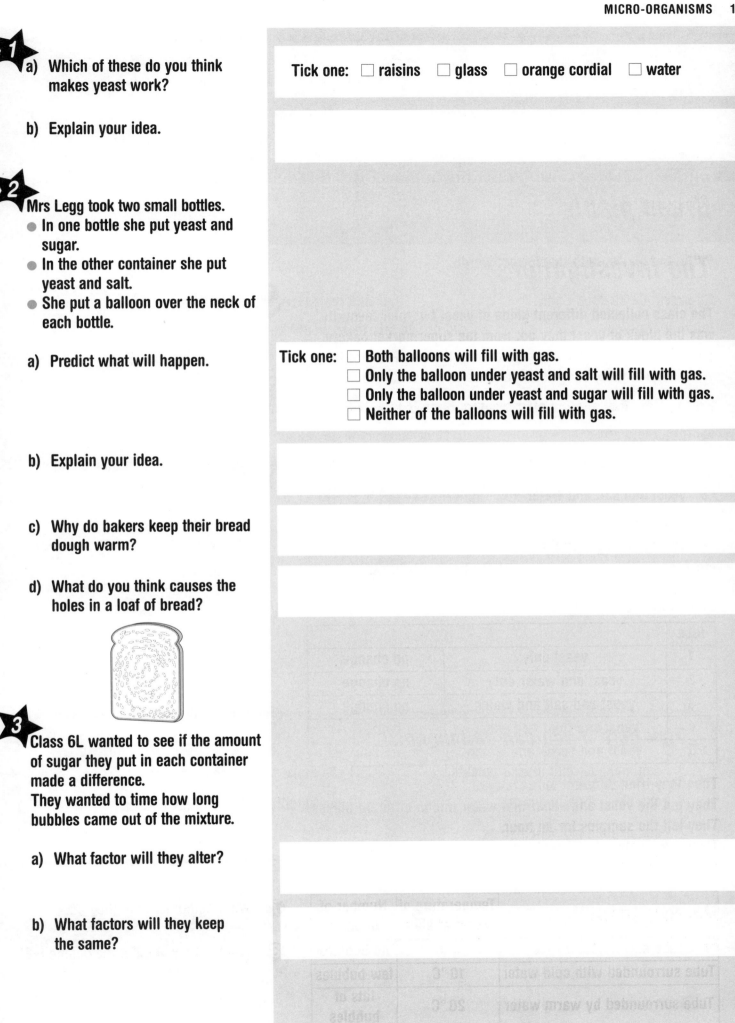

3

Class 6L wanted to see if the amount of sugar they put in each container made a difference.
They wanted to time how long bubbles came out of the mixture.

a) What factor will they alter?

b) What factors will they keep the same?

Interdependence and adaptation– summary

Green plants

Fill in the blanks with the correct words.

All green plants need light, _____, air and the energy from sunlight to grow. If green _____ did not do this there would be very little life on Earth.

Green plants that grow in places where there is little light will be unhealthy. They will grow thin and _____. Their leaves will be yellow. Plants grown in no light will die within a few _____. They may survive on their stores of _____ but without light they starve to death.

Animals depend on green plants to make food for them. Green plants are the start of most food _____ on Earth. Plants are the _____ of the food eaten by animals. In food chains animals are _____.

Tick here if you can do this now!

☐ I can make careful measurements.   ☐ I can make careful observations.

☐ I can show data in charts.   ☐ I can identify patterns in my results.

☐ I can explain my conclusions.

Did you know?

★ Bacteria are the basis of many food chains. They can eat the chemicals in rocks! They are the basis of some special food chains in caves and in the deep oceans where green plants do not grow.

Micro-organisms – summary

Yeast

Yeast is a micro-organism. It is a form of fungus. Other fungi include mushrooms and toadstools. All fungi need a source of food. They may look like plants but they are not able to make their own food from air, water and sunlight. Most fungi need food in the form of dead or decaying plant or animal material. A few even feed on living plants and animals. Most fungi like to grow in dark, damp and warm places.

Many fungi give people problems. Some plant diseases are caused by fungi. This can lead to famines when food plants like potatoes are affected. People put fungi to uses. These include:

- yeast to make bread rise
- yeast to brew beer and wine
- penicillin fungi that are used to make antibiotics

1 Add a title to each of the paragraphs.

2 In which of these places would fungi grow best?
   Tick one:
   ☐ a desert
   ☐ a jungle
   Explain your answer.

3 In which of these places would fungi grow best?
   Tick one:
   ☐ a damp cellar
   ☐ a dry attic
   Explain your answer.

Tick here if you can do this now!

☐ I can make careful measurements.   ☐ I can show data in charts.

☐ I can identify patterns in my results.   ☐ I can explain my conclusions.

Did you know?

★ Athlete's foot is caused by a fungus that lives on your skin.
  It loves the warm, damp and dark conditions inside your socks!

More about dissolving – dissolving faster

Class 6L have been studying the way that sugar dissolves in water

The investigation

The class were experimenting with the speed at which sugar dissolved when they stirred and when they did not stir.

They found that a spoon of sugar took hours to dissolve completely if it is not stirred. They found that it dissolved quickest if the solution was stirred all the time.

They wanted to find out the effect of using water at different temperatures.

- They used water from the hot and cold taps to get different temperatures.
- They used two teaspoons of sugar each time.
- They used 50 ml of water in each test.
- They stirred the mixture once every 10 seconds.
- The same person stirred each time.
- They timed how long it took for the sugar to disappear completely.

The class predicted that the sugar would dissolve twice as fast in hot water as it did in cold water.

These are the results:

Temperature of water	Time to dissolve (seconds)
10 °C	150
20 °C	120
30 °C	80
40 °C	35

Approaching the investigation

1. **What did the class want to find out?**
   They wanted to see if sugar dissolved faster in hot water than in cold water.

2. **What did they predict?**
   They predicted that it would dissolve twice as fast in hot as in cold.

3. **Was their prediction correct?**
   Their prediction could not be tested because they didn't say what 'hot' water was.

4. **Which variables did they try to keep the same?**
   Volume of water
   Number of stirs
   The person who stirred
   Amount of sugar

5. **Which variable did they alter?**
   The temperature of the water.

6. **What did they measure?**
   The time it took for the sugar to dissolve.

7. **What equipment did they use?**
   A stopwatch
   Measuring jug
   A spoon

8. **What conclusion did they come to?**
   Sugar dissolves much faster in hot water than in cold water.

Investigate! Hints and tips

Do this investigation yourself.
★ Be careful with hot water.

★ Mix hot and cold water to make the different temperatures of water.

★ Take care that the thermometers do not roll off the desk.

1

The children measured 50 ml of water each time.

a) Which size measuring jug should they use?

Tick one: ☐ 100 ml   ☐ 200 ml   ☐ 500 ml

b) Explain your idea

c) Why do you think the children did not use water hotter than 40 °C?

d) Why did the children test the temperature at the beginning of each test?

e) Why did they not think it sensible to measure it at the end?

Jemma says that it would be better if the sugar was coloured.

f) Why do you think she says this?

2

Jemma wonders if all sugars dissolve at the same rate.
How could she test:
● sugar cubes?
● sugar crystals?
● brown sugar?
● white sugar?

3

Use the results on page 14 to complete this line graph.

a) Predict how quickly the sugar would have dissolved in water at 50 °C.
Show this on the graph with a small cross.
Continue the line to show the trend.

b) What do you notice about the trend of this graph line?

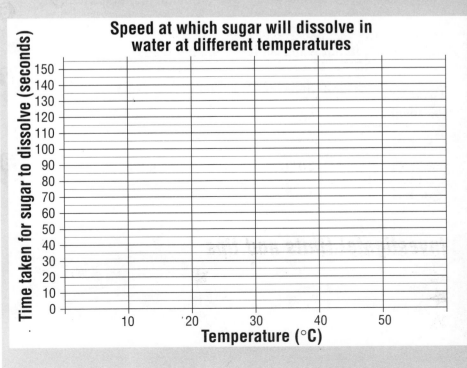

Speed at which sugar will dissolve in water at different temperatures

Time taken for sugar to dissolve (seconds): 0, 10, 20, 30, 40, 50, 60, 70, 80, 90, 100, 110, 120, 130, 140, 150

Temperature (°C): 10, 20, 30, 40, 50

More about dissolving – there is a limit

Class 6L have been studying the amounts of a solid they can dissolve in water.

The investigation

The class were dissolving sugar in water.

- Pat says that you can add more and more and it will dissolve so long as you stir.
- Lena says that water will only dissolve a certain number of spoons of sugar.
- Jo says that there is no limit to the amount you add as the solid disappears.
- Kate says that twice as much water will dissolve twice as much solid.

The class decided to test the predictions.

Mrs Legg said it would be a good idea to use two solids in two different containers.
They decided to use salt and sugar.

They used 50 ml of water.
They made sure that the water was all the same temperature.

These are the results:

	number of spoons of salt that dissolved	number of spoons of sugar that dissolved
50 ml	1	3
100 ml	2	6
150 ml	3	9
200 ml	4	12

Approaching the investigation

1. **What did the class want to find out?**
   They wanted to see if there was a limit to the amount of solid that will dissolve in water.

2. **What did they predict?**
   There were four different predictions.

3. **How did they test the ideas?**
   They decided to measure the number of spoons of sugar and salt that will dissolve in different amounts of water.

4. **What equipment did they use?**
   Spoons
   Measuring jugs
   Stopwatch

5. **What conclusion did they come to?**
   Water will dissolve a certain amount of each solid.
   Twice as much water dissolves twice as much solid.

Investigate! Hints and tips

- When seeing if a material dissolves, you should stir it well.
- Wait a short time and stir again.
- If there is less material each time you stir, it will dissolve in the end.
- Once the powder has dissolved it should not settle on the bottom again.

1

a) Which of the children's predictions were correct?

Tick two: ☐ Pat   ☐ Lena   ☐ Jo   ☐ Kate

b) Tick the one that dissolves most in water.

☐ Sugar   ☐ Salt

c) Which factor did the children have to change in this experiment?

Name one:

d) Which factors did the children have to keep the same in this experiment?

Name two:

2

Kate takes 100 ml of seawater and 100 ml of water from a lake. She predicts that seawater will dissolve salt more quickly than lake water.

a) Is her prediction correct?

☐ Yes   ☐ No

b) Explain your idea.

3

Use the results on page 16 to complete this chart.

Draw in the line for salt first.

Label the line as 'salt'.
Next, draw in the line for sugar.
Label it.

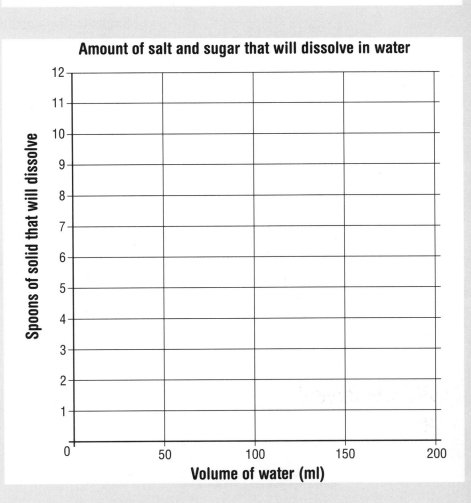

More about dissolving – summary

Dissolving faster

Solids that dissolve are soluble. They form solutions with the liquid.

Sugar dissolves much more quickly in hot water than it does in cold water.

Stirring helps solids to dissolve.

The solute is the solid that is dissolved.

A solvent is the liquid in which a solid is dissolved.

A solution is a mixture of a solute and a solvent.

1 Which is true? Tick one statement: ☐ Sugar is soluble. ☐ Sugar is insoluble.

2 Which is true? Tick one statement: ☐ Sugar is dissolved more slowly in cold water than in warm.
☐ Sugar is dissolved more quickly in cold water than in warm.

3 Which is true? Tick one statement: ☐ A sugar solution is a mix of water and sugar.
☐ A sugar solution is a sweet answer.

4 Which is true? Tick one statement: ☐ Water is the solvent in a sugar solution.
☐ Sugar is the solvent in a sugar solution.

Tick here if you can do this now!

☐ I can make careful measurements.   ☐ I can evaluate my experiments.

☐ I can work safely in experiments.   ☐ I can identify patterns in my results.

☐ I can explain my conclusions.

Did you know?

★ Dry cleaning does not use water but it does use other liquids that can dissolve fat and grease.

There is a limit

There are three ways in which you can tell that a solid has dissolved:

- You cannot see any of the solid.
- None of the solid settles on the bottom of the container.
- You can see through the solution.

When you cannot dissolve any more solid in a liquid you say that the liquid is 'saturated'. We usually talk about being saturated when our clothes are so wet they cannot soak up any more water. In a solution the liquid is full up and it cannot take in any more solid.

To make big crystals of salt you should make up a saturated solution of salt and water. Leave it to evaporate. The water in the solution will evaporate but the salt does not. The salt is left behind. It forms crystals.

Answers these questions on a separate piece of paper.

1 How could we tell that flour does not dissolve in water?

2 Amy adds more clean water to a saturated salt solution. Can she now dissolve any more salt in the solution?

3 Describe how you can make big crystals with bath salts.

Tick here if you can do this now!

☐ I can make careful measurements. ☐ I can show data in charts.

☐ I can identify patterns in my results. ☐ I can explain my conclusions.

Did you know?

★ Crystal growing kits use saturated solutions of different chemicals to make the crystals grow.

Reversible and irreversible changes – heating materials

Class 6L have been studying the way in which different materials change when heated in a flame. They started looking at the way food and other materials change when they put them in a candle flame.

The investigation

The class used a metal spoon. They held the spoon in a wooden peg. They used a small candle to heat the food and other materials. They only used very small pieces of material or food. They wore safety goggles.

The class predicted that all the food would simply burn and go black.

Mrs Legg made sure that people did not have spare paper on their tables.

The children noted what happened after 10 seconds, after 60 seconds and after two minutes of heating.

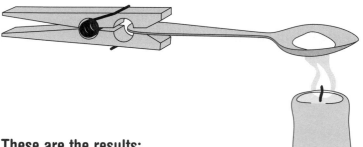

Approaching the investigation

1 **What did the class want to find out?**
The class wanted to find out how things change when heated.

2 **What did they predict?**
They predicted that all the food would go black.

3 **Which variable did they try to keep the same?**
They tried to keep the time and the candle the same.

4 **Which variable did they alter?**
The material.

5 **What did they observe?**
The appearance of the material.

6 **What did they do to protect themselves?**
They wore eye protectors.

7 **What else should they do to make sure they stay safe?**
Tie back hair.
Have no loose clothing.
Make sure there is no scrap paper on the table.

These are the results:

Material	What it looked like at start	What it looked like after 10 seconds	What it looked like after 60 seconds	What it looked like after two minutes
butter	yellow solid	yellow solid	yellow liquid	brown liquid, some smoke
sugar	white grains	white grains	brown liquid, some smoke	black solid
salt	white grains	white grains	white grains	white grains
raisin	brown solid	brown solid	brown solid, some smoke	black ball
bread	white solid	white solid	brown solid, some smoke	black cube
lard	white solid	white solid	clear liquid	clear liquid with smoke
paper	white sheet	white sheet	brown sheet	black sheet

1

a) Which one material did not change at all?

Tick one: ☐ Bread ☐ Salt ☐ Lard

b) Which materials changed as the children predicted?

Tick two: ☐ Sugar ☐ Salt ☐ Lard ☐ Paper

c) Which of the changes was irreversible?

Name one:

The children looked at the changes to lard up to 60 seconds.

d) Tick the correct statement

☐ Jim said the change was reversible because it was just solid to liquid.
☐ Kate said it was irreversible because heat was involved.

2

a) Tick the sentence that describes an irreversible change in wax.

☐ Candles are made by melting wax and pouring it into a shape.
☐ When you burn the candle the wax is changed into gas.

b) Explain how you can reverse these changes.
  ● Boiling water changing to water vapour.
  ● Freezing water to make ice cubes.

3

a) How long did it take the butter to melt?

Tick one: ☐ Less than 10 seconds
☐ Less than 60 seconds
☐ Between 61 seconds and two minutes

b) How long did it take the butter to start smoking?

Tick one: ☐ Less than 10 seconds
☐ Less than 60 seconds
☐ Between 61 seconds and two minutes

Investigate! Hints and tips

Do this investigation yourself.
★ Keep the windows open to give fresh air.

★ Use tiny amounts of each material.
★ Make sure an adult is supervising.

★ Divide up the jobs between a holder, a timer, an observer and a scribe.

Reversible and irreversible changes – burning a candle

Class 6L have been studying the way in which candles burn. They wanted to see how long a candle burnt in a jar.

The investigation

The class collected different sized jam jars. They used the same candle. They turned over the jar and put it over the burning candle. They timed how long the candle stayed alight under the jar.

The class predicted that the candle would burn twice as long in a jar that was twice as big.

Mrs Legg asked the children what they meant when they said the jar was twice as big. She showed them how to use water to measure the volume of the jar.
She asked them to make sure there was fresh air in the jar at the end of each test.

These are the results:

Volume of jar (millilitres)	120	200	500	750
Test 1 Length of time the candle stayed alight (seconds)	4	9	19	30
Test 2 Length of time the candle stayed alight (seconds)	6	10	22	37
Test 3 Length of time the candle stayed alight (seconds)	5	8	19	32
Average Length of time the candle stayed alight (seconds)	5	9	20	33

Approaching the investigation

1 **What did the class want to find out?**
How long candles burnt in different sized jam jars.

2 **What did they predict?**
They predicted that a candle will burn twice as long in a jar that is twice the size.

3 **Why did they do each test three times?**
They wanted to check their results. The average would help them to ignore readings that were too high or too low.

4 **How did they measure the volume of each jam jar?**
The children filled the jam jar with water and then measured the volume of water in a measuring jug.

5 **Why did Mrs Legg tell the children to make sure there was fresh air?**
The children thought that the air would be used up by the burning candle. They noticed that the candle went out straight away if they did not get fresh air inside the jar.

6 **What equipment did they use?**
Jam jars
Stopwatch
Measuring jugs

7 **What did they find out?**
That candles used the air inside a jar. Candles burned for much longer in jars that are bigger.

1

a) On average, how long did the candle burn in the 500 ml jar?

b) Which of these sentences are correct?

Tick one: ☐ 5 seconds   ☐ 9 seconds
           ☐ 20 seconds   ☐ 33 seconds

Tick two: ☐ Candles burn longer in big jars than smaller jars.
           ☐ Candles burn longer in smaller jars than big jars.
           ☐ There is more air in big jars so candles burn longer.
           ☐ There is more space for burning in big jars so candles burn longer.

2

Some miners were stuck in a tiny space underground. There was no air getting in.

a) Should they light a candle?

b) Explain your idea.

☐ Yes   ☐ No

3

Look at the graph.

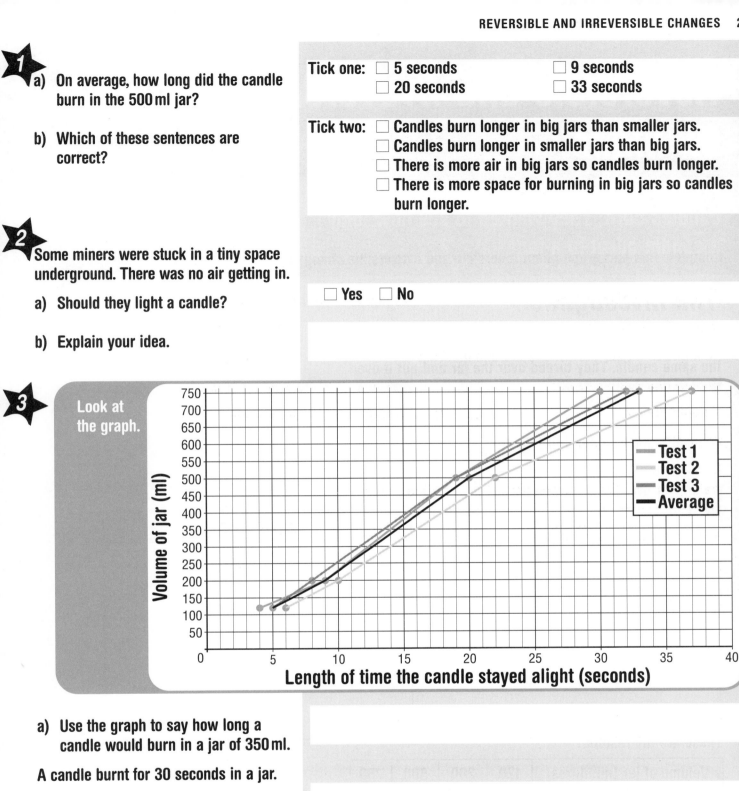

a) Use the graph to say how long a candle would burn in a jar of 350 ml.

A candle burnt for 30 seconds in a jar.

b) Use the graph to work out the volume of the jar.

c) Were the children's predictions correct?

☐ Yes   ☐ No

Investigate! Hints and tips

Do this investigation yourself.
★ Blow into the jar to make sure there is fresh air in the jar each time.
★ Use a short candle so it fits into even a small jar.

★ One person should watch the candle and say when it goes out. Another person should work the stopwatch.
★ Take great care with glass jars. They can get hot.

Reversible and irreversible changes – summary

Heating materials

Complete this paragraph about reversible and irreversible changes.

Melting is the change from _____ to liquid. Evaporation is the change from liquid to _____ . _____ is the change from gas to liquid. Freezing is the change from _____ to solid. Most of these changes are _____ . Burning is where a material is changed into a _____ substance. Burnt paper cannot be made into white paper again. Burning is _____ .

Make your own list of reversible and irreversible changes.

Reversible	Irreversible

Tick here if you can do this now!

☐ I can work safely.

☐ I can make accurate observations.

☐ I can time accurately.

☐ I can explain my conclusions.

Did you know?

★ When paper is burnt the gas carbon dioxide is released. Trees use carbon dioxide to make wood. Wood is made into paper. The changes when we burn paper are reversed by trees!

Burning a candle

Complete these paragraphs about candles.

When candles burn not all the wax is burnt. Some melts and drips down the candle. This change from solid to _____ is a reversible change.

When candles burn they use air. The more _____ there is in a jar the longer the candle will burn. The candle flame burns wax. It is impossible for people to turn burnt wax back into solid wax again. This is an example of an _____ change.

Air is a mixture of gases. The main gases in air are nitrogen and oxygen. When _____ burn they only use oxygen. The flame turns the _____ into carbon dioxide and water. It is very difficult to turn carbon dioxide and water back into wax. This is an example of an _____ change.

Tick here if you can do this now!

☐ I can make careful measurements.   ☐ I can predict what will happen in experiments.

☐ I can use my results to predict what would happen in similar experiments.

☐ I can explain my conclusions.

Did you know?

★ The wax in cheap candles is made from oil. Bees make wax in the hives. This wax can be used to make candles but it is very expensive. Hundreds of years ago candles were very expensive and poor people burnt smelly animal fat in their lamps.

Forces in action – air resistance

Class 6L has been studying the effects of air resistance on pieces of A4 paper. They discovered that paper that was screwed up in a ball fell faster than paper that was dropped 'flat'.

The investigation

Mrs Legg showed the class another way of demonstrating air resistance as a force. She made a 'spinner' from a small piece of paper and attached a paper clip to the bottom.

Then she stood on a chair and held the spinner as high as she could reach above her head. When she dropped it, a pupil timed how long it took for the spinner to hit the ground.

Mrs Legg asked the class a question.

'How does the number of paper clips attached affect the time it takes for the spinner to fall?'

Here are the results of the investigation:

Number of paper clips attached to spinner	Test 1	Test 2
1	4.8 seconds	4.6 seconds
2	4.5 seconds	4.2 seconds
3	3.6 seconds	3.7 seconds
4	3.0 seconds	3.1 seconds
5	2.4 seconds	2.4 seconds
6	1.5 seconds	1.6 seconds

Approaching the investigation

1 **What do the class want to find out?**
How the number of paper clips attached affects the fall of a spinner.

2 **How can they create a fair test?**
By keeping the conditions the same for each test.

3 **What equipment do they need?**
Paper clips, paper spinners, stopwatch, pens and paper.

4 **How will they carry out the test?**
One person drops a spinner with one paper clip from a chair. Their partner records the result. The test is repeated and result recorded. They continue to add paperclips up to a maximum of 6. Each spinner is dropped from the same height.

5 **Can you predict what will happen?**
The spinner will fall faster each time, but how much faster?

6 **How should they record their results?**
For this type of investigation, a table would be best. They can then present the data as a line graph.

7 **What did they find out?**
That the more paper clips that were added, the faster the spinner fell.

8 **Why do you think this is so?**
Air resistance acts on the surface area in the opposite direction to the weight. If the air resistance remains the same but the weight increases, there will be a greater downward force.

1

a) Can you list three things needed to do this investigation?

b) Did the spinner fall faster with one paper clip attached or three?

c) Would it be a fair test if the spinners were dropped from different heights?
Explain your answer.

2

a) Do the results show a fair test?

b) Give reasons to support your answer.

c) How long did it take on average for the spinner to hit the ground with:

d) Can you give one safety tip to anyone doing this investigation?

3

a) Can you use the table of results on page 26 to complete this line graph for Test 2?

b) How can you use the line graph to describe the motion of spinners falling?

1) _____ 2) _____ 3) _____

1) Two paper clips   2) Four paper clips   3) Six paper clips

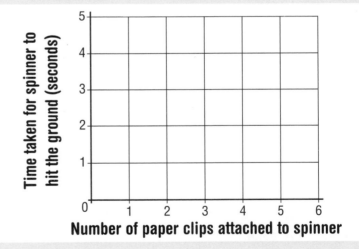

Time taken for spinner to hit the ground (seconds) vs Number of paper clips attached to spinner

Investigate! Hints and tips

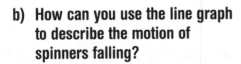

★ Remember, heavy and light objects fall at the same speed. In this investigation it's the air resistance that slows the lighter object by a greater amount.

★ Work in pairs. One person can drop the spinner; the other can accurately time the rate of descent.

★ Be aware of outside influences which could affect the investigation, such as open doors and windows.

Forces in action – gravity

Class 6L have been studying the pull of gravity on masses. They used spring balances to weigh mass.

The investigation

Class 6L predicted that gravity will pull objects down towards the Earth.
They decided to weigh different masses using a spring balance to find the pull of gravity on each one.

Their results are shown in this table:

Mass (g)	Pull of gravity (N)
100	1
200	2
300	3
400	4
500	5
600	6

They drew a quick line graph to see what shape it made.

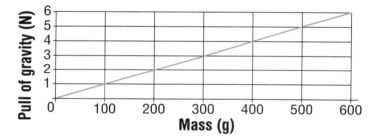

The children then decided to investigate the pull of gravity on an elastic band.
They hung masses from the elastic band and measured the length of the band.

Jim thought the line graph would look like the one for the masses.
Kate thought it would be curved and not straight at all.
Ahmed thought it would be straight for a bit then curved.

Mass (g)	0	100	200	300	400	500	600
Length of rubber band (cm)	12	15	18	21	23	24	24.5
Stretch of band (cm)	0						

Approaching the investigation

1 **What did the class want to find out?**
They wanted to measure how far masses stretched an elastic band.

2 **What did they predict?**
There were three predictions.

3 **Who made the correct prediction?**
Ahmed made the correct prediction. At first the band stretched in a regular way then it stopped stretching so much.

4 **Which variable did they try to keep the same?**
The kept the band the same all the time.

5 **Which variable did they alter?**
The mass they attached.

6 **What did they measure?**
The length of the band.

7 **What equipment did they use?**
Spring balance, ruler and elastic band.

8 **What conclusion did they come to?**
The more masses you add, the more an elastic band stretches.

1

a) How long was the band after 200 g was added?

Tick one: ☐ 20 cm   ☐ 20 N   ☐ 18 cm   ☐ 18 N

b) How much did 400 g stretch the band? (Remember it started at 12 cm long.)

Tick one: ☐ 23 N   ☐ 11 cm   ☐ 23 cm   ☐ 23 ml

2

Lena thinks that thick bands do not stretch as much as thin bands.

a) Design a table that she could use to record her results. It has been started here. Do not show the results.

b) Add the units in the brackets above.

( )	Thick elastic band ( )	Thin elastic band ( )
100		

3

Work out the stretch of the band in the table opposite.
The stretch with 100 g added is 3 cm.

a) Complete the other results in the table on page 28.

b) Use the results to draw this graph.

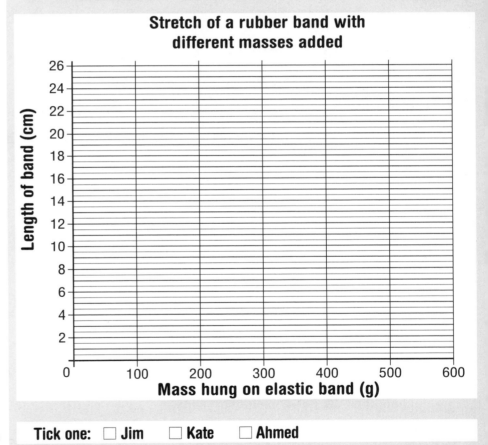

Stretch of a rubber band with different masses added

(y-axis: Length of band (cm), 2 to 26; x-axis: Mass hung on elastic band (g), 0 to 600)

c) Who made the correct prediction?

Tick one: ☐ Jim   ☐ Kate   ☐ Ahmed

Investigate! Hints and tips

Do this investigation yourself.
★ Use bands of different thickness.
★ Use a hanging mass carrier or use a pot with strings and a bent paperclip to hold the masses.

★ Hang the bands from a stick between two desks if you do not have a proper stand.
★ Give each person in the group a job:
– Mass manager   – Scribe
– Ruler holder   – Measuring manager

Forces in Action – summary

Air resistance

Complete this paragraph about air resistance using the words below.

Air resistance is a ⬚⬚⬚⬚⬚⬚⬚. When an object falls, air resistance acts in the ⬚⬚⬚⬚⬚⬚⬚ direction to the weight. This ⬚⬚⬚⬚⬚⬚⬚ down the falling object. The air offers greater ⬚⬚⬚⬚⬚⬚⬚ to objects that have a ⬚⬚⬚⬚⬚⬚⬚ surface area. Looking at our investigation, air resistance pushed ⬚⬚⬚⬚⬚⬚⬚ on the spinners and weight pulled them ⬚⬚⬚⬚⬚⬚⬚.

Air resistance slows the lighter object by a greater amount. That is why the spinners with ⬚⬚⬚⬚⬚⬚⬚ paper-clips took longer to ⬚⬚⬚⬚⬚⬚⬚ to the ground. If two objects of ⬚⬚⬚⬚⬚⬚⬚ weights are dropped when there is no air resistance (such as on the moon) they will reach the ground at the same time.

Tick here if you can do this now!

☐ I can make and repeat measurements.　☐ I can show data in line graphs.

☐ I can identify patterns in my results.　☐ I can use results to draw conclusions.

Did you know?

★ Helicopters, parachutes and hangliders all operate by using air resistance, but the first designs for these inventions were drawn by the Italian genius Leonardo Da Vinci, over 500 years ago...

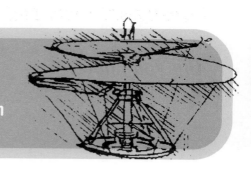

Gravity

The Earth's gravitational pull is strongest on objects with a large mass and weakest on small masses. 100 g is pulled with a force of 1 newton. 300 g is pulled with a force of 3 newtons. This does not mean that 300 g falls faster. Different masses fall at the same rate – you can try this by dropping a paperclip and a big ball of plasticine at the same time. They both reach the ground at the same time.

We are all attracted to the Earth by the pull of gravity. Gravity is a force that can be felt very far away. The gravity pull of the Sun keeps all the planets in orbit. Even Pluto, which is the planet furthest from the Sun, is kept in its orbit by the gravity pull of the Sun.

The Moon is attracted by the gravity pull of the Earth and the Earth is pulled by the Moon. The Moon's gravity pull is most obvious on the seas of the world. The gravity of the Moon causes the tides, which rise and fall each day.

1   How much gravity pull would there be on an object with a mass of 200 g?

2   Which would hit the ground first, a football or a tennis ball?

3   Does gravity work at great distances or only close to the Earth?

4   Which is the most distant planet in the solar system?

5   What object pulls on the seas to make tides?

Tick here if you can do this now!

☐ I can make careful measurements.

☐ I can show data in line graphs.

☐ I can identify patterns in my results.

☐ I can use results to draw conclusions.

Did you know?

★ Gravity is the force that holds our atmosphere close to the Earth's surface. If there were no gravity all the air would spread out into space.

Forces in action – friction

Class 6L have been studying the force needed to pull boxes across different surfaces.

The investigation

Class 6L collected the lids of the boxes in which photocopier paper arrives. They attached a loop of string to each box lid. Each group had their own box lid. They thought they would be able to compare results if they all had the same sort of lid.

They put a 1kg mass in each box. They tested how much force was needed to drag the box lid on different surfaces.

They did each test three times to check their results.

Here are Jim and Lena's results:

	First reading (N)	Second reading (N)	Third reading (N)	Average (N)
table top	4	5	6	
smooth floor	5	7	6	
carpet	8	5	8	
grass	10	8	6	
sand tray	12	14	10	

Later, the children decided to see if they could reduce the friction. They did the test on a table top. They tried:

- rollers made from pencils
- putting the lid on four toy cars
- putting the lid on a skateboard
- adding talcum powder to the table top

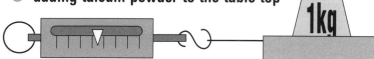

Approaching the investigation

1 **What did the class want to find out?**
They wanted to see what factors affect friction.

2 **In the first investigation on different surfaces, which variables did they try to keep the same?**
They kept three variables the same. They kept the lid, the mass inside and the way it was pulled the same.

3 **In the first investigation on different surfaces, which variable did they alter?**
They altered the surface.

4 **What did they measure?**
The friction between the lid and the surface.

5 **What unit did they use to measure the friction?**
They measured the friction in newtons.

6 **What equipment did they use?**
Spring balance

7 **In what unit did they measure force?**
Newtons

8 **What conclusion did they come to?**
They found that rough surfaces make more friction than smooth surfaces.

Investigate! Hints and tips

Do this investigation yourself.
- ★ Use any sort of box.
- ★ Ask your teacher to show you how to make the hole to attach the spring balance.
- ★ Use a spring balance that is not too strong and not too weak.
- ★ Practise pulling the box with a steady pull. Ignore the jerk just as the box starts moving.

1 Look at the three different tests.

a) On which surfaces were the results most varied?

Tick two: ☐ Table top   ☐ Smooth floor
☐ Carpet   ☐ Grass   ☐ Sand tray

b) Work out the average force needed to move the box on each surface.

Write it in the table.

	Average force needed to pull the box
table top	
smooth floor	
carpet	
grass	
sand tray	

c) On which surface was there most friction?

d) On which surface was there least friction?

2 The children drag the box over sandpaper.

a) Predict the amount of friction.

Tick one: ☐ Less than on the carpet.   ☐ More than on the carpet.
☐ The same as the carpet.

b) Explain your idea.

The children drag the box on rollers.

c) Predict the amount of friction.

Tick one: ☐ Less than on the carpet.   ☐ More than on the carpet.
☐ The same as the carpet.

3 a) Write in the labels for the bars.

b) Write in the labels for the two axes.

Forces in action – floating forces

Class 6L have been studying which things float and which sink. They have been weighing objects in air and in water.

The investigation

Kate and Ali chose five objects that sink in water. They weighed them using a spring balance.

They then hung the objects in a bowl of water. They did not let the objects touch the bottom of the bowl.

The class predicted that the objects would weigh less in water than in air.

These are the results.

	Weight in air (newtons)	Weight in water (newtons)	Difference between the weights
rock	4	3	
potato	2	0.5	
lump of plasticine	2	1	
metal mass	6	4	
tin of cat food	8	4	

They talked about the force that makes objects float. They talked about picking up heavy objects in the swimming pool and how they felt lighter under water. They suggested ways to make objects float that normally sink.

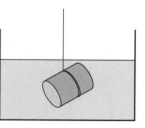

Approaching the investigation

1. **What did the class want to find out?**
   They wanted to see if objects weighed less in water.

2. **What did they predict?**
   They predicted that objects will weigh less in water than in air.

3. **What did they measure?**
   They measured the weight of the objects in air and when they were hung in water.

4. **Why did they make sure the object did not touch the bottom of the bowl?**
   If the object had touched the bottom it would be held up by the bowl and not the water.

5. **What is the name of the force that supports objects in water?**
   Upthrust

6. **What equipment did they use?**
   They used spring balances.

7. **What units did they use?**
   The spring balances were marked in newtons.

8. **What conclusion did they come to?**
   Upthrust supports some of the weight of an object that sinks in water.

Investigate! Hints and tips

Do this investigation yourself.
- ★ Use a variety of objects. Use some that float and others that sink in water.
- ★ Use different spring balances depending on the weight of the object.
- ★ Line up your eye with the scale when reading the weight.
- ★ Tie elastic bands around the objects to make it easy to hang them from the spring balance.

1

a) Which object weighed most
in air?

Tick one: ☐ rock   ☐ potato   ☐ lump of plasticine
☐ metal mass   ☐ tin of cat food

b) Which objects weighed least
in air?

Tick two: ☐ rock   ☐ potato   ☐ lump of plasticine
☐ metal mass   ☐ tin of cat food

Finish the last column of the table
on page 34.

c) Write the name of the object that
lost most weight in water.

2

Kate and Ali weighed objects that
floated in water. They found that all of
them did not weigh anything in water.
Tick the correct explanation.

Tick one: ☐ All objects lose their weight in water.
☐ The water supported all the weight.
☐ Gravity was not working through water.

3

Kate thinks that objects lose half
their weight in water.

a) Is she right?

☐ Yes   ☐ No

b) Explain your idea.

Ali thinks that all objects lose 1N of
weight in water.

c) Is he right?

☐ Yes   ☐ No

d) Explain your idea.

e) Use the table to complete
this chart.

Forces in action – summary

Friction

Friction is the force between two surfaces as they move past each other. Rough surfaces make a lot of friction. Smooth surfaces make less friction. A layer of liquid or fine powder (like water, oil or talc) between surfaces can reduce friction. Rollers reduce friction between two surfaces.

Friction can help us. If there was no friction, anything you touched would slide off the table. If there was no friction, you could not walk anywhere as there would be no grip between your feet and the floor. Without friction, food would simply fall off your fork before you could get it in your mouth.

Sometimes, friction can be a nuisance. Much of the effort of cycling is wasted by friction between the moving parts of the bike. We could save most of the petrol we put in a car if there was no friction between the parts of the engine.

We can move with hardly any friction when we ice skate or ski. There is practically no friction between the blades and the ice so we slide almost effortlessly.

Read these four short paragraphs.

1 Write a title for each paragraph.

Answer these questions on a separate piece of paper.

2 Explain two ways we can reduce friction.

3 Explain how friction helps us slow down a bicycle.

4 Use what you know about friction to explain why ice on roads is dangerous.

Tick here if you can do this now!

- [ ] I can make careful measurements.
- [ ] I can work out averages.
- [ ] I can identify patterns in my results.
- [ ] I can repeat measurements.
- [ ] I can label graphs accurately.
- [ ] I can explain my conclusions.

Did you know?

★ There is more friction between two objects just before they start to move. More force is needed to get an object moving than to keep it going. This accounts for the jerk as something starts moving. Watch the spring balance carefully to see this effect.

Floating forces

Fill in the blanks with the correct words.

Ships float in water because the force of _____ supports them. Metal ships _____ because they are hollow inside. This shape means they can displace a large volume of _____. Submarines are ships that can float and _____ in water. They sink when their tanks are filled with water. This makes them heavier so they sink.

When we swim in water, we float because water holds us up. If we pick up a brick underwater, we can lift it quite _____ because upthrust helps us to support it. Once we lift the brick out of the water it then loses the support of upthrust and feels heavier.

As a boat is loaded with more and more cargo it sinks deeper into the water. The Plimsoll line is a red line _____ on the sides of ships. It shows how much _____ can be safely put on board. Before this line was painted on ships, sailors would drown when waves swamped the ships during storms.

Tick here if you can do this now!

☐ I can make careful measurements.   ☐ I can make accurate observations.

☐ I can identify patterns in my results.   ☐ I can explain my conclusions.

Did you know?

★ The water in the Dead Sea is very salty. This means that it gives a lot of upthrust. People can float so high in the water that they can keep a newspaper out of the water to read it!

How we see things – the size of shadows

Class 6L have been studying the size of shadows. They wanted to see what factors made a difference to the size of shadows.

The investigation

They used a light bulb as a light source.
They used a small matchbox as an object.
They set up a piece of paper as a screen.

They kept the screen and the object in the same place.
(They kept them 3 cm apart.)
They moved the light.
They measured the width of the shadow.

- Jake predicted that the shadow would be widest when the bulb was close to the box.

- Shameela predicted that the shadow would be narrower when the bulb was close to the box.

- Lee predicted that the shadow would not really change much.

These are the results:

Distance of bulb from object (cm)	Width of shadow (cm)
100	4
75	4
25	4.5
5	6
2	10

Approaching the investigation

1 **Who made the most accurate prediction?**
Jake made the most accurate prediction. He said that the shadow would be widest when the light was close to the object.

2 **Which variable did they try to keep the same?**
In this investigation the children kept the distance from the matchbox to the screen the same. The also kept the torch and the matchbox the same.

3 **Which variable did they alter?**
They changed the distance from the torch to the matchbox.

4 **What did they measure?**
They measured the width of the shadow made by the box.

5 **What equipment did they use?**
Ruler
Torch
Matchbox
Screen

6 **What conclusion did they come to?**
The closer the light is to the box, the wider the shadow. This is because more light is blocked out.

a) Was the shadow wider when the light was closer to the matchbox?

☐ Yes   ☐ No

b) How wide was the shadow when the light was 75 cm away from the box?

The children were making shadow pictures of people's heads.

The children talked about the size of the shadow picture.

Whose idea is correct?

Tick one: ☐ Jim said the shadow picture is always the same size as the head.
☐ Kate said the shadow picture is always smaller than the head.
☐ Raifa said the shadow can be larger than the person's head.

3

a) What shape is the line?

Tick one: ☐ straight line   ☐ curve

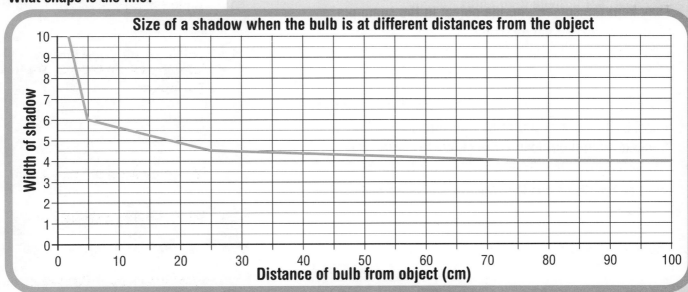

Size of a shadow when the bulb is at different distances from the object

Use the information from the graph.

b) Predict how wide the shadow would be if the bulb was 1 cm away from the box.

Tick one: ☐ 10 cm   ☐ 20 cm   ☐ 7 cm

c) Predict how wide the shadow would be if the bulb was 125 cm away from the box.

Investigate! Hints and tips

Do this investigation yourself.
 It is better to use a torch bulb in a holder than to use a torch.

★ Measure the width or the height.
★ A better word for shadow picture is 'silhouette'.

Changing circuits – dimmer and brighter

Class 6L have been studying the way that bulbs can be made brighter and dimmer in different ways.

The investigation

The children made a series circuit with two batteries and a single bulb. The bulb was very bright indeed.

They added a second bulb to the circuit. They made sure the bulbs were all identical. By adding this second bulb they saw that it made both bulbs dimmer.

They added a third bulb. All three bulbs were very dim indeed.

The class predicted what would happen if they added a fourth bulb. They said that all four bulbs would be so dim it would be difficult to see the glow.

Mrs Legg asked them to complete a table to show what they noticed.

These are the results:

Number of bulbs	Brightness of bulbs ✓✓✓✓✓ = very bight ✓ = very dim
1	✓✓✓✓✓
2	✓✓✓✓
3	✓✓
4	✓

Approaching the investigation

1. **What did the class want to find out?**
   They wanted to add bulbs in a series circuit.
   They wanted to see what happened to the brightness of the bulbs as more were added.

2. **What did they predict?**
   They predicted that the bulbs would get dimmer as more were added.

3. **Which variable did they try to keep the same?**
   The sort of bulb was identical.
   The batteries were the same for each test.

4. **Which variable did they alter?**
   The number of bulbs in the circuit.

5. **What did they observe?**
   They saw what happened to the brightness of the bulbs.

6. **What conclusion did they come to?**
   Bulbs in a series circuit get dimmer as more bulbs are added to the circuit.

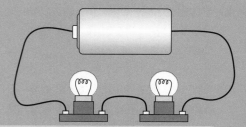

Investigate! Hints and tips

Do this investigation yourself.
★ Test all the batteries before you start the investigation.

★ Test all the bulbs before you start the investigation.
★ Test all the wires to make sure they all work.

★ Look closely to see if there is a dim glow in the filament.

1

a) What trend did you notice in the results?

b) Did the children correctly predict what would happen with four bulbs?

☐ Yes   ☐ No

Imagine there were five bulbs in series.

c) Would there be any glow at all?

☐ Yes   ☐ No

d) Explain your idea.

2 The children decided to experiment with the number of batteries. Explain how they could test different numbers of batteries.

3 Complete these bar charts to show what you think will happen in each case. Each bar chart has four bars.

One bar has been done for you in each chart.

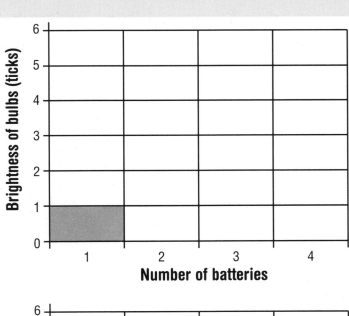

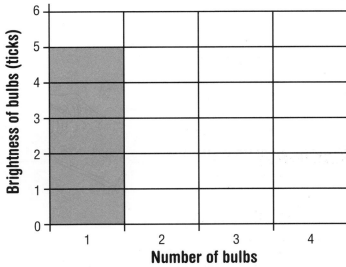

How we see things – summary

The size of shadows

Fill in the blanks using the correct words.

Light travels in _____ lines. Shadows are made when _____ is blocked by an object. Light cannot go through _____ objects, such as our heads. The shadow made by our heads is called a silhouette. If the _____ is made on a piece of paper, it can be cut out to make a shadow picture. The best silhouettes are made when the person is two metres from the paper and the light is four metres away from the person. There should also be no other light _____ in the room. This gives the smallest and sharpest silhouette.

If the light is very close to the person's head, the silhouette is very large indeed. The size of the silhouette gets _____ very quickly as the light gets closer to the head.

Tick here if you can do this now!

☐ I can make careful measurements.   ☐ I can show data in graphs.

☐ I can identify patterns in my graphs.   ☐ I can use my observations to explain scientific ideas.

Did you know?

★ In the cinema, the projector has to be a long way from the screen. This makes the pictures very large. If the projector was very close to the screen the picture would only be the size of a small postcard.

Changing circuits – summary

Dimmer and brighter

The flow of _____ in a circuit is controlled by two main things.

The first is the number of _____ you use. More batteries increase the flow of electricity. _____ batteries mean there is less electricity flowing in the circuit.

_____ bulbs in series increase the resistance of the circuit. This makes it more difficult for electricity to flow. If less electricity flows in a circuit, the _____ will be less bright.

Other factors that will make a difference are:
- new batteries have more stored energy than old batteries
- some bulbs make it harder for electricity to pass through them than others

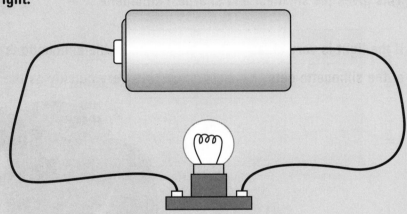

Tick here if you can do this now!
- ☐ I can predict what will happen in experiments.
- ☐ I can make careful observations.
- ☐ I can give scientific explanations of what I see.
- ☐ I can plan good tests.
- ☐ I can identify patterns in my results.

Did you know?
★ Dimmer switches in rooms use resistance. You can make a dimmer for your torch bulbs using a length of propelling pencil lead. The longer the piece of lead the electricity has to pass through, the dimmer the bulb will be.

Answers

Page 9

a) Tick: No

b) The grass had not died quickly and under the mats it was still damp.

c) Tick: There will be no green plants at all.

d) After two weeks the grass and weeds were all yellow. They would die without any sunlight for six weeks.

2 a) They could substitute a clear mat for a piece of carpet to see whether light made a difference to the growth of plants.

b) Cover the area that has weeds with a mat or carpet.

3

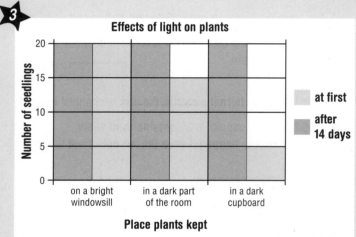

Page 11

1 a) Tick water and orange cordial.

b) Yeast feeds on water and sugar. There is sugar in orange cordial.

2 a) Tick: Neither of the balloons will fill with gas.

b) Yeast needs sugar and water to make gas.

c) Yeast grows best in warm places

d) The holes are caused by bubbles of gas created by the yeast.

3 a) The amount of sugar in each container.

b) The amount of yeast in each container, the temperature of the water, where the container is kept.

Page 12

All green plants need light, WATER, air and the energy from sunlight to grow. If green PLANTS did not do this there would be very little life on Earth.

Green plants that grown in places where there is little light will be unhealthy. They will grow thin and WEAK. Their leaves will be yellow. Plants grown in no light will die within a few WEEKS. They may survive on their stores of FOOD but without light they starve to death.

Animals depend on green plants to make food for them. Green plants are the start of most food CHAINS on Earth. Plants are the PRODUCERS of the food eaten by animals. In food chains animals are CONSUMERS.

Page 13

1   Paragraph 1 – What is fungi?
    Paragraph 2 – Uses of fungi

2   Tick: A jungle. Because fungi grow best in warm, damp conditions.

3   Tick: A damp cellar. Because fungi grow best in dark, damp conditions.

Page 15

1 a) Tick: 100 ml

b) 100 ml jug is closest to the 50 ml they want to measure.

c) Water above 40 °C is too hot to come from taps. It would have to be boiling water. It would also be too dangerous.

d) To get an accurate measure of the temperature.

e) The water would have cooled down by then.

f) The water would then turn a colour when all the sugar had dissolved.

2 Gemma could complete the same test for each of the different types of sugar. Everything should stay the same except the type of sugar.

a)

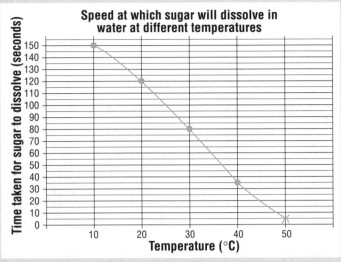

Speed at which sugar will dissolve in water at different temperatures

b) It is approximately a straight line.

Page 17

a) Tick: Lena and Kate

b) Tick: Sugar

c) The amount of water in the container.

d) The temperature of the water, the size of the containers.

a) Tick: No

b) The seawater already has salt dissolved in it. So you would need more seawater to dissolve the salt than lake water. Lake water will dissolve salt more quickly than seawater.

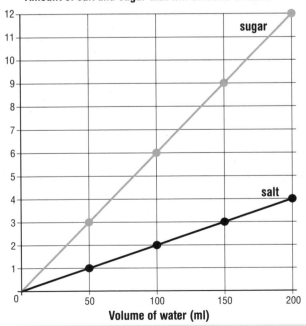

Amount of salt and sugar that will dissolve in water

Page 18

1 Tick: Sugar is soluble.

2 Tick: Sugar is dissolved more slowly in cold water than in warm.

3 Tick: A sugar solution is a mix of water and sugar.

4 Tick: Water is the solvent in a sugar solution.

Page 19

1 Some flour will settle on the bottom of a container when it is added to water.

2 Yes, Amy can dissolve more salt now.

3 Fill a container with water and add the bath salts. Now let the water evaporate and you should get big bath crystals!

Page 21

a) Tick: Salt

b) Tick: Sugar and Paper

c) Any from the table on page 20 except butter, salt and lard.

d) Tick: Jim said the change was reversible because it was just solid to liquid.

a) Tick: When you burn the candle, the wax is changed into gas.

b) Trap the water vapour in a container and allow condensation to happen. Leave the ice cubes out to melt.

a) Tick: Less than 60 seconds.

b) Tick: Between 61 seconds and two minutes.

Page 23

a) Tick: 20 seconds

b) Tick: Candles burn longer in big jars than small jars and There is more air in big jars so candles burn longer.

a) Tick: No

b) The candle will use up air to burn, which would take it away from the miners.

a) 13.5–16 seconds

b) Volume of jar is about 620–750 ml

c) Tick: No

Page 24

Melting is the change from SOLID to liquid. Evaporation is the change from liquid to GAS. CONDENSATION is the change from gas to liquid. Freezing is the change from LIQUID to solid. Most of these changes are REVERSIBLE. Burning is where a material is changed into a NEW substance. Burnt paper cannot be made into white paper again. Burning is IRREVERSIBLE.

Page 25

When candles burn not all the wax is burnt. Some melts and drips down the candle. This change from solid to LIQUID is a reversible change.

When candles burn they use air. The more AIR there is in a jar the longer the candle will burn. The candle flame burns wax. It is impossible for people to turn burnt wax back into solid wax again. This is an example of an IRREVERSIBLE change.

Air is a mixture of gases. The main gases in air are nitrogen and oxygen. When CANDLES burn they only use oxygen. The flame turns the WAX into carbon dioxide and water. It is very difficult to turn carbon dioxide and water back into wax. This is an example of an IRREVRESIBLE change.

Page 27

a) Any three of paper, paperclips, stopwatch, pens and a chair.

b) Three

c) No, because each would be falling from a different distance and it would be impossible to work out which fell fastest.

a) Yes

b) They tried each test twice and dropped each spinner from the same height.

c) 1) 4.35 seconds 2) 3.05 seconds 3) 1.55 seconds.

d) Be careful when climbing up and down on the chair.

a)

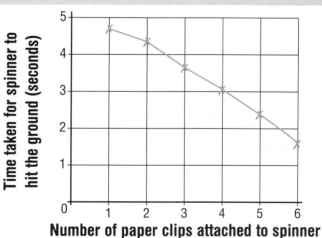

b) The line graph shows that the more paperclips attached to the spinner, the faster the spinner fell.

Page 29

a) Tick: 18 cm

b) Tick: 11 cm

2 a)

b)

Mass (g)	Thick elastic band (cm)	Thin elastic band (cm)
100		
200		
300		
400		
500		
600		

3

Mass (g)	0	100	200	300	400	500	600
Length of rubber band (cm)	12	15	18	21	23	24	24.5
Stretch of band (cm)	0	3	6	9	11	12	12.5

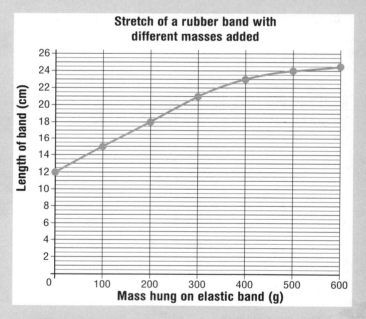

Stretch of a rubber band with different masses added

c) Tick: Ahmed

Page 30

Air resistance is a FORCE. When an object falls, air resistance acts in the OPPOSITE direction to the weight. This SLOWS down the falling object. The air offers greater RESISTANCE to objects that have a LARGER surface area. Looking at our investigation, air resistance pushed UP on the spinners and weight pulled them DOWN.

Air resistance slows the lighter object by a greater amount. That is why the spinners with FEWER paper-clips took longer to FALL to the ground. If two objects of DIFFERENT weights are dropped when there is no air resistance (such as on the moon) they will reach the ground at the same time.

Page 31

1 2 newtons

2 They would both hit the ground at the same time.

3 Gravity works at great distances and close to the Earth.

4 Pluto

5 The Moon

Page 33

 a) Tick: Grass and Sand tray

b) Top to bottom: 5, 6, 7, 8, 12

c) Sand tray

d) Table top

 a) Tick: More than on the carpet.

b) Sandpaper is rougher than carpet so there is usually more friction.

c) Tick: The same as the carpet.

 a) Jim and Lena's results

b)

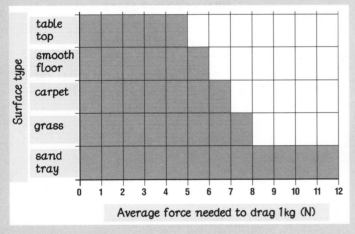

Average force needed to drag 1kg (N)

Page 35

 a) Tick: tin of cat food

b) Tick: potato and lump of plasticine.

c) Tin of cat food

 Tick: The water supported all the weight.

 a) Tick: No

b) Some objects lose half their weight in water but some lose less and some lose more.

c) Tick: No

d) The amount of weight objects lose in water varies.

e)

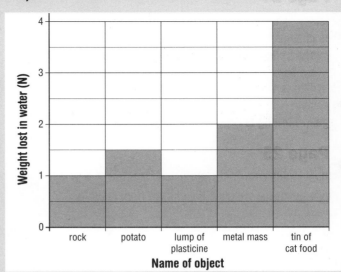

Name of object

Page 36

1 Suggested paragraph titles:
Friction on surfaces
How friction helps us
Problems with friction
No friction

2 Putting liquid or fine powder on surfaces to make them smoother. Use rollers to reduce friction.

3 By pulling the brakes on a bike we increase the friction on the wheels so we slow down.

4 Ice is very smooth so there is little friction. Car wheels are like rollers on the ice so there is almost no friction. The car will skid as there is no friction between the car and the ice.

Page 37

Ships float in water because the force of UPTHRUST supports them. Metal ships FLOAT because they are hollow inside. This shape means they can displace a large volume of WATER. Submarines are ships that can float and SINK in water. They sink when their tanks are filled with water. This makes them heavier so they sink.

When we swim in water, we float because water holds us up. If we pick up a brick underwater, we can lift it quite EASILY because upthrust helps us to support it. Once we lift the brick out of the water it then loses the support of upthrust and feels heavier.

As a boat is loaded with more and more cargo it sinks deeper into the water. The Plimsoll line is a red line PAINTED on the sides of ships. It shows how much CARGO can be safely put on board. Before this line was painted on ships, sailors would drown when waves swamped the ships during storms.

Page 39

a) Tick: Yes

b) The shadow was 4 cm wide when it was 75 cm away from the box.

Tick: Raifa said the shadow can be larger than the person's head.

a) Tick: Curve

b) Tick: 20 cm

c) 4 cm

Page 41

a) The more bulbs on the circuit, the dimmer they were.

b) Tick: Yes

c) Tick: No

d) When there were four bulbs the glow was difficult to see. Adding another one would probably make it impossible to see.

Keep the number of bulbs and the rest of the circuit the same. Add more and more batteries and record whether the bulb got brighter or not.

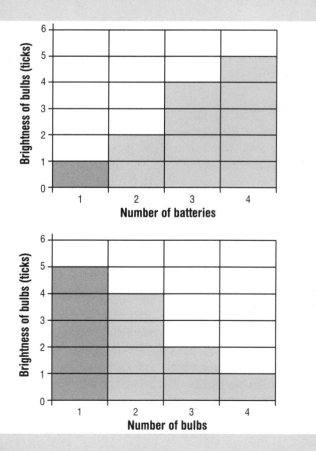

Page 42

Light travels in STRAIGHT lines. Shadows are made when LIGHT is blocked by an object. Light cannot go through OPAQUE objects, such as our heads. The shadow made by our heads is called a silhouette. If the SILHOUETTE is made on a piece of paper, it can be cut out to make a shadow picture. The best silhouettes are made when the person is two metres from the paper and the light is four metres away from the person. There should also be no other light SOURCE in the room. This gives the smallest and sharpest silhouette.

If the light is very close to the person's head, the silhouette is very large indeed. The size of the silhouette gets LARGER very quickly as the light gets closer to the head.

Page 43

The flow of ELECTRICITY in a circuit is controlled by two main things.

The first is the number of BATTERIES you use. More batteries increase the flow of electricity. FEWER batteries mean there is less electricity flowing in the circuit.

MORE bulbs in series increase the resistance of the circuit. This makes it more difficult for electricity to flow. If less electricity flows in a circuit, the BULB will be less bright.